AF553886

Conspiracy Cases in India

Second Nasik Conspiracy Trial, 1911

A Second Nasik Conspiracy Case charged Savarkar with the abetment of murder of Jackson, the Collector of Nasik. The trial opened on January 23, 1911, in which it was contended by the prosecution that the pistol used in the outrage was one of those twenty which Vinayak had been able to send clandestinely to India. It was, therefore, not a difficult matter to find the accused guilty of abetment and Vinayak was awarded on January 30, 1911 a second term of transportation for life.

It may be interesting to note that the two Savarkar brothers had the unique distinction amongst Indian patriots to pass [illegible] portion of their prison life in the Cellular Jail in the Andamans—aptly called "the Indian Bastille". The elder brother, Ganesh, was convicted on June 8, 1909 for composing and publishing a book of [illegible] verses, entitled *Laghu Abhinav Bharat Mela* with a sentence of transportation for life, a punishment reserved for the gravest offences under the Criminal Law of the land.

The Lahore Conspiracy Cases of a later period have been dealt with at appropriate places.

(Courtesy: [illegible] Ganshot—Roll of [illegible] Movement)

Peshawar Conspiracy

[illegible] the Government [illegible] the Government to take [illegible] in [illegible] that Indian [illegible] against any form of communist ideology. It united the propertied classes that supported British [illegible]. British rulers were determined [illegible] to allow communist ideas [illegible] through any land [illegible].

[illegible] ideas cannot be [illegible] till they are [illegible] No walls however high can

Conspiracy Cases *in* India

Editior-in-Chief
O.P. Ralhan

Mahaveer & Sons
(Publishers & Distributors)
New Delhi–110002

Edition 2017

ISBN-978-81-8377-176-4
Rs. 800/-

Published by
MAHAVEER & SONS
3072/28, First Floor, Gola Market, Darya Gang,
(Near Golcha Parking) New Delhi-110002

PRINTED IN INDIA

Published by Sh. Mukul Sharma for Mahaveer & Sons, 3072/28, First Floor, Gola Market, Darya Gang, (Near Golcha Parking) New Delhi-110002 Printed at Himanshu Printers, Delhi.

Dedicated to
the sweet and ever hasting memory
of the Martyrs of Freedom Struggle
who
dedicated their lives for the sake
of Mother India.

back into Punjab in batches or singly, they were arrested and conspiracy cases were launched against them.

These conspiracy cases were launched, not on the basis of any concrete action of theirs in the British Indian territory in the Punjab against the British raj but on the basis of having come into contact with Soviet ideology and the Russian revolution. It was pure and simple communist thought, which these muhajirs had learnt in Soviet Russia which the British India rulers were prosecuting in their courts of justice (?).

The British rulers did not want to take any chance by allowing the muhajirs to move about freely in the Punjab, talk about the victorious Soviet revolution and what it was all about. They arrested them as soon as they set foot in the Punjab and booked up conspiracy cases against them and passed heavy sentences on them. What for, [illegible]

The first conspiracy case judgement was given on 31 May 1922 and the last one ended in 1927. In between this period about five Bolshevik or Moscow conspiracy cases were launched and heavy sentences were pronounced against the accused. For instance, Akbar Khan was given seven years rigorous imprisonment including three months in solitary confinement, Mohammed Hussain, five years rigorous imprisonment including 3 months in solitary confinement, and Ghulam Mehboob (Peshawar) five years rigorous imprisonment including three months in solitary confinement. This was the second case tried by the session judge Fraser who delivered the judgement on 2[illegible] April 192[illegible].

Shaukat Usmani was arrested on 8 May 1923. The *London Times* on 12 May 1923 wrote malignantly about Bolshevik activity in India saying that an alleged agent of Moscow had been arrested and conspiracy case had been started against him under Section 121A (waging war against the king emperor to overthrow him) and to

Preface

Conspiracy cases in India is a history of the Revolutionary Movements and the role of revolutionaries who fought against the introcities, brutalities and ruthless repression and exploitation and divide and rule policy of the British Raj in India. It is a history of those revolutionaries who laid down their lives for the sake of their motherland. They were hanged, they were killed in police encounters, they died in Jails, they scarified their lives observing hunger strikes for months together in various jails. The long felt desire of this book specifically on conspiracy cases in India in the Research fields, was need of the hour. Ironically no one has attempted till now to collect material on this matter. Being in the library profession and amidst the scholars. I have attempted to collect material from various sources. Though it may not be complete in itself, what I am sure this book fill up the lacuna in this regard will help support the scholars working in this field.

I am really indebted and gratefull to all authors/Publishers/ Printers of those books, I have taken the material with courtesy, because to approach everyone was not possible for me. I am quite hopeful the scholar community will definitely be benefited by this venture.

—Editor

Conspiracy Cases in India

Conspiracy Cases (1908-1911)

Besides proceeding against persons alleged to be connected with individual overt acts, the Government started big conspiracy cases to rope in as many persons as it thought to be "undesirable" from its point of view. A few typical cases are enumerated here that took place between 1908-1911 to give an idea of the nature and scope of such trials.

Akali Conspiracy Case, Hoshiarpur

In the Hoshiarpur Akali Conspiracy Case, the arrest warrants of Kishan Singh Gargaj (1819-1926) were issued. To evade arrest, he became a fugitive and started working underground.

(Eminent Freedom Fighters of Punjab– Fauja Singh, p. 159)

Akalgarh Riot Case (Gujranwala District) 1919

Akalgarh is a small town in the district of Gujranwala. There was complete hartal on April 6, 14 and 15, 1919. Meetings were held and processions were taken out. On April 15 the mob marched towards the railway station and attempted to set fire some of the bridges on the railway line. About six persons were held and charged with offences under Sections 121, 124-A, 147, 426, 431 and 435 I.P.C. and a few boys of 15 years of age were severely whipped.

Alantaung Rebellion Case

One comprehensive case for incidents occurring between December 22 and December 31, 1930, was started in Tharrawaddy before a Special Tribunal with thirty-seven rebels as accused. The court sentenced eleven persons to death. An appeal was preferred before the High Court and it confirmed the death sentences of nine commuting the punishment of two to transportation for life.

Amritsar Assault Case (1919)

Miss Sherwood, a middle-aged lady, was Superintendent of a Mission School in Amritsar. She was also a lady doctor. On April 10, 1919, when she was going on her cycle she encountered a mob which raised slogans of "kill her, she is English". She wheeled round and tried to escape, but the mob overtook her and struck her on the head with lathis. In this case seven persons were sentenced to death and eight persons were sentenced to transportation for the life and their property was forfeited.

Amritsar Girls' School Case (1919)

On April 10, 1919, some nationalists attacked and fired at the Girls Mission School but could not find the four lady missionaries who had hidden themselves somewhere in the building. On arrival of the police the people had dispersed. In this case, 9 men were held and out of them 6 were sentenced to transportation for life and forfeiture of their property.

Amritsar Leaders' Case (1919)

A few nationalists organized a revolutionary party

after they had returned from Germany. They spread their revolutionary ideas against the British Government and the Rowlatt Bills. On April 9, 1919, on the occasion of Ram Naumi festival a procession was taken out as the result of which the Government ordered the arrest of Dr. Kitchlew and Satyapal. The news of the arrest of these two popular leaders caused a strong feeling against the Government and on April 10, 1919, some public buildings were sacked and burnt. Railway lines and bridges were destroyed, telegraph communication was interrupted and some of the Europeans were injured and murdered. In this case, about 17 important leaders were held and tried before Mr. Justice Broadway's Commission Dr. Kitchlew, Dr. Satyapal, Badr-ul-Islam Ali Khan, Mohd. Bashir, Kotu Mal, Narain Das Khanna, Gurdial Singh, Bhawan Nand, Dina Nath, Gurbaksh Rai, Ghulam Nabi, Ghulam Mohd., Abdul Aziz, Mohd. Ismail and Moti Ram Mehra were charged with offences under Sections 121-121A, 124-A, 396, 147, 302, 326, 50, 426, 124-A, 147, 436, 302, 120B and 506 I.P.C. The allegation against these persons was that they were the leaders of the whole movement which culminated on the 10th April in the act of waging war against the British Government. Dr. Kitchew and Dr. Satyapal were sentenced to transportation for life. Dr. Mohd. Bashir was sentenced to death.

Anarkali (Lahore) Case (1919)

In the Anarkali Case, one Arjan Singh was tried, convicted and sentenced to death.

Bhagatanwala Case (Amritsar) (1919)

On the afternoon of April 10, 1919, a mob sacked the Post Office near the Golden Temple at Amritsar. Then the crowed moved on to Bhagtanwala Railway Station where they cut the telegraph wires, looted the godown and set the station building on fire. In this case about 15 persons were convicted under Section 121 IPC and were sentenced to transportation for life.

Burma Conspiracy (1915)

The revolutionary stirrings in India did not fail to influence the tenor of Burmese political life in a considerable degree. There had been no time when Burma was completely free from attempts, however feeble, to drive away the foreigners and to revive kingship in their ancient land.

The first organised effort by the Indian revolutionaries to introduce sedition and something more became noticeable during the World War I and contact was firmly established between the two countries through secret channel. Taking advantage of the War and War preparations, the Indian revolutionaries made serious attempts at establishing centres in and outside India, and Burma was reckoned by them as a convenient place not up to then turned very much into a beehive of the police and its spies.

In Burma, the main programme in 1914, was to cause defection in and stir up mutiny among the military forces thereby making the overthrow of the Government possible from inside its own ranks.

There had been Bengali revolutionaries in Burma a few years before the World War I who had been establishing contact with the local people for the dissemination of ideas subversive of Government authority through literature and holding public meetings wherever possible.

Arrival of seasoned revolutionaries and literature from the U.S.A. added strength to the hands that had been silently working against odds. Gradually infiltration of a larger number through the eastern borders brought together a band of young men of exceptional ability, resourcefulness and culture with whom no risk was too great where the freedom of the country was concerned. The main stream of revolutionary ideas flowed from the organisation in U.S.A., the *Ghadr* party, and its members entered Burma from the Far Eastern countries especially through Thailand (Siam) and the movement got its support from its headquarters in Bangkok.

The mouthpiece of the movement was the *Ghadr* newspaper which was sent free to all Indians, especially to those residing at Bangkok. More copies than one were sent to the same person subscribing to the idea with a request of the reader that his copy should be passed on to others after he had finished with it.

One of the recipients of such bundles was 'Arya Prince Charlie at Bangkok', an assumed name no doubt, and his share used to be a roll comprising fifty copies of each issue which were meant obviously for distribution.

Gradually censorship was introduced over entry of foreign newspapers and other articles coming through post and the number decreased with complete stoppage by interception.

Another Paper doing its bit was the *Jahan-e-Islam* started in Constantinople in May 1914, which contained articles in Arabic, Hindi and Turkish. Due to its violent attack on the British and her allies, this was also dealt with in the same manner as the *Ghadr,* but not before it had succeded in its mission exceedingly well. The Urdu section of the Paper published in its issue of November 20, 1914, a speech of Enver Pasha of Egypt to the effect that declaration of independence should not be delayed any further. In his language it was:

"The magazines of the English should be plundered, their weapons looted and they should be killed therewith. The Indians number thirty-two crores at the best and the English are only two lakhs; they should be murdered: they have no army. The Suez Canal will shortly be closed by the Turks, but he who will die and liberate the country and his native land will live for ever. Hindus and Muhammadans, you are both soldiers of the army and you are brothers, and this low degraded English is your enemy. You should be *ghazis* by declaring jehad, and by combining with brothers murder the English and liberate India." (*Report of the Sedition Committee,* 1918, p. 169).

The conspiracy organised in Burma had the support of the Turkish Government and persons with extreme detestation for the British were placed in positions at the disposal of the Turkish Government whose Consul in Burma at the time proved to be of immense help to movement.

The attempt to spread disaffection amongst the army stationed in Rangoon, particularly the 130th Baluchis succeeded to a certain extent and there was open revolt against the Government in January, 1915. The rising was brought under control after both the originators and participants had paid for the miscalculated revolt with their lives. The number of persons punished with varying terms of imprisonment was more than two hundred. The other insurrections were caused by the Malay State Guides and the 5th Native Light Infantry.

The organisers took immense trouble and risk inasmuch as one of them reached Mandalay by way of Manila and Singapore and others from Bangkok *via* Siamese frontier. The centre of revolution in Burma kept itself busy in collecting money and arms as best as it could and it had been humming with activity of grave portents.

By the month of April 1915, the Government obtained evidence of a *Ghadr* plot in Burma and serious steps were taken to tackle in with vigour. *Ghadr* literature was found in several places, particularly in

Myawaddy near the Siamese forntier. Enlistment of supporters had been going on apace mainly amongst the Sikhs and the Punjab Mahome-dans.Many names, very prominent in subsequent trials, came to the knowledge of the police. The main offence attributed to the prisoners was waging war against the King, tampering with the loyalty of the Army, and spreading inflammatory reports to assist the King's ememies. There was open exhortation done through a pamphlet, *A Message of Hope to Military Brethrem,* to the native officers of the military police who "were invited not to be tempted by medals and badges of slavery but to throw them away, wash out the old stain of servitude and adorn their breasts with the insignia of freedom."

It subsequently became known that brisk preparations had been going on from 1911, mostly by some young men coming from distant Punjab. At least two of these had knowledge of manufacturing bombs; another possessed materials for the purpose. They rented a house in Rangoon where frequent meetings were held with the common object of overthrowing the Government.

The *Ghadr* paper was duplicated in this premises. They maintained regular contact with workers in Bangkok and in India. Subscriptions were collected for the advancement of the cause and their activities grew in volume. Some of them sincerely believed that an all-out rebellion was imminent and success was bound to come.

The conspirators had not been depending solely on their own resources. The German Government took a good deal of interest in the affairs of the *Ghadr* Party in U.S.A. They undertook the training of Indians "returning to India to the use of arms in places along the railway which was being in Northern Siam in the direction of Burma largely by German Engineers and

Punjabi workmen and to invade Burma and foment rebellion by Indian troops and the military police."

In the Far East intense revolutionary activity requiring great tact, intelligence and other resources was noticeable at various places. Bangkok was one of the important centres where representatives of the secret society from India met those coming from San Francisco and from the different centres in Burma, working hand in hand with different groups of Indians. The British Government became extremely alert and adopted measures to meet the emergency. Because of its early knowledge the rising contemplated in October, 1915, on the *Bakr-id* Day was easily foiled by the police. The Military Police Battalion at Pyowbe incited to the point of action also failed at the scheduled time due to defections in the ranks and by prompt Governmental action. The extent of the preparation in this particular case, with revolvers, dynamite and other explosives, was bigger than in most other places. The revolutionaries had shown their mettle in a risky game, but a few timid and covetous souls brought failure and dismay to what might have proved a grand *finale* to a glorious chapter in the history of Burma, attaining with India, independent status during the World War I.

Burma Conspiracy Case (1915-1916)

In accordance with the resolution taken in U.S.A. amongst the members of *Ghadr* Party several persons entered Burma by different routes, particularly by way of whom were highly educated.

A batch of Punjabis, some of whom were highly educated, influential and held positions of trust and responsibility in the society, reached Burma in 1915 with the express object of starting a revolution. They set to work without delay and rented several premises in Rangoon. They visited different parts of Burma, openly preached sedition, mixed with all sorts of Burmese people, particularly with those having sympathy for the nationalist cause, introduce the topic of rising in rebellion wherever possible, take steps for smuggling the *Ghadr* inside Burma. When police vigilance was intensified and the newspaper could no longer be imported, they made arrangements for its duplication locally. At times they openly advocated mutiny and would say that arrangements had been completed for receiving foreign aid and mass support from the revolutionaries in India.

The centres of activity were scattered over a wide area and one who would join in Singapore would at once establish communication with another in Rangoon. One of the accused left Singapore after the mutiny and went over to Rangoon at the end of February, 1915. Gradually Burma, particularly Mandalay and Rangoon, became the two important cities in the Eastern countries where an all-out attempt was made for a future rising. Arms and ammunitions, dynamites and other explosive materials were collected to the extent allowed under the peculiar circumstances of the case. One of the accused, closely associated with Sohanlal, came to Burma with materials for waging war against the British.

Preparations had been nearing completion when the police came into possession of the fact, swooped upon the organisation, and arrested seventeen Punjabis. In due course the accused were placed before a Special Tribunal at Mandalay on March 6, 1916, for trial.

They were accused under the omnibus charge of waging war against the King, making preparations for an uprising, helping the enemy with material information, seducing the military police from allegiance of the authorities, conspiracy, sedition (121, 121-A, 122, 124-A, Rule 25 of the Defence of India Consolidation Rules 1915, etc.).

On July 31, 1916, judgment was delivered when sentences of death were passed on

(i) Harnam Singh
(ii) Challia Ram
(iii) Narian Singh
(iv) Basswa Singh
(v) Narinjan Singh
(vi) Palla Singh
(vii) Another.

The rest excepting one was awarded transportation for life.

On August 16, 1916, the local Government passed an order remitting the sentence of forfeiture of property of all the convicted persons. Harnam Singh, Challiaram and Narain Singh did not submit any petition for consideration of their cases and the question of reducing their sentence did not arise.

Three other prisoners' appeal for mercy was rejected. The seventh accused escaped death with transportation for life. There was one other accused Bhai Balwant Singh, whose appeal for mercy was also rejected. All the condemned persons were executed between August 19 and 22, 1916, in Burma.148

Burma Executions

In connection with the Tharrawaddy Rebellion in Burma, the Home Member, Burma Government, stated on February 24, 1933, that 274 persons were sentenced to death of whom fifty-one had already been executed and the number of persons undergoing transportation for having taken part in the rebellion was 535.

THE DYNAMITE CONSPIRACY

Two important leaders of the Chittagong Uprising, Anant Singh and Ganesh Ghosh, were arrested within six months of the date of the rising. The First Armoury Raid case trial started against about 36 revolutionaries including these two. Masterda, Nirmalda, Ambicada and several active soldiers of the revolutionary army were in those days hiding in the rural areas of Chittagong district. A few days before the beginning of the trial five of the accused, including myself, were unexpectedly released on bail. However, a condition was imposed on us five to the extent that we should be present in the dock along with the other accused in the Jail from 10 a.m. to 5 p.m. on every day of trial. The real purpose of thus releasing us on bail was to keep a strict surveillance on us, naturally expecting we or any other among us would try to contact Masterda, and as soon as we secured Masterda's contact to secretly follow us and arrest him.

At that time there were military camps in almost every village of the Chittagong district and there was strict military and police guard at every cross-roads and at every important centre of the Chittagong town. Even then the authorities could not rest in peace. That was because there were important leaders of revolution. Anant Singh, Ganesh Ghosh, Lokenath Bal and others in Chittagong Jail facing trial, and very experienced leaders of revolution like Masterda Surya Sen, Ambica Chakravarthy and Nirmal Sen along with their several armed and dedicated followers still outside leading an absconding life.

As it was Chittagong Jail was well-guarded and quite safe. Yet, after the three important leaders of the uprising. Anant Singh, Ganesh and Lokenath Bal—were arrested and brought in there, stricter security arrangements were made to ensure maximum safety in the prison.

The Indian Superintendent, Jailor and warders of the Jail were changed and Europeans inducted in their place. Breaking all the rules and norms of the Jails, armed soliders with rifles in their hands were deployed to guard the undertrial ward in which the Armoury Raid Case undertrials were lodged. Barbed wire fencing was erected all around the jail walls, military outposts were establishing at every corner and the Eastern Frontier Rifles \and the Gorkha Regiment were entrusted with the task of guarding the Jail from outside. Arrangements were made for the stationing of Gorkha military guards with machine guns on the roof of the Jail Office. As a matter of fact, the Chittagong Jail was converted into, and looked like, a well-defended fortress.

A few days after our trial had started, I received an urgent message from Masterda to go and meet him at a specified place. Accordingly, one day after dusk I manage to evade the surveillance of the C.I.D. agents, crossed to the other side of the Karanphuli river and reached the village Saroyatoli, at a distance of 10-12 miles from Chittagong, by midnight. There I met Masterda in his secret shelter. After talking for a few minutes Masterda finally told me in a calm, courageous and charming tone:

> Today I am entrusting a very risky and quite responsible job to you. Now the conditions are not opportune for waging open battles like those at Jalalabad or Kalarpole. Armed Police and military contingents have spread over the entire district, and so we should now carry out our activities and actions in a guerilla way. In this situation you should act as my link with the leaders in the Jail to facilitate our efforts to formulate a new martial strategy and tactics.

Thereafter Masterda and Nirmalda had decided within a few days that arrangements should be made to rescue the undertrial revolutionaries. Either an attack should be mounted on the armed police escort party while the revolutionary undertrials were being brought to the court for trial and our comrades be freed from their stronghold, or if that was not possible the Jail walls were to be blown up by explosives and the revolutionary prisoners were to liberated. It was further decided that landmines should be planted secretly at several important centres of the Chittagong town, and simultaneously with the blasting away of the Jail walls exploisons should be effected at these various places. Thus the entire administration of Chittagong had to be paralysed and terrorised at one stroke.

After contacts between the Jail comrades and the undertrial prisoners had been established through me, Masterda and Nirmalda from outside and Anantda and Ganeshda from within the Jail had collectively chalked out a plan for a second round of the Chittagong Uprising. Anantda and Ganeshda were entrusted with the responsibility of directing all activities inside and outside the Jail in regard to the proposed plan. I was to consult them and take their advice every day when we were all together in the dock and accordingly direct and supervise the actual work outside.

Immediately after the plan was finalised, as per the advice and directions of the revolutionary leaders we had quite clandestinely, and with great caution, prepared several landmines. These landmines were filled up with gun-power specially preapred by us for that purpose. About 10 seers of gun-powder was stuffed in each landmine. Every landmine was connected by long electrical wires. These wires were taken from under the ground for quite a long distance and arrangements were made to connect them with motor-batteries so as to ignite and cause explosions when needed. The revolutionary leadership had decided that the main wall of the Jail should be blasted off at some points by means of landmines and dynamites ignited from inside the prison, and the undertrial revolutionaries were to be rescued. The moment the Jail wall was blown up by the explosions, some comrades from outside would throw some powerful hand-bombs at the two guard out-posts at the two corners of the wall and also fire at the guards there in order to terrorise them and engage them in an exchange of fire and make them run or fight for their lives. Taking this opportunity the revolutionary prisoners were to come out of the Jail through the breach in the wall and quickly depart to the rural areas for hiding. It was arranged and fixed that on the D-Day Rabi Ray and Dwijen Das would come with a motor vehicle and wait outside near the Jail. Immediately as the revolutionary would come running out these two were to pick them up in their vehicle and take them quickly to the bank of the river to the prescribed *ghat.* At the *ghat* Sukhendu Dastidar and Mahindra Mazumdar would be waiting with a small boat (*sampan)* and as soon as the rescued revolutionaries turn up they would take them into the boat and quickly row it to the other bank and then take them to some safe shelters in some village.

Meanwhile Anant Singh and Ganesh Ghosh had befriended two European warders, Mr. Bloomfield and Mr. Wright, by occasionally but liberally bribing them. Slowly they were converted completely to our side and began to help us actively. Within a few days I had, through that medium, smuggled three army revolvers, plenty of cartridges, a few hand-bombs, two dozen very powerful dynamites of foreign make secured from the armoury of the Maharaja of Agartala by Indumati Singh, about a half maund of gun power for filling up the landmines, ten big torches, ten big daggers, about 50 yards of electrical wire, some excellent gun-cotton, a powerful magnifying glass, several big batteries of the torch lights, electric bulbs and various sorts of other useful instruments and tools into the Jail. Inside the

Jail Subodh Choudhury, Phanindra Nandi, Ananda Gupta, Subodh Roy (Jhunku), Sahayram Das, Ranadhir Dasgupta, Sukhendu Dastidar, Subodh Biswas, Nani Dev and others had, under the direct supervision of Anant Singh and Ganesh, made arrangements with great competence to plant dynamites and landmines underneath the soil at various specified places near the main wall of the Jail.

Along with the smuggling of things and messages into the Jail, in accordance with the plan to paralyse the administration of Chittagong and destroy the centres of authority, the following steps were taken:

1. In the well-protected court-building situated upon a hillock we intended to blow up only that portion which housed the Offices of the Chittagong Divisional Commissioner and District Magistrate. Accordingly, and to that extent, seven landmines were secretly set up beneath the soil in spite of the night curfew and the heavy guard around the Court Bungalow. The first explosion was intended to be off when the Divisional Commissioner's or District Magistrate's car passes by the road leading to the court bungalow so that either of them could be killed. At that place intended for the first explosion we had set up two sets of landmines with different wire connections so that explosion could be caused a second time too when desired. After the first explosion in which the Commissioner or the District Magistrate might be fatally injured, topmost officers of the Chittagong district administration as well as several top officers of the police and the military were sure to arrive there to inspect the place. At that exact juncture the second set of landmines was to be set off giving rise to tremendous explosions killing all the officers and personnel present there.

2. Inside the town the Judge of the Tribunal, top military officers and other high European officers were

generally using a road called the Lab Line. Beneath that road three landmines were planted at various places and their electric wire connections were taken to a considerable distance to be connected to a motor-battery. When needed the European officers along with their vehicles could be blown up by setting off the landmines at the right time.

3. Three landmines were buried under the road slopping downwards from the Police Superintendent's Bungalow. The S.P.'s vehicle used to travel by that road only. Long electric wire connections were provided connecting the landmines to a battery so that the explosions could be set off when needed. The S.P. along with his vehicle was to be blown up at the right time.

4. A separate enclosure with wooden stands was arranged in the Chittagong Cricket Ground for the European officers to watch the game. Four landmines were set up beneath the ground under these wooden stands with long wire connections to a battery cancealed at a considerable distance. It was proposed to blow up the Stands thereby killing or critically injuring all the Europeans watching the game by setting off the explosions at the needed time.

5. In those days the Divisional Commissioner of Chittagong, the District Magistrate, the Superintendent of Police, top officers of the Army and other high European officers used to meet at the Circuit House for their secret consultations. Arrangements were made to set up three powerful landmines under the road leading to the Circuit House Gate.

6. There was a desolate house near the Askhar Khan Tank in Chittagong. Inside, and in the premises of, that house three powerful landmines were planted beneath the ground. They were connected with long electric wires which were to be joined to a battery concealed at a considerable distance. According to the plan a bomb was

to be exploded in that house. Naturally top police and military officers and administrative officials would rush there for investigation. These three landmines were to be exploded when the house and the premises would be full of these officers and the accompanying personnel, in order to kill most of them at one blow. The revolutionary leadership had decided that about 10 *maunds* of gun-powder for landmines need to be manufactured. Also one *maund* of acid was to be brought from Calcutta. To give actual shape to the plan a lot of money was also needed in addition to the above material. Masterda had collected the entire money and gave it to us.

Comrades Apurba Sen, Nibaran Ghosh, Prafulla Mallik, Pramod Dasgupta (Bhulu), Prabhat Dutt, Arun Dastidar and some other young men, of tender age but of uncommon daring and patriotism, had, with great alertness and tact coupled with a death-defying spirit and in spite of the night curfew in force in entire Chittagong, planted the landmines at the different specified places assiduously digging up the soil and then deftly covering the landmines again with the soil.

To implement such an extensive and gigantic plan of a second round of the Chittagong Uprising, so many tender-aged, hard-working and patriotic spirited youths carried out a variety of activities so assiduously and at such a heavy risk that there seems to be hardly a parallel to this in the entire history of the Bengal revolutionary movement. The following young comrades of ours—Kalikinker Dey, Anil Rakshit, Ashu De, Rikhal Sakha Basak, Anil De, Apurba Sen, Sushil Sen, Prafulla Mallik, Rabi Sen and others—had worked day and night with great industry and determination for about 7-8 months to manufacture the needed 10 *maunds* of gun-powder and succeed in their task.

Comrades Fakir Roy Choudhury, Benu Ghosal, Ramani Banerji, Chitta Sen. Madhu Guha, Bankim

Mazumdar, Bishweshwar Choudhury, Sarat Kanungo, Rabi Acharya and the like had also made considerable contribution towards the implementation of this extensive plan during 1930-31. At that time the entire responsibility for the town organization devolved on the shoulders of Sachin Sen (Manda). He played quite an important role in all these activities. As per the advice of Masterda he used to select hard-working and appropriately talented youths and hand them over to me for the work of implementing the plan.

At the end of 1930 Kebalda (Manoranjan Sen) had very secretly procured 8 TNT bombs, some gun cotton and some amount of money from Calcutta and brought them over to Chittagong. I had taken him to the secret shelter of Masterda. Kebalda gave all these things to Masterda and told him that Kalpana Dutt, Pritilata and a few other girls were quite eager to actively participate in revolutionary work. Among them Kalpana had especially come along with him to Chittagong enthusiastic to take up some responsibility. With Masterda's permission. Kalpana wanted to leave Calcutta with out delay and join the Chittagong College. At that time, despite the uncommon repression and surveillance by the military and the police, no particular suspicions were as yet entertained on women. As such several important tasks in connection with the proposed second round of the uprising could be performed by girls. Hence Masterda decided to take work from girls too and asked Kebalda to keep Kalpana in contact with me. As per Masterda's direction Kalpana left Bethune College in Calcutta and joined Chittagong College. She had played an active part in the preparatory activity in connection with the proposed second round of Chittagong Uprising through my medium.

Kalpana Dutt was entrusted with the task of procuring the much-needed Nitric and Sulphuric acids for the manufacture of gun-cotton and explosives. She too, defying all dangers and risks, had collected and brought to Chittagong about one *maund* of the required acids from Calcutta. Renu Roy and Kamala Banerji had actively helped Kalpana in procuring the acids. Under the directions of Kalpana Dutt, and in her company. Nibaran Ghosh and Nani Das had successfully evaded police surveillance and brought all those acid bottles neatly packed inside a trunk to Chittagong.

At the same time we assiduously engaged our selves in the work of manufacturing ammunition (gun powder) for the landmines, and also the landmines, amidst the intense surveillance and searches conducted by the Army, the Police and the Intelligence personnel all over Chittagong. We used to manufacture these in a desolate house near the Patharghat Brick-field, in the house of Subodh Roy in the village Kumira, in the village house of Rakhal Sakha Basak on the other side of the Karnaphuli river, and especially in the house of Kalikinker Dey and his paternal uncle, Nisi Dey, in the southern side of the town. We had received unparalleled active cooperation from the inmates of the houses referred to. And then, Binodini *mashima* (martyr Rajat Sen's mother) and Manorama *mashima* (martyr Debu's mother) had extended whole-hearted cooperation and rendered active help in all our revolutionary work. At that time we used to keep many fire-arms and explosives in Binodini *mashima's* house in her safe custody.

Inspector Killed in Mistake For the I.G.P.

While our case was under trial Anantda, and Ganeshda received the news that Mr. Craig, the Chief of Bengal police, had come to Chittagong and that he would be leaving Chittagong by train on 1 December 1930. Immediately as they received this news both of them, when we all met in the court, directed me to contact Masterda forthwith and convey their message to him that they desired that Mr. Craig should not be allowed to go back to Calcutta alive and accordingly requested Masterda to make arrangements immediately for an attack on Mr. Craig. As per their instructions I went to meet Masterda the same night in a very secret manner and conveyed the message to him. As per the plan prepared by the Jail comrades and Masterda, Ramkrishna Biswas and Kalipada Chakravarthy had come to Chittagong town after dusk the following day itself. Both were absconding rebels—proclaimed offenders—on whose heads the government had already announced handsome rewards. Arrangements were made to send them unseen by anybody by a train bound for Calcutta from a small Railway Station outside Chittagong town. They managed to board the train harmlessly and right in the compartment adjacent to that in which Mr. Craig was travelling.

In the early hours of 1 December 1930 at about 4 a.m. the train halted at Chandpur Railway Station. There was a dense fog in that cold winter night and it was difficult to see things even from a little distance. Darkners all round added to it. Ramakrishna and Kalipada quickly came near the compartment of Craig as soon as the train stopped, and stood ready with loaded revolvers in their hands on the railway platform. Within a few moments an officer exactly resembling Mr. Craig and wearing a uniform quite all that of Craig, got down from that compartment. Immediately Ramakrishna and Kalipada fired at him and quickly fled away from the place vanishing in the darkness. That officer, Tarini Charan Mukherji. Inspector of Police and body-guard of Mr. Craig, was fatally injured and fell down on the spot. Ramakrishna and Kalipada managed to go out of the town to the rural areas, but in vain. They were caught within a few hours. They were not sent to Chittagong, but to Calcutta Jail. A Special

Tribunal which tried them awarded capital punishment to Ramakrishna Biswas and life imprisonment to Kalipada Chakravarthy. Ramakrishna Biswas was hanged on the gallows in the Alipore Central Jail on 8 August 1931.

Sarat Chandra Bose's Contribution

Sarat Chandra Bose, elder brother of Netaji Subhas Chandra Bose, a renowned. Advocate and a highly revered leader, had taken up the cudgels of our defence and came to Chittagong a few times in 1930 to argue for us in the Armoury Raid case. One day he told me very secretly that he had a proposal to be conveyed to Masterda Surya Sen. It was as follows: It was incumbent on all of us to protect the life of so important a leader as Masterda. Hence if Masterda consented he (Sarat Bose) would certainly make the necessary arrangements to send him safely out of India to a safe place in some foreign land. I conveyed that proposal of Sarat Chandra Bose to Masterda. On hearing that Masterda replied:

> Please convey my reverent greetings to Sarat Babu. Then tell him that our goal is still quite far off. I have till now sacrificed 20 colleagues of mine at the altar of the motherland and do not know how many more may be sacrificedl in the days to come. In such a situation it is impossible for me to leave Chittagong, the field of my activity, and to go anywhere else for my safety. I have decided to go on fighting here only till the end of my life.

I duly conveyed this reply of Masterda to Sarat Chandra Bose who was non-plussed and greatly impressed by it. So much so that when he came to Chittagong for the last time he took out 4 fresh TNT bombs and two thousand rupees from his suitcase, handed them over to me and said: "Please give these to Masterda and tell him that this is but a token-gift of mine for him on being greatly impressed by his reply my proposal. Please convey my profound regard for him." On receiving this present Masterda became spell-bound and asked me to convey his boundless regard for the profound patriotism and uncommon daring of Sarat Bose.

From September 1930 to May 1931 we were completely engaged in intense activity in connection with the proposal for a second round of Chittagong Uprising, and almost the entire work in connection with it was completed by us with great perseverance, exclusive attention and assiduous labour. Some time in May the date and time for the proposed attack was also decided upon. The landmines placed under the ground at various places were connected with long wire connections to be joined to the batteries at considerable distances. But unfortunately on one afternoon towards the end of May 1931 when all the revolutionary prisoners were gone to the court for trial, the District Magistrate, the Superintendent of the jail the Superintendent of Police and several other officers searched the whole Jail premises thoroughly, dug up the ground at many places and seized all the landmines and other things hidden under the soil by the revolutionaries in their attempt to effect a jail-break as a part of the second round of Chittagong Uprising.

Then, in the early hours of 3 June 1931 Nibaran Ghosh was unfortunately caught with a landmine in his possession. Consequently the police made hectic investigations conducted extensive searches all over the town and unearthed one by one all the landmines which were planted at various places. The following day the police surrounded Nisi Dey's house in the early hours and arrested Sushil Sen, Prafulla Mallik and myself. However, Apurba Sen and Kalikinker Dey managed to escape from the police dragnet. With that the plan to terrorise and paralyse the district administration by simultaneous explosions of several landmines at various centres of the town was foiled.

It was true that all the efforts of the revolutionaries had, in the end, gone futile, but the imperialist authorities too had become quite panicky and terrified on considering the entire sequence of events and the probable consequences that might have ensued had not the plan, fortunately for them, been foiled at the eleventh hour. They realized that the policy of violent repression adopted by them would only provoke the revolutionaries to further and defiant resistance. Hence before instituting a case on us they met Anantda and Ganeshda in Jail, talked quite sweetly with them and put forward a compromise proposal on their own. On considering that proposal our leaders submitted a counter-proposal. After a few days of deep consideration the government authorities of the district consented to our leaders, counter proposal and a compromise was arrived at. As a result only eight among us twelve accused in the Dynamite Conspiracy case were convicted, that too to short terms of imprisonment, after a nominal trial by the Special Tribunal. [As a part of the Compromise Deal, none among the accused in the First Armoury Raid Trial were sentenced to death, mainly because the prosecution did not plead for the award of the same—Ed.]

[*Courtesy: Smaranika*, Calcutta, 18 January 1987.]

(Courtesy– Easter Rabellion in India. The Chittagong Uprising—by I. M. Sharma– Marxist Study Forum, Hydrabad, 1993)

Dynamite Conspiracy Case Judgment

Special Tribunal - Chittagong

Emperor
Versus

1. Nibaran Ghosh
2. Chandra Kumar Bose
3. Ardhendu Sekhar Guha
4. Prafulla Ranjan Mallik
5. Sushil Kumar Sen
6. Nishi De
7. Rabindra Narayan Sen
8. Prabhat Ranjan Dutta
9. Hriday Ranjan Das
10. Ashutosh De
11. Anil Kumar Rakshit

Charges: Sec. 120 (b) I.P.C.
Sec. 4 (b) & 5, Explosive Substances Act

Finding—The Sentences

Each of the accused Nibaran Ghosh, Rabindra Narayan Sen, [Ardhendu Guha, Sushil Sen, Prafulla Mallik], Prabhat Ranjan Dutta and Anil Kumar Rakshit plead guilty to the two charges framed u/s 120(b) I.P.C. & read with Sec. 5 of the Explosive Substances Act (Act VI of 1908). We accept their plea of guilty and find each of the aforesaid accused guilty on the said two charges and convict them thereon. The accused stated that they did not wish to be defenced by any pleader but the learned P.P. very fairly placed before us certain arguments and facts whereby he urged that the sentences on these accused should not be severe. He has commented on the fact that the accused are all of immature age and that no actual loss of life or damage to property had been caused; he prays that the accused may be given a chance to mend their ways and become useful citizens. We have carefully considered all the elements of the case and the arguments of the learned P.P. Although there has been no actual loss or damage to property, nevertheless we cannot ignore the seriousness of the conspiracy or shut our eyes to the terrible consequences which would have resulted but for the timely and smart arrest of the accused Nibaran. In our opinion the accused Nibaran Ghosh and Rabindra Narayan Sen were deeply involved and Ardhendu Guha was the leader of this conspiracy. We accordingly sentence each of them to undergo R.I. for a term of 3 years on each of the aforesaid two charges. The sentences shall run concurrently. Of the four remaining accused it appears that Prabhat and Anil Rakshit took a very minor part whereas Sushil Sen and Prafulla Mallik were more involved. We accordingly sentence Sushil Sen and Prafulla Mallik to undergo R.I. for two years on each of the said charges, the sentences to run concurrently. The accused Prabhat Dutta and Anil Rakshit are sentenced to undergo R.I. for a term of 8 months on each of the said charges, the sentences to run concurrently.

The learned P.P. prays for permission to withdraw from the prosecution of the charges against the accused Chandra Kumar Bose, Nishi De and Ashutosh De. He has placed certain facts before us and we are of opinion that the evidence against them justifies us in according this permission. We therefore give him permission to so withdraw. The accused Chandra Kumar Bose, Nishi De and Ashutosh De are acquitted of the Charges framed against them. We direct them to be set at liberty forthwith.The trial shall proceed against the accused Hriday Ranjan Das.

Sd/-A.N. Sen, President. ; Sd/- Abu Ali Choudhury.
Sd/- Bipin Behari Mukherjee

Commissioners, Special Tribunal, Chittagong

Dated, Chittagong, the 29th September 1931.

Chittagong Uprising: Roll of Honour

Glory be to the patriotic sons of our motherland—the great revolutionaries of Chittagong who fell martyrs!

S.No.	*Name*	*Age*	*Date of Death*	*Short Biographical Sketch*
1.	Pramod Ranjan Choudhury	25 yrs.	28 Sept 1926	Born in 1901 at Kelisahr, Dt. Chittagong. Son of Ishan Chandra Choudhury. Though in Anushilan he was an intimate colleague of Masterda aslo. Arrested and imprisoned in the Dakshineshwar Bomb Case, he along with Anant Hari Mitra and others attacked and killed the notorious Special Superintendent of D.I.B., Bhupendranath Chatterji in the Presidency Jail (New Central Jail) on 28.5.1926. Charged for murder, sentenced to death and hanged along with Anant Hari Mitra and Birendra in Alipore Central Jail on 28.9.1926.
2.	Anurup Chandra Sen	34 yrs.	1928	Of the same age as and an intimate colleague of, Surya Sen. He founded and organized the revolutionary party in Chittagong in 1918 along with Surya Sen and three others. He wrote the constitution of the Chittagong Revolutionary Organization. He was an Assistant Head Master in a High School at Barul, 24 Paraganas. Masterdra used to take his advice regarding all important matters. He was arrested by the Government of Bengal in 1926 and interned in an unhealthy village in North Bengal for about 2 years. He was afflicted with a dangerous. Disease while interned there but his repeated petitions for release from internment on health grounds were dismissed offhand and he was transferred to Kashi instead. There he died due to the disease in 1928.

3.	Sukhendu Dutt	16 yrs.	October 1929	Son of Sarada Charan Dutt. Was quite an intelligent student in School. Became a member of Masterda's revolutionary party in 1928. Was stabbed and got seriously injured by goondas at the time of the elections to the District Congress Committee of Chittagong in 1929, and was immediately taken to, and got admitted in, Belghachia Hospital on the instructions of Subhas Babu. Expired in October 1929 in the same Hospital.
4.	Hari Gopal Bal (Tegra)	14 yrs.	22 April 1930	Born at Village Kanungopara, Dt. Chittagong. Son of Pran Krishna Bal; brother of Lokenath Bal. Was a student of 9th Class in school when he participated in the Uprising. Washetfind and youngest martyr to fall in the battle of Jalalabad on 22.4.1930. His final words were: "Comrades! I am passing away. But you continue the fight!"
5.	Tripura Sen	17 yrs.	22 April 1930	Born on 12 May 1913. Resident of Comilla. Son of Nibaran Chandra Sen (Gupta). Was a Lieutenant in the Congress Volunteer Corps in Chittagong which was actually organized by the revolutionary party. Participated in the Uprising on 18 April, 1930. Fought heroically in the battle of Jalalabad firing unintermittently at the enemy, but was unfortunately hit by the enemy bullets and died on the spot.
6.	Nirmal Lala	14 yrs.	22 April 1930	Born at Village Haola, Chittagong Dt. Son of Jatra Mohan Lala. Was of the same age as Tegra and a school pupil like him. Participated in the Armoury Raid on 18 April. Fell in the battle of Jalalabad on 22 April.
7.	Bidhu Bhushan Bhattacharya	24 yrs	22 April 1930	Was a gold-medalist of Chittagong Medical School having passed the Doctor's course with distinction. He was firmly and untiringly

				firing at the enemy in the battle-field of Jalalabad, **when suddenly** several machine gun bullets hit him on the legs and different parts of the body. He immediately called out his younger brother and comrade-in-arms, Naresh, saying: "I am passing away. You take my position!" Within a few moments thereafter he embraced death.
	Naresh Roy	24 yrs.	22 April 1930	Resident of Village Noapara, Chittagong dt. Son of Girish Chandra Roy. Passed the Doctor's course from Chittagong Medical School. Was one of the leaders of the squad sent to attack Chittagong European Club on the night of the uprising on 18 April. He was till then in-charge of the revolutionary party's counter-intelligence wing. He laid down his life in the battle of Jalalabad.
9.	Sashanka Sekhar Datta	18 yrs.	22 April 1930	Born at Village Dengapara, Chittagong dt. Son of Nabin Chandra Datta. Was a first Year Student in Chittagong College. Participated in the attack on the Police Lines Armoury on the night of 18 April. Fell in the battle of Jalalabad.
10.	Madhusudan Dutt	24 yrs.	22 April, 1930	Born at Village Bidgram at Chittagong. Son of Manindra Kumar Dutt. Was the organizer of the revolutionary party in the rural areas. He had brought the gun of his father along with him and participated in the 18 April Uprising. Fell a martyr in the battle of Jalalabad on 22 April.
11.	Pulin Chandra Ghosh	18 yrs.	22 April, 1930	Born at village Gossaidanga, dt. Chittagong, Son of Jagat Chandra Ghosh. Participated in the raid on Police Lines. Laid down his life in the battle of Jalalabad.
12.	Jitendralal Dasgupta	19 yrs.	22 April 1930	Born at village Dhalghat, dt, Chittagong. Participated in the raid on the Police Lines Armoury on 18 April. Killed by enemy bullets in the battle of Jalalabad.

14.	Matilal Kanungo	18 yrs.	23 April 1930	Born in 1913 at village Kanungopara, dt. Chittagong. Son of Durga Mohan Kanungo. Participated in the attack on the Police Lines Armoury. Was quite seriously injured in the battle of Jalalabad and was lying unconscious even on the next day when the British authorities without properly checking whether he died or not had consigned his body to flames along with ten other dead comrades in a mass cremation on the top of the Jalalabad hill.
15.	Ardhendu Dastidar	20 yrs.	24 April 1930	Born at village Dhalghat, dt. Chittagong. Son of Chandra Kumar Dastidar. A few days before the uprising he had been injured in an accidental explosion while engaged in the manufacture of bombs. But even though he was not all well he enthusiastically participated in the raid on the Police Lines Armoury on 18 April. He was very critically injured in the battle of Jalalabad and was lying unconcious atop the hill when the British forces coming the next day found him alive and sent him to Chittagong Sadar Hospital for treatment. However, he breathed his last in the Hospital on 24.4.30.
16.	Himangshu Sen (Andu)	15 Yrs.	1 May 1930	Born in 1915 at Barahatia, dt. Chittagong. Son of Chandra Kumar Sen. Was a student of 9th Class in school. He was one among the four young men who attacked the Police Lines Armoury on the night of 18 April 1930 under the leadership of Anant Singh and Ganesh Ghosh. Within a short time thereafter he also went along with Anant Singh in a car to the A.F.I. Armoury at Pahartali in order to aid the squads under Lokenath Bal and Nirmal Sen there. Then, on return to the Police Lines Armoury from there he went forward to set fire to the broken arms heap after pouring petrol on it and in that course got quite seriously burnt. It was in an effort to immediately hospitalize him that Anant Singh, Ganesh Ghosh

				and two others got separated from the main revolutionary army in that night (and, alas, could never join it again). Himangshu could, however, not recover. He was arrested from a house at Chandanpura, Chittagong, and imprisoned. Died in the Chittagong District Jail Hospital on 1 May 1930.
17.	Amarendralal Nandi	20 yrs.	24 April 1930	Born at Dengapara, dt. Chittagong. Son of Rasiklal Nandi. Was selected and taken in the squad sent to attack the European Club on the day of the uprising. Was sent by Masterda to the town to collect some important information as well as to try contact the separated Comrades—Anant Singh, Ganesh Ghosh and others. However, could not again contact Masterda and join the revolutionary army. Was hiding in the town when he was suddenly surrounded by the enemy. Fled and hid in a culvert, but found out there also. Refused to surrender and committed suicide.
18.	Swadesh Ranjan Roy	20 yrs.	6 May 1930	Resident of Dacca. Worked as a private contractor in Chittagong. Was not among the comrades initially selected for participation in the uprising but was inspired and moved to action by reading the leaflets distributed on the night of the uprising came running to the Police Lines and joined the revolutionary army on his own. Thereafter participated actively in the battle of Jalalabad too. He laid down his life in the clash of arms at Kalarpole on 6 May 1930 along with three other comrades-in-arms.
19.	Rajat Kumar Sen	19 yrs.	6 May 1930	Born 1911. Son of Ranjanlal Sen. Was first year student in Chittagong College when he plunged into the uprising. Was selected for the raid on the Auxilliary Force Armoury. Participated in the battle of Jalalabad on 22 April too. Fell in the encounter at Kalarpole on 6 May.

20.	Debaprasad Gupta	20 yrs.	6 May 1930	Born in December, 1911, at Chittagong. Son of Jogendranath Gupta. Second year student in Chittagong College. Was one among the first six-man assault squad on the Police Lines Armoury in Chittagong on 18 April 1930. Participated in the battle of Jalalabad on 22 April and laid down his life in the clash of arms at Kalarpole on 6 May.
21.	Manoranjan Sen	19 yrs.	6 May 1930	Born in 1911 at village Barma, dt. Chittagong. Son of Rajanikanta Sen. Actively participated in the uprising on 18 April and also in the battle of Jalalabad on 22 April. Died in the encounter at Kalarpole.
22.	Jibanlal Ghoshal (Makhan)	18 yrs.	2 September 1930	Born in 1912 at Sadarghat, Chittagong. Son of Jasoda Ghosal. Participated in the uprising on 18 April. Escaped from Police clutches in the shoot-out at Feni on (22/23 April) along with Anant Singh, Ganesh Ghosh and Ananda Gupta. Was killed in the Chandannagar encounter with police led by Mr. Tegarin the early hours of 2 September.
23.	Subodh Dey	18 yrs.	15 April 1931	Born 1913 in Chittagong. Died in Calcutta Presidency Jail as a result of police torture on 15.4.31.
24.	Ramakrishna Biswas	21 yrs.	4 August 1931	Born 1910. A meritorious student receiving scholarship of Chittagong College. Could not participate in the uprising on 18 April since he was injured in an accidental bomb-explosion a short period prior to that while he was clandestinely manufacturing bombs. Along with Kalipada Chakravarthy, shot at and killed Inspector Tarini Mukherji at Chandpur Railway Station in mistake for the I.G.P. on the night of 1.12.1930. Tried for the murder, sentenced to death and hanged on the gallows at

				Alipur Central Jail on 4.8.31. Was a great source of inspiration and example to Pritilata Waddedar, the first woman-martyr of *Agni Yug*.
25.	Apurba Sen (Bhola)	17 yrs.	13 June 1932	Born at village Chhatradandi, dt. Chittagong. Son of Harish Chandra Sen. Was a reliable follower and body-guard of Masterda. Actively and dedicatedly participated in the Dynamite Conspiracy. Was killed by military bullets while he was leading Masterda and Pritilata out of enemy encriclement at Dhalghat on the night of 13.6.32.
26.	Nirmal Kumar Sen	31 yrs.	13 June 1932	Born in 1900 at village Guchhi, dt. Chittagong. Son of Rasik Sen. Was a first-rank member of the Chittagong revolutionary organization since the time of its inception in 1918. Went to Burma in 1920 for securing arms and ammunition. Took part in the Non-Cooperation Movement (1921). Was arrested and detained under the Bengal Ordinance in 1925 and released in 1928. Was one of the main leaders of the Chittagong Uprising. The raid on the Auxiliary Force Armoury at Pahartali was successfully accomplished under the joint leadership of Lokenath Bal and Nirmal Sen on the night of 18 April. Participated in the battle of Jallalabad on 22 April and rendered precious help to the fighters by repairing, cleaning and lubricating the jammed muskets with skill and perserverence. Afterwards led an underground life along with Masterda and was a right-hand man of his in all activities. Shot at and killed Captain Cameron in Dhalghat when suddenly surrounded by the military under him. However, himself got fatally hit by enemy bullets in that process.

27.	Pratilata Waddedar	21 yrs.	24 Sept. 1932	Born on 5 May 1911 at village Goalpara, dt. Chittagong. Daughter of Jagat Bandhu Waddedar. Was a member of the women's organization known as Dipali Sangha at Dacca and Chhatri Sangha at Calcutta. First woman-martyr of the *Agni Yug*. Met Ramakrishna Biswas in the condemned cells in Alipore Jail several times before his hanging and was inspired by his example for self-immolation in the cause of revolution. Surrounded by the military in the house of Savitri Chakravarthy at Dhalghat, along with Surya Sen and others. Escaped arrest along with Masterda and remained underground. Led the attack on the European Club at Pahartali on the night of 24.9.32 successfully and immediately thereafter committed suicide by consuming nectar (potassium cyanide). Her dead body found lying at the Club Gate by the police who also recovered 'An Appeal to Women' from her person.
28.	Manoranjan Dasgupta	20 yrs.	19 May 1933	Became active after the uprising and led an underground life due to police hunt. Was hiding in Gahira along with Tarakeshwar Dastidar and Kalpana Dutt when their shelter was suddenly surrounded by Jat military. Was the first to notice encirclement and warn comrades. Heroically participated in the ensuing encounter but was fatally shot at while trying to break out of the cordon. Died on the spot.
29.	Purna Talukdar	60 Yrs.	19 May 1933	Old man of 60 yrs. age belonging to a prosperous peasant family of village Gahira. Taking all risks sheltered Tarakeshwar Dastidar, Kalpana Dutt and others in his house. Shot dead in cold blood by the military in the morning of 19.5.33 in the encounter between the revolutionaries and the military.

30.	Saileshwar Chakravarthy	....	10 August 1932	Born at village Dewanpur, dt. Chittagong. Son of Ratneshwar Chakravarthy. Participated in the Uprising on 18 April. Also fought in the battle of Jalalabad on 22 April. Was entrusted with the leadership of the squad meant to attack the Pahartali European Club on 10 August 1932. However, the attack did not materialize at all and overcome by a sense of remorse and anguish he committed suicide the same night.
31.	Nityaranjan Sen	17 Yrs.	7 January 1934	Was an intelligent school pupil prior to the Uprising on 18 April. At that time efforts were made to recruit him into the revolutionary party but in vain, since at that time he was mere concerned about his future career. However, the subsequent uprising and the heroic sacrifices of several martyrs inspired him greatly and the once unwilling gem of a boy now began to take all interest and totally dedicated himself to the work of the party. Was one among the squad of four revolutionary young men who attacked top European officers in a Cricket Ground in Chittagong with bombs and a revolver. Was shot dead by the military at the scene of attack.
32.	Himangshu Chakravarthy	....	7 January 1934	Joined the revolutionary party in his school days inspired by the heroic Chittagong Uprising on 18 April. In order to avenge the sentence of death passed on Masterda and Tarakeshwar Dastidar he along with three other comrades attacked top European officers with bombs and a revolver in the Chittagong Cricket Club Ground on 7 January 1934 five days prior to Masterda's hanging. Was shot dead at the scene of action.
33.	Surya Ranjan Sen	40 yrs.	12 January 1934	Born at Noapara, dt. Chittagong. Son of Rajmani Sen. Graduate in Arts. Worked as a teacher in the Umatara High School, Chittagong. Great Leader of the Chittagong Rebellion; a top leader of Indian.

Armed Revolutionary Movement; First President of the Provisional. Revolutionary Government of Free Chittagong. Born 22 March 1894. One of the founders of the Chittagong Revolutionary Organization in 1918. Was arrested encounter at Nagarkhana Hill in 1923, but later released due to lack of evidence against him. After release foiled the efforts of the Police to re-arrest him under Bengal Ordinance and escaped to Calcutta. In 1925 he was surrounded by the police while taking shelter in the Shobabazar den but managed to escape with the help of other comrades. Like this he was underground for about 2 years conducting organizational activities in different districts of Bengal and sometimes outside Bengal too. He was arrested in 1926, detained under Regn. III of 1818 and released in the end of 1928. After release participated in the Calcutta Congress and there after took the reins of Chittagong District Congress in his hands. Organized a Congress Volunteer Corps in Chittagong too, but with a view to utilize the picked cadets in it for an armed uprising. Gave his consent to the plan for an armed revolt already worked out by Anant Singh and Ganesh Ghosh. Was the Supreme Commander of the Chittagong Uprising of 18 April 1930. Directed Lokenath Bal to command the revolutionary army in the battle of Jalalabad and himself discharged a very important and risky job during that battle on 22 April. After that battle caused the dispersal of the revolutionary army in the rural areas in small squads and directed a long-drawn struggle for preservation of the movement and directed occasional guerilla attacks by the revolutionaries. Led a long underground life in that process and managed to escape along with Pritilata in the Dhalghat Encounter on 13 June 1932 in

				which his close comrade-in-arms, Nirmal Sen, and reliable follower and bodyguard, Bhola, were killed. Finally arrested at Gairala on 16 February 1933. Tried along with Tarakeshwar Dastidar and Kalpana Dutt in the Chittagong Armoury Raid Supplementary Case and sentenced to death along with Tarakeswar. Hanged along with Tarakeswar on 12 January 1934 in Chittagong Jail.
34.	Tarakeshwar Dastidar	26 yrs.	12 January 1934	Born 1908 at village Saroatali, dt. Chittagong. Son of Chandramohan Dastidar. Was a responsible organiser of the revolutionary party both before and after the Uprising on 18 April. Was seriously injured in an accidental explosion while manufacturing bombs a few days prior to the uprising and hence could not participate in the uprising. All the responsibilities of the revolutionary party devolved on his shoulders after the arrest of Masterda which he discharged with commendable efficiency. Was arrested in the Gahira encounter on 19 May 1933. Was hanged along with Masterda on 12 January 1934.
35.	Krishna Gopal Choudhury	22 yrs.	5 June 1934	Born in 1912 at Kelisahar, dt. Chittagong. Son of Hemendra Choudhury. Participated in the raid on Police Lines Armoury on the night of 18 April. Fought in the battle of Jalalabad on 22 April also. Led the attack by four member squad on the Europeans in the Cricket Club Ground in Chittagong on 7 January 1934. Injured in the shoot-out, caught, tried for the attack and hanged along with another comrade-in-arms, Haren Chakravarthy, on 5.6.34.
36.	Harendra Chakravarthy	16 yrs.	5 June 1934	Born at village Gairala, dt. Chittagong. Son of Kalikumar Chakravarthy. While studying in school was inspired by the 18 April Uprising and joined the revolutionary party. Participated in the attack on Europeans in the Cricket Ground on 7 January 1934

				in order to avenge the death sentences on Masterda and Tarakeshwar Dastidar. Was seriously injured by enemy bullets in that course, caught, tried and hanged along with Krishna Choudhury on 5.6.34.
37.	Biren Dey	21 yrs.	March 1931	Born in a very poor family. Participated in the attack on Telephone Bhavan under the leadership of Ambica Chakravarthy on the night of 18 April 1930. Also participated in the battle of Jalalabad on 22 April. Afterwards led an underground life in the rural areas in contact of Masterda and was training new members in the use of arms. In this course he was seriously injured one day while teaching a boy how to use a fire-arm. Lack of proper and prompt treatment resulted in septicity and ultimately led to his death in March 31. He thus laid down his life on the alter of freedom largely unknown to the people.
38.	Sukumar Kanuago	16 yrs.	August 1931	Tender aged school pupil. Came into contact with the underground revolutionaries after the Uprising and joined the revolutionary party. In August 1931, while target-practising with a revolver a bullet pierced into his head due to a slight negligence. He at once dropped dead on the spot. His young comrades-in-arms who were present there took away his dead body to a desolate place on a hill and buried it there.
39.	Yashoda Pal	...	March 1928	Born at Comilla. Served in the Bengali Platoon during First World War. After War she imparted training in arms to the Chittagong revolutionaries. She was arrested in 1924 on the charge of manufacturing powerful bombs at Manicktala and was convicted to 7 years imprisonment. Was afflicted with T.B. in jail. Breathed her last in March 28.

No.	Name	Age	Date	Details
40.	Rajani Sen	60 yrs.	September 1931	Was an attorney in Chittagong Court. Father of Martyr Manoranjan Sen who laid down his life in the clash of arms at Kalarpole. After the murder of the atrocious D.S.P., Ahsanullah, the police surrounded their house, caught hold of Chittaranjan, younger brother of Rajat Sen, and began to severely beat him up. This old father could not tolerate it and firmly objected to the devillish conduct of the police whereupon he himself was heavily struck on the chest by the European Sergeant Kelly. His old physique could not withstand that heavy blow and Rajani Sen immediately dropped down in agonising pain. The very next day he expired.
41.	Sarojkanti Choudhury	...	1932	A calm and clever school pupil. Inspired by the Chittagong Uprising he joined Masterda's revolutionary party. He served as a link between Masterda and the revolutionary organization in Chittagong town. Suspecting his secret activities police used to harass him by repeasted interrogation in police lock-up. Finally one day in 1932 he was taken to the police station and tortured so severely that each and every limb of his body was battered. Thereafter sensing that he was about to die police took his half-dead body and threw it away in front of his house. Within an hour or so of that he breathed his last.
42.	Dhirendralal Badua	...	1932	Belonged to a middle class family in Chittagong. A school pupil and a follower of Buddhism and *ahimsa*. Yet under the inspiration of the Chittagong Uprising joined the revolutionary party. Was arrested in 1931 and imprisoned. Resisted the atrocities inside the jail and broke the jail rules. For that he was severely tortured inside jail and as a consequence succumbed to the physical injuries sometime in 1932.

43.	Shyam Kumar Nandi	...	27 Nov. 1932	Killed by the police on 27.11.32.
44.	Suresh Banik	...	1933	His house was a safe shelter for all underground revolutionaries of Chittagong. Masterda used to fondly call hm 'Passenger'. He was arrested and convicted on the charge of giving shelter to the revolutionaries. While in jail he was seriously afflicted with small-pox. Instead of arranging for his treatment the jail authorities callously consigned him to a dungeon. This aggravated his condition and in a short time he succumbed to the disease. This was a case of intentional murder by the British authorities.
45.	Phanindra Bhushan Bhattacharya	...	1934	Belonged to village Durgapur. Was an important organizer in Durgapur area. Was arrested on the charge of sheltering absconding revolutionaries of the Chittagong Uprising. Died in jail in 1934.
46.	Bipin Chandra Das	...	1934	Village Nawabpur, Chittagong district. Was a genuine sympathiser of the revolutionaries. Sheltered several underground revolutionaries in his house. Was arrested on the same charge in 1934 and was severely tortured in the police lock-up. As a result died in police custody.
47.	Sahay Sampad Choudhury	...	1934	A school pupil. Joined the revolutionary party being inspired by the heroic 18 April Uprising. Arrested in 1930 and thrown into jail. Died in imprisonment in 1934.
48.	Ashwini Kumar Guha	...	26 June 1934	Born at village Noapara, Chittagong district. Was a school teacher. Joined the revolutionary party and became a good organiser. Arrested in 1931 and imprisoned. Developed symptoms of insanity in jail and hence transferred to the Ranchi Lunatic Asylum. Committed suicide there on 26.6.34.

49.	Rohini Badua	20 Yrs.	18 Dec. 1935	Belonged to a Buddhist family of Chittagong. Born in 1915. He was detained without trial in 1932 first in jail and then in a detention camp. Later interned in a village under Goyalandghat P.S., Faridpur dt. Harassed and humiliated by the Sub-Inspector of Police in charge of that P.S. Attacked and killed that S.I., Syed Ershad Ali, in the office room of the Goyaland P.S. on 15 June 1935. Tried for that murder, boldly confessed and sentenced to death. Refused to pray for mercy. Hanged in Faridpur Jail on 18.12.35.
50.	Nirendralal Bhattacharya	...	27 Feb. 1936	Born at village Jaishthapura, Chittagong dt. Son of Sashi Kumar Bhattacharya. Was a student of 10th Class in the Saroyatali High School. Was arrested for sheltering and aiding in various ways, the underground revolutionaries of Chittagong. Detained in 1933. Exasperated by the atrocities in the detention camp committed suicide in Hijli Detention Camp on 27.2.1936.
51.	Brajendralal Choudhury	18 yrs.	1936	Born in 1918 at village Kanungopara, Chittagong dt. Son of Chaitanya Kumar Choudhury. Joined the revolutionary party inspired by the 18 April Uprising. Was arrested under the Bengal Ordinance on the charge of sheltering, and actively aiding, the underground revolutionaries of Chittagong. Committed suicide in Berhampore Jail being exasperated by the atrocities of the Jail Officers (in 1936).
52.	Mahendralal Biswas	60 yrs.	1936	Born at Khodurkhil, Chittagong dt. Head of a middle class family. His house served as a reliable den for Masterda and his comrades. Police raided it several times but were never able to arrest any underground revolutionary. Out of this anger he was arrested and imprisoned. In jail he went on hunger-strike for some just demands. Died in the course of that fast.

53.	Ramakrishna Chakravarthy	...	1937	Born at village Dhalghat, Chittagong dt. Son of Nabin Chakravarthy. Tender aged school pupil when he was attracted by the revolutionary movement. The only son of a widow-mother. A historic encounter occurred between the revolutionaries and the British forces at his house on 13 June 1932 in which Captain Cameron of the military and Nirmal Sen and Bhola of the revolutionaries were killed, and Masterda and Pritilata managed to escape. Arrested thereupon for giving shelter to Surya Sen and others, along with his mother Savitri Chakravarthy. Both were sentenced to 4 years' R.I. for that offence. Adolescent Ramakrishna was given the hardest job of extracting oil inside the jail. Due to excessive work burden and inferior quality of food given to ordinary convicts Ramakrishna's health got spoilt and he was afflicted with T.B. Succumbed to that dreaded disease in Midnapore Central Jail some time in 1937.
54.	Beharilal Badua	...	27 Nov 1937	Died in prison after police torture on 27.11.37.
55.	Mahesh Chandra Badua	30 yrs.	Jan. 1938	Born in 1908 at village Satbaria, dt. Chittagong. Son of Gour Kishore Barua. Took part in the Non-Cooperation Movement (1921) and Civil Disobedience Movement (1930). Joined the revolutionary party inspired by the Chittagong Uprising. Arrested for taking part in the Bathua political dacoity in 1933. Sentenced to transportation for life and deported to the Andamans. Repatriated in August 1936 and confined in the Rajshahi Central Jail. Died in Jail in January 1938.
56.	Phanindra Lal Nandi	...	1940	Born at village Dengapara, dt. Chittagong. Son of Banga Chandra Nandi. Participated in the raid on Paharatali A.F.I. Armoury on 18 April, Fought in the battle of Jalalabad. Later proceeded for an

				attack on Europeans at Sadarghat, Chittagong, along with Swadesh Roy and four others on 5 May 1930. The action could not take place and Dhani Nandi was caught near Kalarpole on their way of escape. Sentenced to transportation for life in the Chittagong Armoury Raid case and deported to the Andamans in March 1932. Afflicted with T.B. and repatriated. Intense efforts were made to secure his release on medical grounds and for good treatment but in vain. The British Government did not release him and due to the inferior quality of treatment in jail he died in prison in 1940.
57.	Haripada Mahajan	...	1940-41	One of the front-rank fighters who attacked the Police Lines Armoury on 18 April 1930. Participated in the battle of Jalalabad too. Led an underground life for about 10 years after the uprising in the adjoining territories of Burma. Died in an accident in 1940-41.
58.	Prabodh Kumar Majumdar	...	1942	Born at village Durgapur, dt. Chittagong. Member of the revolutionary party. Died in prison in 1942.
59.	Nani Bhattacharya	...	1943	Younger brother of Haripada Bhattacharjee who was transported to the Andamans for the murder of Ahsanullah. As a school pupil participated in the Quit India Movement in 1942 and was arrested and imprisoned. Contacted a dreaded disease in Dacca Jail due to the negligence of the Jail authorities and succumbed to it in 1943.
60.	Lalmohan Sen	32 yrs.	19 Oct. 1946	Born in 1914 at Musapur, Sandip, Noakhali district. Led a band of fighters to remove railway lines and cut off telegraphic wires near Dhoom Railway Station some 55 miles from Chittagong as a very

necessary preliminary operation for the Uprising on 18 April. Arrested, tried in the Chittagong Armoury Raid case along with Anant Singh, Ganesh Ghosh and others, sentenced to transportation for life on 1 March 1932 and deported to the Andamans. Participated in the two hunger-strikes in 1933 & 37 in the Cellular Jail; participated in another hunger-strike in Alipore Jail in July 1939 (for 45, 37, & 36 days respectively). Released on 31.8.1946. Within a short period thereafter while he was on a mission in the riot-torn areas of Noakhali district, killed by a frenzied communal mob on 19.10.46. Total jail period–more than 16 years.

(Courtesy–Easter Rebellion the Chittagong Uprising, by I.M. Sharma, Marxist Study Forum, Hyderabad, 1993).

Inter-Provincial Conspiracy Case

Name	*District*	*Province*	*Sentence*
Prabhat Chandra Chakrabartti.	Tippera and Calcutta	Bengal	Transportation for life. Jitendra Nath Gupta
	Faridpur and Calcutta	Bengal	Transportation for life.
Sitanath De	Faridpur	Benga	Transportation for life.
Narendra Prosad Ghosh	Mymensingh	Bengal	14 years' transportation.
Dhirendra Nath Bhattacharji	Tippera	Bengal	14 years' transportation
Purnananda Das Gupta	Dacca	Bengal	14 years' transportation
Kishori Mohan Das Gupta	Noakhali and Calcutta	Bengal	7 years R.I.
Manindra Lal Chaudhury	Chittagong	Bengal	7 years' R.I.
Paresh Guha	Dacca	Bengal	7 years' R.I.
Satyandra Narayan Majumdar	Jessore and Calcutta	Bengal	7 years' R.I.
Pravat Kumar Mitra	Hooghly and Calcutta	Bengal	7 years' R.I.
Jotin Chakrabartti	Tippera and Calcutta	Bengal	7 years' R.I.
Dwigendra Nath Talapattra	Rajshahi & Calcutta	Bengal	7 years' R.I.
Haripada De	Dacca and Calcutta	Bengal	7 years' R.I.
Niranjan Ghoshal	Faridpur	Bengal	7 years' R.I.
Amulya Chandra Sen Gupta	Dacca	Bengal	7 years' R.I.
Amiya Kumar Pal	Dacca and Calcutta	Bengal	7 years' R.I.
Hem Chandra Bhattacharji	Chittagong and Calcutta	Bengal	6 years' R.I.
Jyotish Chandra Majumdar	Tippera and Calcutta	Bengal	6 years' R.I.
Bimal Bhattacharji	Mymensingh and Calcutta	Bengal	6 years' R.I.
Surendra Dhar Chaudhuri	Tippera and Calcutta	Bengal	6 years' R.I.
Abani Mohan Bhattacharji	Tippera and Calcutta	Bengal	5 years' R.I.
Sudhir Chandra Bhattacharji	Tippera	Bengal	3 years' R.I.
Shyam Behari Lal Sukla	Shahjahanpore and Calcutta	Bengal and U.P.	3 years' R.I.
Santosh Chatarji	Faridpur and Calcutta	Bengal	3 years' R.I.
Sushil Kumar Roy Chakravarty	Faridpur	Bengal	3 years' R.I.
Indu Bhushan Majumdar	Barisal and Calcutta	Bengal	3 years' R.I.
Probodh Kumar Ghosh	Calcutta	Bengal	3 years' R.I.
Abani Ranjan Sarkar	Khulna	Bengal	1 year's R.I.

Political Trouble in India—H. W. Hale, Chug Publication, Allahabab, 1974, pp. 186-224.

Accused in the Main Inter Provincial Cases Mainpuri Conspiracy Case

Accused

Name	*District*	*Province*	*Sentence*
Gopi Nath	Jasrana	U.P.	7 years
Karhori Lal	Bewar	U.P.	3 years
Sidh Gopal	Chandrika	U.P.	5 years
Prabhakar	Alipur	U.P.	5 years
Chandradhar	Mainpuri	U.P.	5 years
Dammi Lal	Alipur	U.P.	7 years
Raja Ram	Deokali	U.P.	3 years
Kali Charan	Shahjahanpur	U.P.	Acquitted
Sheo Charan Lal	Etah	U.P.	5 years
Fateh Singh	Cawnpore	U.P.	5 years
Makundi	Etawah	U.P.	3 years
	Approvers		
Somdeo Sharma	Fyzabad	U.P.	
Dalpat Singh	Mainpuri	U.P.	

Kakori Case

Offences

1. Conspiracy.
2. Bamrauli dacoity.
3. Bichpuri dacoity.
4. Dwarkapur dacoity.
5. Kakori train dacoity.

Ram Prasad Bismil	Shahjahanpur	U.P.	Hanged
Ashfaqullah Khan	Shahjahanpur	U.P.	Hanged
Rajendra Nath Lahiri	Benares and Pabna	U.P. and Bengal	Hanged.
Roshan Singh	Shahjahanpur	U.P.	Hanged.
Jogesh Chandra Chatterji	Dacca	Bengal	Transportation for life.
Sachindra Nath Bakhshi	Benares and Jhansi	U.P.	Transportation for life.
Sachindra Nath Sanyal	Benares and Allahabad	U.P.	Transportation for life
Makundi Lal	Etawah	U.P.	Transportation for life
Govind Charan Kar alias D. N. Chaudhri	...	Bengal	Transportation for life
Manmotho Nath Gupta	Benares	U.P.	14 years' R.I.
Raj Kumar Singh	Cawnpore	U.P.	10 years' R.I.
Ram Kishan Khattri	Chanda	C.P.	10 years' R.L.
Suresh Chandra Bhattachariya	Cawnpore and Benares	U.P.	10 years' R.I.
Vishnu Saran Dublis	Meerut	U.P.	10 years' R.I.
Banwari Lal	Rae Bareli	U.P.	5 years' R.I.
Bhupendra Nath	Benares and	U.P.	5 years' R.I.

Sanyal	Allahabad.		
Prem Kishan Khanna	Shahjahanpur	U.P.	5 years' R.I.
Ram Dulare Trivedi	Cawnpore	U.P.	5 years' R.I.
Parnawesh Kumar Chatterji	Jubbulpore	C.P.	4 years' R.I.
Ram Nath Pande	Benares	U.P.	3 years' R.I.

Approvers

Benarsi Lal	Shahjahanpur	U.P.
Indu Bishan Mitra	Shahjahanpur	U.P.

Absconding

Chandar Shekhar	Benares	U.P.

Lahore Conspiracy Case No. 1 of 1930.

Accused

Bhagat Singh	Lahore	Punjab	Hanged.
Sukh Dev, *alias* Dyal, *alias* Swami, *alias* Villager, son of Ram Lal	Lyallpur	Punjab	Hanged.
Shivaram Rajguru *alias* "M", *alias* Ramguru *alias* Raghunath.	Benares	U.P.	Hanged
Kishori Lal Rattan *alias* Deo Datt Rattan, *alias* Mast Ram Shastri.	Hoshiarpur	Punjab	Transportation for life
Jai Dev *alias* Harish Chandra	Hardoi	Bengal	Transportation for life.
Sheo Varma *alias* Parbhat *alias* Ram Narain *alias* Ram-Narain Kapur.	Hardoi	Bengal	Transportation of life
Gaya Parshad *alias* Dr. B. S. Nigham *alias* Ram Lal *alias* Desh Bhagat.	Cawnpore	U.P.	Transportation for life.
Mahabir Singh *alias* Partab of Shahpur Tehla	Etah	U.P.	Transportation for life.
Bijoy Kumar Sinha *alias* Bachu.	Etah	U.P.	Transportation for life.
Kanwal Nath Trivedi *alias* Kamal Nath Tewari	Champaran	Bihar	Transportation for life
Kundan Lal *alias* Partap has proved to be Bhagwan Das Mahor *al.* Gunthala arrested at Bhusawal.	Benares	U.P.	7 years' R.I.
Prem Dutt *alias* Master *alias* Amrit Lal	Gujrat	Punjab	5 years' R.I.

Absconders

Chandar Shekhar Azad *alias* Panditji	Benares	U.P.	**(Shot dead in Feb, 1931)**

alias Quick-Silver.			
Kailash Patti *alias* Kali Charan	Azamgarh	U.P.	Arrested in Delhi.
Bhagwati Charan *alias* B. C. Vohra.	Lahore	Punjab	(died as result of bomb explosion in May 1930).
Yashpal	Dharmsala	Punjab	(arrested in U.P.
Satgur Dayal Awasthi.	Cawnpore	U.P.	Arrested.)

Approvers

Jai Gopal *alias* Harbans Lal *alias* Gopal *alias* Kishan Chand	Gujranwala	Punjab	
Phonindra Nath Ghosh *alias* Dada.	Champaran	Bihar.	
Manmohan Bannerji *alias* Manohar Bannerji	Champaran	Bihar	
Lalit Kumar Mukarji	Allahabad	U.P.	
Hans Raj Vohra *alias* Tarlok Chand	Lahore	Punjab	
Ram Saran Dass	Kapurthala State	Punjab	(Ram Saran Das and Brahm Dutt were later convicted to 1½ years R. I. each for perjury).
Braham Dutt *alias* Manmohan	Cawnpore	U.P.	

Lahore Conspiracy Case, No. 2 of 1930

Accused

Inderpal	Kangra	Punjab	Transportation for life.
Rup Chand	R. Pindi	Punjab	Transportation for life.
§Jahangiri Lal	Sheikhupura	Punjab	Transportation for life.
Gulab Singh	R. Pndi	Punjab	Transportation for life.
Kundan Lal	Benares	U.P.	Transportation for life.
Nathu Ram	R. Pindi	Punjab	7 years' R. I.
Sardar Singh	Muttra	Punjab	4 years' R. I.
Gurbakhsh Singh	Gujranwala	Punjab	4 years' R. I.
Bhim Sen	Sheikhupura	Punjab	4 years' R. I.
Sukh Dev Raj	Gurdaspur	Punjab	3 years' R. I.
Sita Ram	Jhelum	Punjab	2 years' R. I.
Kundan Lal	Sheikhupura	Punjab	2 years' R. I.
Hari Ram	R. Pindi	Punjab	2 years' R. I.
Gokal Chand	Sheikhupura	Punjab	2 years' R. I.

Krishen Lal	Jhelum	Punjab	2 years' R. I.
Harnam Singh	R. Pindi	Punjab	2 years' R. I.
Bishen Dass	R. Pindi	Punjab	(Died during course of trial).
	Absconders		
Yash Pal	Kangra	Punjab	Arrested U.P.
Hansraj (Wire less)	Lyallpur	Punjab	Arrested Sind.
Lekh Ram	Hissar	Punjab	
Prem Nath	Lahore	Punjab.	
Mussumat Prakasho	Lahore	Punjab	Arrested Delhi.
‡Mussumat Durga Devi	Lahore	Punjab	Arrested Punjab
Chandra Shekhar Azad	Benares	U.P.	(Killed in Allahabad while offering resistance to police).
‡Mussumat Soshila	Gujrat	Punjab	
‡Prof. Sanpuran Singh Tandon.	Lahore	Punjab	Arrested Punjab
‡Chailbihari	Delhi.		

* To run concurrently with 3 years R. I. awaeced in a separate case under the Arms Act.

§Brothers.

‡Surrendered, but no proceedings were coaducted against them.

Delhi Conspiracy Case

Accused

On withdrawal of case

Name	*District*	*Province*	*Sentence*
1. Vidha Bhusan	Chapra	Bihar	Interned under Reg. III of
2. Khiali Ram	Agra	U.P.	1818.
3. Dhanwantri	Gurdaspur	Punjab	Tried u/s 307, I. P. C. and 19, Arms Act, and sentenced to 7 years' R. I.
4. N. K. Nigham	...	Delhi	Tried u/s 20, Arms Act, and sentenced to 2 years' R. I.
5. Vishwanath Rao Vashampayan	Jhansi	U.P.	Tried u/s 46 & 5, Explosive Act and sentenced to 2 years' R. I. but acquitted by High Court.
6. Potdar			
7. Sachchindananda Watsayana	Jullundur	Punjab	Tried u/s 46, Explosives Act, but acquitted by High Court.
8. B. P. Jain	Meerut	U.P.	Tried u/s. 46, Explosive Act, Sentenced 3 years.

9. Babu Ram	Etah	U.P.	Tried u/s 6, Explosives Act, Acquitted by High Court.
10. Kapur Chand	...	Delhi	Tried u/s 46, 5, Explosive Act, and 19 Arms Act, 3 years R.I.

Deoghar Conspiracy Case 1924

Sailendra Nath Chakravartti	Allahabad	U.P.	7 years' R. I.
Upendra Kumar Dhar.	Sylhet and Comilla	Assam-Bengal	7 years' R. I.
Surendra Nath Bhattacharya	Dacca	Bengal	7 years' R. I.
Birendra Nath Bhattacharya	Dacca	Bengal	5 years' R. I.
Sukhendu Bikas Dutt	Chittagong	Bengal	5 years' R. I.
Prasad Chandra Chattarji	Hooghly and Howrah	Bengal	5 years' R. I.
Sushil Kumar Sen	Barisal and Hailakandi	Bengal-Assam	5 years' R. I.
Bijon Kumar Bannerji	Howrah	Bengal	5 years' R. I.
Atul Krishna Dutt	Khulna	Bengal	3 years' R. I.
Lakshmi Kanta Ghose	Howrah	Bengal	3 years' R. I.
Biswa Mohan Sanyal	Nadia	Bengal	3 years' R. I.

Gaya Conspiracy Case

Shyama Charan Barthwar	Gayan and Benares	Bihar and U.P.	Seven years' R. I. and fine of Rs. 200 in
Dr. Kesho Prasad	Gaya	Bihar and	default 6 months' R.I.
Biswanath Prasad	Darbhanga, Gaya and Benares	U.P.	
Sahadeo Singh	Gaya	Bihar	Five years' R.I. and
Satrughana Saran Singh	Gaya	Bihar	fine of Rs. 200 in
Jagdeo Lohar	Gaya	Bihar	default 6 month's R.I.
Mithilesh Kumar Singh	Gaya	Bihar	Four years' R.I. and
Pramatha Nath Mukharjee	Hooghly and Daltonganj	Bihar and Bihar	fine of Rs. 200 in default 6 month's R.I.
Lala Prasad	Gaya	Bihar	
Jagatdeo Malaviya	Allahabad	U.P.	Three years' R.I.
Kedar Nath Malaviya	Allahabad	U.P.	
Mahant Bhagwan Das	Gaya	Bihar	Two years' R.I. and
Ganesh Prasad Varma.	Gaya and Daltonganj	Bihar	fine of Rs. 150 in default 6 months' R.I.
Radha Mohan	Gaya	Bihar	Two years' R.I.
Bijay Kumar Das Gupta	Chittagong and Benares	Bengal and U.P.	
Deodhari Prasad Jadav	Gaya	Bihar	One years' R.I.

Inter-Provincial Conspiracy Case

Prabhat Chandra Chakrabartta	Tippera and Calcutta	Bengal	Transportation for life
Jitendra Nath Gupta	Faridpur and Calcutta	Bengal	Transportation for life
Sitanath De	Faridpur	Bengal	Transportation for life
Narendra Prosad Ghosh	Mymensingh	Bengal	14 years' transportation
Dhirendra Nath Bhattacharji	Tippera	Bengal	14 years' transportation
Purnananda Das Gupta	Dacca	Bengal	14 years' transportation
Kishori Mohan Das Gupta	Noakhali and Calcutta	Bengal	7 years' R.I.
Manindra Lal Chaudhury	Chittagong	Bengal	7 years' R.I.
Paresh Guha	Dacca	Bengal	7 years' R.I.
Satyandra Narayan Majumdar	Jessore and Calcutta	Bengal	7 years' R.I.
Pravat Kumar Mitra	Hooghly and calcutta	Bengal	7 years' R.I.
Jotin Chakrabartti	Tippera and Calcutta	Bengal	7 years' R.I.
Dwigendra Nath Talapattra	Rajshahi and Calcutta	Bengal	7 years' R.I.
Haripada De	Dacca and Calcutta	Bengal	7 years' R.I.
Niranjan Ghoshal	Faridpur	Bengal	7 years' R.I.
Amulya Chandra Sen Gupta	Dacca	Bengal	7 years' R.I.
Amiya Kumar Pal	Dacca and Calcutta	Bengal	7 years' R.I.
Hem Chandra Bhattacharji	Chittagong and Calcutta	Bengal	6 years' R.I.
Jyotish Chandra Majumdar	Tippera and calcutta	Bengal	6 years' R.I.
Bimal Bhattacharji	Mymensingh and Cacutta	Bengal	6 years' R.I.
Surendra Dhar Chaudhuri	Tippera and Calcutta	Bengal	6 years' R.I.
Abani Mohan Bhattacharji	Tippera and, calcutta	Bengal	5 years' R.I.
Sudhir Chandra Bhattacharji	Tippera	Bengal	3 years' R.I.
Shyam Behari Lal Sukla	Shahjahanpore and Calcutta	Bengal and U.P.	3 years' R.I.
Santosh Chatarji	Faridpur and Calcutta	Bengal	3 years' R.I.
Sushil Kumar Roy Chakravarty	Faridpur	Bengal	3 years' R.I.
Indu Bhushan Majumdar	Barisal and Calcutta	Bengal	3 years' R.I.
Probodh Kumar Ghosh	Calcutta	Bengal	3 years' R.I.
Abani Ranjan Sarkar	Khulna	Bengal	1 years' R.I.

Karachi Conspiracy Case 1932

1. Gurbaksh Singh	Ichra, Lahore	Punjab	2 ½ years' R.I.
2. Birji	Karachi	Sind	1 years' R.I.
3. Munshiram	Narawal, sialkot	Punjab	1 years' R.I.
4. Fatehraj	Jodhpur	—	2 ½ years' R.I.
5. Boor Singh	Jermiasingh, Gurdaspur	Punjab	6 months' R.I.
6. Mukandalal	Punjab and	Karachi	1 years' R.I.
7. Sadhu Singh	Jermiasingh, Gurdaspur	Punjab	1 years' R.I.
8. Diwan Chand	Budha Tola, Sialkot	Punjab	1 years' R.I.
9. Birendra Nath Pande	Cawnpore	U.P.	Acquitted
10. Doctor Moolraj	Multan	Punjab	Acquitted
11. Hari Singh (Appcover)	Muttra	U.P.	Pardoned.

(*Terrorison in India–1917–1936*)

A 'Capital' Conspiracy (1912-1915)

The spirit of revolt against British rule in India that had gripped the imagination of the Bengali youths was not slow to affect the minds of the valiant Punjabis. In the early months of 1907, as the Lieutenant Governor noted in his report:

"Everywere people were sensible of a change, of a 'new air' which was blowing through men's minds, and were waiting to see that would come of it." *Report of the Sedition Committee, 1918, p. 141 et seq.*

The said report further stated that

"in the big cities in the centre of the Province the agitators seriously try to arouse feelings of disloyalty. ....In certain important towns such as Rawalpindi, Sialkot and Lyallpur an active anti-British propaganda is being openly and simultaneously preached. In Lahore, the Capital of the Province, the propaganda is virulent and has resulted in a more or less general state of serious unrest."

The number of supporters of extremist views had been growing fast. A riot broke out over the conviction of the *Punjabee* for sedition. Scant courtesy was shown to Europeans whom the common people had hitherto looked upon with awe and unwilling respect. The educated extremist agitators carried on a campaign of hate by means of speeches at public meetings and spread a definite anti-British propaganda in the villages more particularly where widespread and deep dissatisfaction over legislation proposing modifications of Canal Colony tenures and a projected raising of canal rates in the Bari-Doab, prevailed. Special care was taken to inflame the passion of the great Sikhs and goad them into action.

Attention was directed to the police who were branded as traitors to their fellow countrymen and advised to quit the service of the Government. The Indian soldiers, otherwise loyal, were invited to join the people by leaving their ranks. The movement was to proceed towards the objective of bringing the Government machinery to a standstill preferably by stirring up a strong feeling of racial hatred.

When these methods succeeded in their mission exceedingly well it was then a question of months if not days when an overt act of a violent nature was to take place anywhere within the Province. Punjab was compared to a heap of dry gunpowder when a small spark would result in a terrible explosion. And it so happened in the heart of the Capital of India.

It was the daring outrage on Lord Hardinge, the Viceroy of India, on December 23, 1912. The occassion was the Viceroy's state entry to Delhi for initiation of the new Imperial Capital of India. The special train conveying His Excellency steamed into the central station. The State functions arranged for the occassion at the place were gone through with unusual pomp and grandeur. Hardinge mounted a tusker and the procession started moving. When the procession was in the centre of Chandney Chowk just beyond the Clock Tower and in front of the Punjab National Bank buildings, a bomb burst with deafening report on the rear part of the *howdah* between Hardinge and one of the attendants, Jamadar Mahabir Singh of Balarampur State, holding the umbrella. The full effect of the explosion on the Viceroy was prevented by the Viceroy's seat, the back of which was wrecked. The whole of the metal work of immense weight and great thickness of silver was blown off. A portion of the projectile hit Hardings's back and passed upwards his shoulder causing a wound four inches long and exposing the shoulder blade. There were multiple injuries on the right side of the neck and on the right hip.

The incident is better described in the words of Lady Hardinge who was accompanying her august husband in the procession. She expressed it as a 'terrible experience' for her and certainly it was. But it seems that she was able to maintain her composure as best as was possible under the circumstances and guided the nearest attendants to the Viceroy to remove His Excellency to a place where succour would be readily available. She wrote:

"Passing down the Chandney Chowk where the cheering was on all sides, I suddenly felt an upheaval and was thrown forward. When I recovered my place, I felt rather dazed and most decidedly deaf with loud singing in the head. The Viceroy turned to me and said, 'I am afraid, that was a bomb.'

"The elephant had stopped. Then he called out: 'Go on' and the procession started again. My impression was perfect stillness from the crowds until then, but when were restarted, there were voices raised and I heard 'bravo' amongst them.

"I then began noticing more details; for instance that the *howdah*- back had gone and the Viceroy looked pale. I said, 'Are you sure that you are not hurt?'

"He answered, 'I am not sure. I had a great shock, but I think I can go on.'

"A few seconds afterwards, I stretched back, and through a slit of the uniform near his right shoulder (the farthest from me) I could see red flesh appearing.

"Then I thought that shall I tell him he is wounded, which will frighten him, or to take the risk of the harm the jolt of the elephant may do him. I looked round again and noticed the legs of a man who was hanging backwards and dead.

"Then I quietly said, 'Do let me stop the procession as I fear the man behind is dead.' (We have moved on 150 yds.)

"He said: 'Of course we cannot go on under these circumstances.'

"I stopped the elephant and signed to Col. Maxwell on the elephant on the front. He ran up and the Viceroy said, 'Can you do anything for the poor man behind?'

"And I said: 'Would you like Col. Roberts to come? I think the Viceroy's shoulder is hurt'.

"Just then the Viceroy had a little convulsion and was rapidly losing consciousness. Regaining consciousness, he gave all instructions for the full carrying out of the ceremony.

"After this there is nothing to tell excepting a history of the difficulties of getting him off the *howdah* and his clothes taken off. He was bleeding profusely from about six wounds. No one was in the house, but the staff did everything and managed him beautifully."

(A letter read in a meeting at the Town Hall, Bombay, on January 8, 1913).

Nobody could be arrested in spite of declaration of rewards from the Government and the Native Chiefs who showed a greater concern than those who could be really interested in the case. The amounts assumed a fantastic figure and there was doubt whether these would be available when occassion would demand it.

The Government of India on January 24, 1913, declared that a reward of Rupees one lakh will be paid to anyone giving information leading to the arrest and conviction of the person or persons responsible for the act. The declaration cancelled all previous notifications of reward by the Government or of anybody else.

The only theory that could be established at the time after prolonged investigation was that the bomb, a composite percussion type, was similar to those used in previous outrages in Bengal. It was made of a cigarette tin which contained picric acid, fulminate of mercury and jute combs (sharp iron spikes, technically known as 'pins' and attached to the rollers of jute machines).

The idea of the cigarette tin, used at Delhi, with

the cigarette label in tact, was to enable the culprit to carry the machine without causing suspicion.

There were the usual arrests and investigations were carried with the zeal befitting the occassion. Nothing could be established, the Delhi police felt dismayed and the matter rested there for the time being.

Before six months had elapsed from the date of attempt on the Viceroy, Lahore gave an indication of revolutionary activities in the Province. The Lawrence Garden was the scene of an outrage that had apparently failed in its objectives on May 17, 1913. A *chaprasi* of the Gymkhana Club was found dead on the road about one hundred yards from the Montgomery Hall. He had terrible wounds in the left leg and right knee, while his chest and body were pierced as if by some sharp nails. A lamp-post on the side of the road opposite to where the *chaprasi* was lying prostrate, was found smashed to pieces.

The culprits could not be traced. During investigations it transpired that a bomb had been placed on the road by which the unfortunate *chaprasi* had been passing on his cycle when he stumbled against it and caused the explosion.

News had reached from Bengal to Lahore that Gordon of the Maulavai Bazar fame had been transferred to Kasur, a District of Lahore, to make him safe against the vendetta of the Bengal group of workers. Close watch was kept over his movements and it came to the knowledge of Bengali's counterpart in Punjab that Gordon would be present on May 17, 1913, at the Club, and steps had to be taken to murder him when coming out of the Club room. As with the Delhi outrage, the Police were unable to discover any clue whatsoever relating to the outrage.

Signs of revolutionary activity became gradually pronounced in Delhi and elsewhere. Leaflets containing exhortations to young men for revolutionary actions were distributed especially amongst the students. One of this extolled the attempt on Hardinge's life on December 23, 1912, in the following language:

"The *Gita,* the Vedas and the Koran all enjoin us to kill all the enemies of our Motherland, irrespective of caste, creed or colour....Leaving other great and small things, the special manifestation of the Divine Force at Delhi in December last proved beyond doubt that the destiny of India is being moulded by God Himself."

Baffled in their attempt to arrest anybody in connection with the past two serious outrages, the police diverted their attention to the probable source of seditious literature, particulalry of the issues of the *Liberty* which were in secret circulation or pasted at different parts of the city from time to time.

On and from February 16, 1914, a considerable number of houses were searched at different places. The police took action partly on warrants under the Press Act by the Deputy Commissioner of Delhi, for the seizure of proscribed leaflets of inflammatory nature. Connection with Bengal was sought to be established by a government statement to the effect that some copies of the seized leaflets had already been produced as evidence in the Raja Bazar Case. Most of the men who later figured as accused in the Delhi Conspiracy Case were arrested during the course of these searches.

It came to be known that the *Liberty* was printed either in Jullundur, at least its first two issues, or in Calcutta, particularly the third and the fouth. In one of these it published a list of heroes who had been executed for murder or who had been imprisoned for violent crimes. These men were described as 'Workers of God, and that they had been working under heavenly guidance'. The motive must be love for doing God's work. Sacrifice of life was indispensable. It concluded: "Be

God's instruments. Die and build your nation. *Bande Mataram.*"

The connecting link of the two wings of the revolutionary party in Punjab and Bengal was Rash Behari Bose who had been mainly instrumental in infusing life to the organisation functioning in Northern India. The object of the movement as stated by Rash Behari himself was "by the commission of outrages to awaken the masses to the fact that they are living under a foreign yoke. Then a strong desire will burst among the masses for open revolution."

Rash Behari acted not only as the link between Bengal and Punjab but as the Director of operations in the whole of Northern India. He selected some able lieutenants who were prepared to undergo any amount of suffering and face any risk unto death.

Amongst those was Abadh Behari. He attended the Lahore Central Training College, but lived at Delhi and was an intimate friend of Amir Chand since 1908. He met Rash Behari at Agarwal Ashram in 1912. Abadh Behari was made the head of the revolutionary activities in U.P. and Punjab. He had a hand in every department of the organisation and was capable of managing even intricate jobs with comparative ease. Once he wrote to a friend of his:

"Death is for all and we shall die the death of a hero .....The Bengal spirit should be implanted in Punjab."

Abadh Behari was arrested on February 19, 1914. In his room was found a few copies of *Liberty* pamphlet, a manuscript copy of a Paper called *Talwar*, the original of which was first published in Berlin on March 19, 1910. The title page displayed a picture of Madan Lal Dhingra as its hero and exemplar. A Hindi manuscript dealing with the uses of poisons for political purposes and a document advocating general massacre of Europeans formed part of the seized documents from his room. Amongst other articles were a cap of bomb and a bottle of petrol.

Amir Chand was for some time employed in the Cambridge Mission High School, and at the time of his arrest was the Headmaster in the Sanskrit School, Charkhewalan. He was the central figure in the group of 'the workers of God'. Teaching of youngmen, particularly in the revolu-tionary cult was his life's mission. The experience of his age and the undoubted talents were an asset to the organisation.

During the search of Amir Chand's house some brown papers of a very distinctive character were found. Amongst the papers was a cover containing a Hindi pamphlet dealing with the use of poison. There were a few copies of the *Liberty* and a document containing a list of names with an *alias* and a letter of the alphabet opposite each name; a list of places, each also with a special letter denoting places of meeting. Amir Chand's house was called Rs. 100, Abadh Bihari's Rs. 400/-, etc. Annas and Pies indicated time. Another manuscript headed *Love of Liberty* advocated a general massacre of Europeans, especially the English. There was a mass of other incriminating documents.

A biscuit box containing a quantity of cottton wool with some slight yellow stains on it was also found in another room. Amir Chand and his nephew were put under arrest on February 19, 1914.

Balmokand, together with Abadh Behari, was expecially deputed for the preparation and dissemination of seditious literature and was trained in the throwing of bombs. In February 1914, Balmokand unsuccessfully tried at Jodhpur, where he acted as a private tutor, to secure a pass for gaining entrance into the Viceregal enclosure. He was put in charge of operations in Punjab, especially for Lahore.

Balmokand was entrusted by Rash Behari for finding an employment for Basant Kumar Biswas so that he might be readily available when there was demand on his services.

Basanta *alias* Bishan Das served in The Popular Dispensary, Sutramand, Lahore, a job secured through the good offices of Balmokand. While not unmindful of his duties to his masters, he could always manage to eke out time and opportunity to carry out the plan and programme of his political leader. He rendered a very good account of himself in connection with the attempt on the Viceroy's life. He was successful in evading arrest in a remarkable manner. The story goes that his effeminate features and puny size came very handy to dress in female attire and get himself mixed up with the ladies taking their stand in the Punjab National Bank Building in Chandney Chowk, for witnessing the show. When at his suggestion the ladies around him diverted their attention to a particular part of the procession, he managed, it is alleged, to throw the bomb unobserved and during the commotion caused by the violent explosion deftly slipped out of the building and got mixed up with the crowd on the streets.

He was selected with Abadh Behari to conduct the operations for the murder of Gordon and but for the indiscretion in placing the bomb in a pathway not frequented by the European members of the Club, he might have added another feather to his cap of exploits.

Basanta Biswas left Delhi and went to his native village Paragacha in the Nadia District, Bengal, to perform the *sradh* ceremony of his father where he was arrested on February 26, 1914.

Rash Behari Bose, one of the principal accused, could not be found anywhere and a reward of Rs. 5,000 was offered by the Government on March 14, 1914, for his apprehension. He was declared a proclaimed offender and all his properties were confiscated to the State.

He was described in a circular as a man "of about thirty years of age, fair complexioned and tall, has large eyes, and that the third finger of one hand is stiff and scarred due to some accident." One of the prosecution witnesses, the approver, in the Delhi Conspiracy Case, deposed:

"He is strongly built, neither very fair, nor very dark. He looked like a Bengali or a Punjabi according to how he was dressed. He had a small wound in the third finger knuckle, owing to his finger being crushed in the door of a railway carriage during the last visit to Bengal. The wound was of the size of a four-anna bit. He has broad eyes."

On March 16, 1914, Amir Chand, Abadh Behari, Basanta Biswas, Balmokand and seven others were placed before the Delhi Magistrate for trial. The accused were variously indicted in groups for conspiracy, sedition, murder, possession of explosives, etc. Against all the accused the common charge was that they had conspired together for commission of murder and in furtherance of their common object, some of the accused were in possession of explosives in contravention of the Explosive Substances Act. The prosecution alleged that certain of the accused had actually committed murder, viz., at Lahore when a *chaprasi* was killed on May 17, 1913. Some others happened to be members of a conspiracy having distributed or being in possession of literature which contained deliberate incitements to murder.

The Magistrate framed charges against all the accused, eleven in number, for conspiracy to murder. Amir Chand, Abadh Behari, Balmokand and Basanta Biswas were further charged under the Explosive Substances Act, Basanta Biswas and Abadh Behari for the murder of a *chaprasi* on May 17, 1913, at Lahore.

The Sessions Trial opened at Delhi on May 21, 1914, and the omnibus charge ran thus:

"That you....between October, 1910 and March, 1914, both at Delhi and at other places in British India, did conspire with one another and with other persons (the approvers etc.) and other persons unknown, to commit the offence of murder (302 I.P.C.) which offence was committed on May 17, 1913, at Lahore and thereby committed an offence under Section 120B and 302. I.P.C."

The charge was amended on May 25, by substitution of the word "agree" for "conspire".

On October 5, 1914, judgment was delivered in which Amir Chand and Abadh Behari were sentenced to 20 years' transportation under the Explosive Substances Act, Basanta Biswas to transportation for life for conspiracy in consideration of his tender age; Abadh Behari, Amir Chand and Balmokand were further sentenced to death.

On October 22, 1914, appeals were preferred in the Punjab Chief Court on behalf of Amir Chand, Abadh Behari and Balmokand. The prosecution Counsel prayed for confirmation of the sentence of the three appellants and enhancement of sentence of Basanta Biswas. It was contended that he was twenty-two years of age and was fully conscious of the consequence of his action. On February 10, 1911, all the accused, including Basanta, were condemned to death. Three others were given varying terms of imprisonment.

The Secretary of State was moved to stay execution for a short time to enable the condemned men to move the Privy Council. On March 1, 1915, the request was rejected.

The accused fought against time and paucity of resources and anyhow managed to submit an appeal with the Privy Council. The judgment of the Judicial Committee rejecting the appeal came to be known in India on April 29, 1915. There was a little loss of time and all the four.

(i) Amir Chand (ii) Balmokand
(iii) Abadh Behari (iv) Basanta Biswas.

were executed on May 11, 1915, in the Ambala jail. (A Lahore message, dated May 12 published in *The Pioneer* on May 14, 1915, stated "all the four accused.....have now been executed").

The four great heroes of India who with unflinching devotion had worked jointly in life against enormous odds, sacrificed their lives together on the gallows and marched together towards the Martyrs' Paradise to enjoy a nation's gratitude raised from below.

Though not quite known to the world at large the name of a silent Martyr in connection with the Delhi Conspiracy executions should be recorded with deserving respect. Balmokand paid the highest penalty of the law for the love of his country. When the news of his execution reached his home, Ramrakhi, the devoted wife of Balmokand, in spite of all persuasions to the contrary stopped taking food and drink and in the course of a few days she followed her husband with a cheerful mind with the blessings of all who gathered around her during the last few days of her mortal existence. Blessed be her name!

Conspiracy in the South (1897-1910)

Secret organisations had their inception in the Western India much earlier than anywhere else. The Government came to realise more fully the influence they wielded over young minds and the extent of their preparation after the murder of Rand. It took some further time to get ready for conspiracy cases as such after the assassination of Ashe. As a result some cases such as Gwalior, Nasik, Satara, etc., were started in 1909-1910, a little after the Alipore Conspiracy Trial had ended.

The Tinnevelly Conspiracy Case was started almost along with the trial for the murder of Ashe. Altogether thirteen accused were placed on trial for murder, conspiracy and abetment of murder. Judgment was delivered on February 15, 1912, by the High Court in which nine accused were convicted and sentenced to rigorous imprisonment ranging from one to seven years. The third judge differed with the other two and convicted only four instead of seven. The case was referred to Full Bench of the High Court and hearing was held in March 1912. The original judgment was not materially altered.

Chaur Tribal Revolt–1777 and 1779

Dacca Conspiraccy Case 1910: Exasperated at the failure in protecting the property of the citizens of East Bengal, the police took recourse to the most easy step of starting a big case in which there were no less than 55 accused, young and old, students, the leaders of men, persons most respected in the profession of whom 44 were in custody.

Preliminary enquiry for commitment was started on August 8, 1910, and a Special Magistrate began sitting from September 30. The accused were committed to Sessions on November 22. Before the Additional District Judge the case commenced on January 3, 1911, and the Judge delivered his judgment on August 7. Three were sentenced to transportation for life, eighteen to ten years' and fourteen to seven years' and one to three years' rigorous imprisonment.

Eight were acquitted. In the appeal before the High

Court in October 1911, the sentences of fourteen accused were confirmed and the rest were set at liberty.

Dakshineswar Bomb Case (1925)

It is called Dakshineswar Bomb Case because at this place Anantahari Mitra prepared the bombs. Mitra died on gallows in the Alipur Central Jail in September 28, 1926.

Danda Fauj Case (Lahore) (1919)

A large number of nationalists paraded the streets of Lahore on the evening of 11th and the morning of 12th April, 1919. Chanan Din, the main organiser, made inflammatory speeches and proclaimed that he and his colleagues were rebels and did not recognize. His Majesty as their King. Chanan Din and some of his companions were arrested and convicted.

Dedaye Rebellion Case

A miniature rebellion was started at Dedaye, a township in the Pyapon district on January 7, 1931, by a band of rebels apparently under the orders of Saya San, their leader. The fight lasted for nearly an hour and a half when about thirty to forty rebels were killed on the spot.

A large number of survivors and their supporters were arrested in due course and before the Special Tribunal seventy-two accused were placed on trial under the omnibus charge of waging war against the King, conspiracy, etc. of which eighteen were sentenced to death. The High Court confirmed the sentence of fifteen. Petitions for mercy were submitted to the Government, all of which were granted excepting four who were executed in due course.

Delhi Conspiracy Case

Accoused

Name	District	Province	On withdrawal of case Sentence
1. Vidha Bhusan	Chapra	Bihar . .	Interned under
2. Khiali Ram	Agra	U.P.	Reg. III of 1818.
3. Dhanwantri	Gurdaspur	Punjab	Tried u/s 307, I. P. C. & 19, Arms Act, & sentenced to 7 years' R. I.
4. N.K. Nigam	..	Delhi	Tried u/s 20, Arms Act, & sentenced to 2 years' R.I.
5. Vishwanath Rao Vaishampayan.	Jhansi	U. P.	Tried u/s 46 & 5, Explosives Act & sentenced to 2 years' R. I. but acquitted by High Court.
6. Potdar	..	..	
7. Sachchidananda Watsayana.	Jullundur	Punjab	Tried u/s 46, Explosives Act, but acquitted by High Court.
8. B. P. Jain	Meerut	U.P.	Tried u/s 46, Explosives Act. Sentenced 3 years.
9. Babu Ram Gupta	Etah	U.P.	Tried u/s 6, Explosives Act. Aquitted by High Court.
10. Kapur Chand	..	Delhi	Tried u/s 46 5, Explosives Act, and 19, Arms Act 3 years' R. I.

Deoghar Conspiracy Case—1927

It seems that the leaders of the Jugantar and Anushilan parties attempted to form a coalition about this time, but in the circumstances, the scheme was short lived. Other raids by the police in August and

September removed bomb-making materials from the possession of members and resulted in some convictions. By July, however, a new leader had appeared, who claimed to have established touch with revolutionaries in Assam and the United Provinces. He was also in touch with Indra Chandra Narang, a Punjab student in Calcutta, and Bengali members of the Hindustan Republican Association in Calcutta. This man was making rapid strides towards establishing his leadership, when he was arrested in Deoghar, in possession of two Mauser pistols and cartridges. He gave his name as Birendra Nath Bhattacharji of Kalagaria, Dacca. Amongst the papers seized was a notebook containing in cypher, group by group, names and addresses, with their code introductions and passwords, of 68 members of the revolutionary party in Bengal, Assam, Bihar and Orissa, the United Provinces, and the Punjab. The cypher book also contained the names of eighteen intended victims. This led to searches in many places. One of the most productive of these was at the house of Sailendra Nath Chakravarti at Allahabad where two revolvers, two hundred cartridges, gunpowder, explosive substances, cypher addresses, a false beared, entrenching tools, three pairs of handcuffs and a mass of literature including military books, prescribed books and revolutionary pamphlets were found. Amongst these were copies of the 'Yellow' and 'White' leaflets which had figured so prominently in the Kakori Conspiracy Case. Other searches produced similar finds, but not in such large quantities. Accordingly a case was instituted against 19 Bengalis and one Punjabi at Deoghar, which ended in the conviction of eleven to sentences ranging from three to seven year's rgorous imprisonment. In addition Surendra Nath Bhattacharji and his brother Brindra were sentenced to three year's rigorous imprisonment under the Arms Act. The

Punjabi, who had been studying at Calctutta, was acquitted on appeal to the High Court.

The Deoghar Case was a very decisive blow to the revolutionary parties, and the broken up caused by the Criminal Law Amendment Act arrests, the successful bomb finds and this Case, was now completes. The detenus under Regulation III of 1818, the 1924 Ordinance and the Bengal Criminal Law Amendment Act, were released, mostly in 1928, and all by restriction orders.

Deoghar Conspiracy Case

Name	District	Province	Sentence
Sailendra Nath Chakra-vartti.	Allahabad	U.P.	7 years' R. I.
Upendra Kumar Dhar	Sylhet and Comilla	Assam Bengal	7 years' R. I.
Surendra Nath Bhatta-chary.	Dacca	Bengal	5 years' R. I.
Birendra Nath Bhatta-chariya.	Dacca	Bengal	5 years' R. I.
Sukhendu Bikas Dutt	Chittagong	Bengal	5 years' R. I.
Prasad Chandra Chattarji	Hooghly and Howrah	Bengal	5 years' R. I.
Sushil Kumar Sen	Barisal and Hailakandi.	Bengal Assam.	5 years' R. I.
Bijon Kumar Bannerji	Howrah	Bengal	5 years' R. I.
Atul Krishna Dutt	Khulna	Bengal	3 years' R. I.
Lakshmi Kanta Ghose	Howrah	Bengal	3 years' R. I.
Biswa Mohan Sanyal	Nadia	Bengal	3 years' R. I.

Deplorable Incident (1913-1915)

The political character of the occurrence at Nimej in the Beaur Sub-Division of the Shahabad District can be attributed only to the motive of the action. One of the principal accused used to preach amongst his followers that any action including which high hopes were placed for an armed rising in India was frustrated without achieving result of any moment.

While preparations for a formidable rising had been going on both within and outside India, outbursts of revolutionary violence involving lives of servants of the Government and agents and spies in the employ of the police occurred here and there in various parts of Bengal.

Dhundia Wagh

Dhundia Wagh, Chief of Bednore, Mysore, a Mahratta by birth, rallied a strong force, mainly drawn from Tipu's forces, around him and successfully ravaged the Karnatak under both the British and the Mahratta troops and killed Dhondu Pant Gokhale. He remained a real terror to the British forces for a fairly long time but was defeated in the battle fought on the right bank of Malprabha. Ultimately he was overcome and killed on September 9, 1800, at Kongal.

East Khandesh, Sholapur and Aundh Conspiracies —1910

During the year 1910 three seditious conspiracies of minor importance came to light, known as the East Khandesh, Sholapur and Aundh Conspiracies. The second of these was discovered at Pandharpur, the place where the missionary body was assaulted in 1908; the members of the Conspiracy were described as a very insignificant lot of youths, and the District Magistrate remarked regarding them, "These youths would seem to have had no definite purpose, though their ideas were revolutionary. They were without funds, as they had to pilfer the material they used in the bombs, and the prices they gave for the "arms" which they collected did not exceed a few annas. "In the Aundh Conspiracy, which was hatched in the Native they state of that name, three persons were mainly concerned; were convicted and sentenced to terms of imprisonment of 8., 5, and 3 ½ years respectively. These cases, though of considerable local importance, were of the main line of revolutionary Conspiracy; at the same time they indicated that a good deal of underground plotting was going on.

(Political Trouble in India—1907-1917 by James Compbel Ker, 1917) p. 540.

5th Native Light Infantry Revolt (1915)

During World War I, the insurrection by the 5th (Native) Light Infantry Regiment, stationed at Singapore in 1915, was one of the worst that the British administration had to face.

Inspired by Sohanlal and others some were successful in sowing seeds of discontent in 'the Regiment' which was in addition to one that had been lurking in the minds of the troops due to arbitrary promotions and indiscreet deployments. When the particular Regiment, about 900 in number, was asked to get ready for proceeding to Hong Kong, the simmering fire burst into flame and they openly refused to obey.

The army authorities were completely taken unawares, their espionage system having failed miserably. The revolt broke out without warning at 3 p.m. on February 15, 1915, the Chinese New Year's Day, and it at once assumed serious proportions. The rebels tried to influence the entire force comprising the Regiment and some amongst the loyal element having refused to join were shot dead or ordered not to interfere with their action in any way.

According to premeditated plan settled in consultation with the revolutionaries primarily responsible for the outbreak, the insurrectionists opened fire on the sentries and guards round the

German concentration camp and those who were not killed or wounded fled leaving the prisoners an easy chance of escape. The rioters then started for the town. A number of houses by which they passed in their march were sacked and burnt.

Gadodia Stores, Delhi Dacoity—1930

On 6th July 1930? Chandershekar Azad, Kailashpati Dhanwantri, Lekh Ram and Kashi Ram committed an armed decoity at the Gadodia stores in Delhi city, and carried off some Rs. 14,000 in cash in a motor-car, firing in the street as they left in order to discourage pursuit. This loot was distributed to various centres, and with the Delhi allotment, a bomb factory disguised as a soap factory was opened.

(Political Trouble in India 1917-1937 by H.W. Hale. Allahabad, Chugh Pub. 1924)

Gujranwala Leader's Case (1919)

A serious outbreak occurred on 14th April 1919. On that day a general *hartal* took place; a mob proceeded to the station and stopped a train; and the guard and the driver were assaulted; a bridge near Gumkul on Wazirabad side was set on fire; telegraph and telephone wires were cut off and the Kachhi Bridge on the Lahore side was also set ablaze and thus Gujranwala was practically isolated. The Superintendent of Police, Mr. Heron, was assaulted. A meeting was organised in front of the residence of Amar Nath, a local Congress leader. In this meeting speeches were made condemning the Rowlatt Act. While the meeting was in progress, the police opened fire wounding a few persons. A large number of participants proceeded towards the Civil Lines, and the Post Office, Dak Bungalow, law Courts, the Railway Station and the goods sheds were burnt down. All these acts of violence were directed against the Government and the European officials. No property belonging to an Indian was damaged. In this case, about 15 persons were held and charged under Section 121 IPC. Out of this, two were sentenced to death and eight to transportation for life and the forfeiture of their property.

Gujarat Case (1919)

On the morning of 14th April, 1919 after the news of the firing in Gujranwala had been received, seditious hand-bills were distributed in Gujarat announcting a rebellion and *hartal*. The shops were closed and the mob had promenaded the city. On the morning of 15th, the mob re-assembled with black flags and a picture of Mahatma Gandhi. They then proceeded to the Mission High School and when the Head Master refused to close it, broke in and smashed the windows and furniture. The mob afterwards marched towards the Railway Station where it wrecked the telephone and telegraph instruments. At this juncture, the police fired the crowd. A number of arrests were made.

Gaya Conspiracy Case

Shyama Charana Barthwar	Gaya and Benares.	Bihar and U. P.	Seven years' R. I. and fine of Rs. 200 in default 6 months' R. I.
Dr. Kesho Prasad	Gaya,	Bihar	
Biswanath Prasad	Darbhanga, Gaya and Benares.	Bihar and U. P.	
Sahadeo Singh	Gaya	Bihar	Five years' R. I. and fine of Rs. 200 in default 6 months' R.I.
Satrughana Saran Singh	Gaya	Bihar	
Jagdeo Lohar	Gaya	Bihar	
Mithilesh Kumar Singh	Gaya	Bihar	Four years' R. I. and fine of Rs 200 in default 6 months' R. I.
Pramatha Nath Mukharjee	Hooghly and Daltonganj.	Bengal and Bihar	
Lala Prasad	Gaya	Bihar	
Jagatdeo Malaviya	Allahabad	U. P.	Three years' R. I.

Kedar Nath Malaviya	Allahabad	U.P.	
Mahant Bhagwan Dass	Gaya	Bihar	Two years' R. I. and
Ganesh Prasad Varma	Gaya and Daltonganj.	Bihar	fine of Rs. 150 in default 6 months' R. I.
Radha Mohan	Gaya	Bihar	Two years' R. I.
Bijay Kumar Das Gupta	Chittagong and Benares.	Bengal and U.P.	
Deodhari Prasad Jadav	Gaya	Bihar	One year's R. I.

Gumanpura Railway Derailment Case (Amritsar) (1919)

On the evening of 12th April, 1919, Lal Singh Lambardar of Sanghna, a village some four or five miles from Amritsar, visited the neighbouring village of Gumanpura and Basahe where he urged the people to rise in revolt. He also advised them to destroy the railway line. A large number of nationalists within an hour removed several railway lines along with their wooden sleepers. As a result of this sabotage, the engine and eight wagons of the goods train were derailed. In this case, about 16 persons were arrested and convicted. Lal Singh was sentenced to death and his property was forfeited.

Gwalior Conspiracy Case

An important ramification of the Nasik Conspiracy extended to the state of Gwalior, and came to light in connection with the arrest of Ganesh Savarkar at the end of February, 1909. The branch at Gwalior was called the Nava Bharat (New India) Society, the same thing as the Abhinav Bharat, and 22 persons were tried by a special tribunal appointed by His Highness the Maharaja Scindia. In August 20 of them were convicted; the ringleaders G.L. Desai, a photographer who produced seditious pictures, and T.G. Sadawartwala were sentenced to seven years transportation, and the remainder to minor punishments in proportion to their participation in the Conspiracy. A copy of the rule was found during the investigation, and a translation reproduced in the judgement of the special tribunal. The rules as usual enjoined secrecy and implicit obedience, and provided for the use of false names and cipher codes of which specimen were found.

Objects of the Gwalior Conspiracy

The accused were charged with an convicted of exciting disaffection against the British Government, but their aim as set forth in the rules was to establish a republican form of government "Since all Native Princes are mere puppets," and accordingly, as the learned Chief Justice remarked, "the conduct of the accused who joined the ranks of that society and took the oath is nothing short of conspiring to wage war against his Highness."

The following extract from the rules, as reproduced in the judgment of the special tribunal, explains the methods approved by the Conspirators:

"Section IV—Now there are two ways of carrying out the advice for attaining liberty; education and agitation. There will be through consistency between the two. Education includes swadeshi, boycott, national education, entire abstinence from liquor, religious festivities, lectures, sermons, Kathas (legends related with music and singing) establishment of institutions, libraries, different occasion of pan-supari (social gatherings) etc, while agitation comprises target-shooting, sword, exercise, preparation of bombs, dynamite, procuring revolvers, taking gymnastic exercises, running races, learning and teaching the use of weapons and missiles, travelling in different provinces and countries and getting information thereof. Those lovers of the country who are deported should establish an association for propagation of national religious duties. Should an occasion for a general rising in any province at a proper time arrive, all should help that cause and attain liberty.

Gwalior Conspiracy

The *Abhinav Bharat Society* spread its ramifications far and wide and almost every important place in the whole of Western India enjoyed the distinction of having a branch in it. Bombay, Nasik, Poona, Pen, Aurangabad, Hyderabad and even the State of Gwalior did not fail to offer their young men in the fight for freedom.

The *Nav Bharat Society* in Gwalior chalked out a programme of action for attainment of liberty. It was mainly divided into two sections, viz., (i) Education including *swadeshi,* boycott, national education, entire abstinence from liquor, religious festivities, lectures, libraries, etc., and (ii) Agigtation, aimed at "target shooting, sword exercise, preparation of bombs, dynamite, procuring of revolvers, learning and teaching the use of weapons and missiles." It further directed that

"should an occasion for a general rising in any province at a proper time arise, all should help that cause and attain liberty. ....Confidence, itself is a means to shake off servitude; we are fully convinced that if thirty crores of people are prepared to fight, none can thwart them in their desire. First, education will be given to prepare the mind, and then a rebellion raised; the war of independence will be carried on by resorting to cunning and craft."

Signs were not lacking at the time of secret societies extending their activities to a wider area. They had been gaining experience by practising acts of daring and resourcefulness. Ahmedabad was not very slow to come and in November 1909, it manifested its preparedness through an overt act by throwing a bomb at the car of the Viceroy, Lord Minto, which fortunately for him failed to explode at the time. After the procession had passed off two cocoanut bombs were discovered on the road and an unsuspecting public lost one of his hands by explosion while picking up one of them.

The materials collected during police investigation in connection with the activities of *Abhinav Bharat Society* contained correspondence between the revolutionaries working in Nasik and the State of Gwalior. In collaboration with the Government of India, the State started conspiracy cases before a Tribunal constituted for the specific purpose with 22 accused of the *Nav Bharat* and 19 belonging to the *Abhinav Bharat Society* resulting in the conviction of more than half of the accused.

The charges against all the accused were that they at Nasik and at other places in British India and Vinayak Damodar Savarkar in London (i) attempted to wage war, (ii) conspired among themselves to wage war, (iii) conspired amongst themselves to commit offences punishable under Sec. 121 I.P.C., (iv) conspired to deprive the King Emperor of the sovereignty of British India, (v) conspired amongst themselves to overawe either by criminal force or show of criminal force the Government or the Government of Bombay, (vi) collected arms and ammunition with the object of waging war, and (vii) concealed by an illegal omission the existence of a design to wage war, (Sections 121, 121A, 122, 123, and 125 I.P.C.).

Hafizabad Case (Gujranwala District) (1919)

In different public meetings in Hafizabad the local leaders strongly condemned the Rowlatt Bill and urged the people to take strong action in emulation of what had taken place elsewhere. On the morning of 14th April, 1919, a meeting was organised near the railway station. The crowd attacked a train and broke all the windows and shutters on the platform side with *lathis* and stones. About 19 persons were held and charged under Sections 121, 147, 307, 436, 149 I.P.C. Sentence of death was pronounced on Mangal Singh who was the principal speaker of the meeting. Kesar Mal and Karam Chand who were prominent amongst the leaders were also prosecuted on 24th May, 1919.

Htihlaing Rebellion

For a none too-important uprising in Htihalaing twentyseven rebels were placed on trial of which two were sentenced to death. The High Court on the appeal before it remarked that the case against U.Thathalawka had been amply proved and his appeal was dismissed. The appeal of the other persons met with the same fate.

Horawh Gang Case: A very big case was started before a Special Tribunal at the Calcutta High Court under Sections 121, 122, 123, I.P.C. on Dec. 1, 1910. The prosecution tried to rope in all persons suspected of complicity in almost all political events of a revolutionary nature including Chingripota, Netra, Haludbari and other dacoities, tampering with the loyalty of the 10th Jats, then stationed at Alipore, murder of Government pleader and police officers, etc. Selected men of as many as twelve political groups were placed among the accused. Judgment was delivered on April 19, 1911. Of the 46 accused originally placed on trial five were discharged and case against one was dropped. One died. Thirty-three were acquitted and six were further convicted over their sentence in connection with the Haludbari Dacoity Case.

There were several other cases relating to different incidents under the cover of 'conspiracy'. Some of these were the Midnapore (1908), Madaripur (1913), Barisal (1913-14), Raja Bazar Bomb (1914-15), and several others, till the end of the British rule in India.

The history of the revolutionary movement if ever written out in detail, is bound to bring into prominence the contact that was established and the mutual help rendered to different organisations in Northern India under the Punjab and Bengal leaders. This would be an important and interesting subject deserving special attention.

Inter Provincial Conspiracy Case—1932

It had been known that Prabhat Chakravarti and Jiten Gupta had been leading a very strong and active group of the Anushilan. Jiten had escaped from the Buxa internment camp in February 1932, but was re-arrested on 28th December 1932. Prabhat Chakravarti had absconded from his place of domicile in January 1932, and was arrested on the 14th January 1933. A loaded revolver and important papers, including cypher addresses of connections all over Bengal and other parts of India were found on him. Enquiries were made at all the addresses and many searches and arrests were made. A videspread conspiracy was revealed, with ramifications in many provinces, but especially in the Punjab, where a connection with the Hindustan Socialist Republican Army had been attempted. A mass of material was collected and eventually no less than forty persons were put on trial in what is known as the Inter-Provincial Conspiracy case. Two of the accused, Jitendra Chandra Naha and Hrishikekesh Das Gupta on being tendered pardons became approvers, and many witnesses were examined who had been for a time revolutionaries or bad, at some time or other, tried with the idea of becoming revolutionaries. This branch of the Anushilan was shown to have made extensive preparations for the enlargement and strengthening of the group and for the Commission of outrages. In fact, some of the accused had already been convicted for their part in offences already committed.

The effect of this case was very damaging to this branch, which was one of the most active and widespread of the Anushilan party. Apart from those actually accused and sentenced, many persons who had been connected with the movement were called in evidence, and the result was that, apart from the leaders who were sent to prison, a large number of the more lukewarm sympathisers and dabblers, were discredited. This, combined with sucesses in other smaller cases and the ceaseless vigilence of the police, brought about an easier situation, although it was impossible to relax the extraordinary precautions for safeguarding the lives of officials and their families in Bengal, or to decrease the intensive intelligence organization which had been rendered so necessary by the events of the foregoing years. There was, however, a growing believe in some quarters, or perhaps little more than a hope that public opinion was slowly turning against terrorism and that in their effects to crush it Government and its officers had earned a steadily increasing amount of sympathy and support from the community at large.

(Political Trouble in India 1917-1937 by H.W. Hale, Chugh Publications, Allahabad, 1974, pp. 40-43)

THE REVOLUTIONARY

An organ of the Revolutionary Party of India
India—Ist january 1925
Vol. I.

Manifesto of the Revolutionary Party of India.

"Chaos is necessary to the birth of a new star" and

the birth of life is accompanied by agony and pain. India is also taking a new birth, and is passing through kthat inevitable phase, when chaos and agony shall play their destined role, when all calculations shall prove futile, when the wise and the mighty shall be bewildered by the simple and the weak, when great empires shall crumble down and new nations shall arise and surprise humanity with the splendour and glory which shall be all its own.

This new power, which is shaking the world from its very depths, this new spirit, which is working miracles behind the scen, is also manifesting itself in the young blood of India is taking the shape of a movement which is despised and ignored by the wise and the learned, and is being described as the wild dreams of a few mad men. This remarkable movement is the revolutionary movement of young India.

This revolutionary movement has unnerved the weak, has inspired the robust and the healthy and has confounded the wordly wise and the learned. This movement can never be crushed just as mcuh as the coming of the spring can never be thwarted. It will never die out until it has fulfilled the mission for which it has taken its birth. Tyrants will oppress it, the fatihless will taunt it, and the crushed by the sword, and the noble impulse that takes birth in the very depths of our being can neither be ignored nor taunted.

This revolutionary movement is the manifestation of the new life that has taken birth in the nation. To denounce this life is to denounce one's own understanding.

Twenty years of ruthless repression has not been able to crush it. Scathing denunciations by the renowned public leaders have not bee able to arrest its steady growth. The movement stands mightier to-day than what it was before. The prospects of this revolutionary party were never so bright a they are today. The future is assured.

Let no Indian deny the existence of this revolutionary party in order to denounce the repessive measures of the foreign rulers. The foreigners have no right to rule over India and therefore they must be donounced and driven out, not tha they have committed any particular act of violence or crime. These are the natural consequences of a foreign rule. This foreign rule, must be abolished. They have no justification to rule over India except the justification of the sword, and therefore the revolutionary party has taken to the sword. But the sword of the revolutionary party bears ideas at its edge.

The immediate object of the revolutionary party in the domain of politics is to establish - Federal Republic of the United States of India by an organised and armed revolution. The final constitution of this Republic shall be framed and declared at a time when the representatives of India shall have the power to carry out their decisions. But the basic principles of this Republic shall be universal suffrage, and the abolition of all systems which make the exploitation of man by man possible; *e.g.*, the railways and other means of transportation and communication, the mine and other kinds of very great industries such as the manufacture of steel and ships, all these shall be nationalised. In this Republic the electors shall have the right ot recall their representatives if so desired, otherwise the democracy shall become a mockery. In this Republic, the legislation true shall have the power to control the executives and raplace them whenever necessity will arise.

The revolutionary party is not national but international in the sense that its ultimate object is bring harmony in the world by respecting and guaranteeing the diverse interests of the different nations; it aims not at competition but at co-operation between the different nations and states, and in this respect it follows the footsteps of the great Indian Rishis of the glorious Past and of Bolshevik Russia in the modern age. Good for huminity is no vain and empty word with the Indian revolutionaries. But the weak, the coward and the powerless can do no good either to themselves or to humanity.

With regard to the communal questions, the revolutionary party contemplates to grant whatever rights the different communities may demand, provided they do not clash with the interests of other communities and they lead ultimately to harty and organic union of the different communities in the near future.

In the domain of economic and social welfare the party will foster the spirit of co-operation in as large a scale as possible. Instead of private and unorganised business enterprises the party prefers co-operative unions.

In the spiritual domain the party aims at establishing the truth and preaching is that the world is not "Maya"—an illusion to be ignored and despised at but that it is the manifestation of the one indivisible soul, the supreme source jof all power, all knowledge, and all beauty.

This revolutionary party has its own policy and its own programme. It cannot for obvious reasons divulge all its secrets. But when it will become quite sure that the government happens to know more than our own people, then the public will also be informed of its plans and methods without and hesitation at all.

This revolutionary party pursues the policy of co-operation when possible and dissociation where necessary with the Congress and its different parties. But this party views all constitutional agitations in the country with contempt and ridicule. It is a mockery to say that India's salvation can be achieved through constitutional means, where no constitution exists. It is well-deception to say that India's political liberty can be attained through peaceful and legitimate means when the enemy is determined to break the peace at his convenience and the line pharse "legitimate" looses all its charm and signifleance when one pledges himself to maintain peace at all costs.

Our public leaders hesitate to speak in clain terms that India wants complete autonomy free from foreign control. They perhaps are ignorant of the fact that nations are born through the inspitations of great ideals. The spirtual ideal which hesitates to accept this spirit of complete appear the most sablime. The time has come to speak the truth in the most unmistakeable terms and to place before the nation an ideal worth the name.

The ideal before us is to serve humanity in an organised way. This ideal can never be realised by India so long as she remains in bondage and slavery, so long as India remains British India. In order that India my realise her ideals she must have a separate and independent existence. This independence can never be achieved through peaceful and constitutional means. Even a child can understand that the laws that govern British India are not made by the Indians jnor can they have any control over them. British India can never be transformed into a Federal Republic of the United States of India through the British laws and constitutions. Young Indians ! Shake off yourg illusions, face realities with a stout heart, and do not avoid struggles, difficulties and sacrifices. The inevitable is to come. Do not be misguided any more. Peace and tranquility you cannot have and India's liberty can never be achieved through peaceful and legal means. The following memorable words of a great English author Mr.

Robertson may serve to make the wise men of India wiser still.

"The movement and programme of reform was mainly the achievement of Irish and Protestant leaders, to whom British statesman had revealed the fatal secret that England could the bullied but not argued into justice and generoslty". (England under the Hanoverians, p. 197). Indian public leaders are still ignorant of this "fatal secret', or else they are foolishly wise to ignore it.

The wise men of India say that it is absured to cherish the hope that India can be re-conquered by the force of arms, though they forget that it is equally of more absured to believe that a handful of Englishmen have kept under subjugation by the force of arms, onefifth of the whole human race. Posterity may well doubt the authenticity of his fact that a handful of Englishmen over ruled over the Indian continent, it is so inconceivable.

A few words more about terrorism and anarchism. These two words are playing the most mischevous part in India today. They are being invariably misapplied whenever any reference to the revolutionaries is to be made, because it is so very convenient to denounce the revolutionaries under that name. The Indian revolutionaries are neither terrorists nor anarchists. They never aim at spreading anarchy in the land, and therefore they can never properly be called anarchists. Terrorism is never their object and they cannot be called terrorists. They do not believe that terrorism alone can bring independence and they do not want terrorism for terrorism's sake, although they may at times resort to this method as a very effective means of retaliation. The present government exists solely because the foreigners have successfully been able to terrorise the Indian people. The Indian people do not love their English masters, they do not want them to tbe here; but they do help the Britishers simply because they are terribly afraid of them; and this very fear resists the Indians from extending their helping hands to the revolutionaries, not that they do not love them.

This official terrorism is surely to be met by counter terrorism. A spirit of utter helplessness pervades every strata of or society and terrorism is an effective means of restoring the proper spirits in the society without which progress will be difficult. Moreover the English masters and their hired lackeys can never be allowed to do whatever they like, unhampered, unmolested. Every possible difficulty and resistance must be thrown in their way. Terrorism has an international bearing also, because the attentions of the enemies of England are at once drawn towards India through of the acts of rerrorism and revolutionary demonstrations and the revolutionaries are thereby able to form an alliance with them, and thus expedite the speedy attainment of India's deliverance. But this revolutionary party has deliberately abstained itself from entering into this terrorist campaign at the present moment even at the greatest of provocations in the form of outrages committed on their sisters and mothers by the agents of a foreign government, simply because the party is waiting to deliver the final blow. But when expediency will demand it the Party will unhesitatingly enter into a desperate dempaign of terrorism, when the life of every officer and individual who will be helping the foreign rulers in any way will be made intolerable, be he Indian or European, high or low. But even then the party will never forget that terrorism is not their object, and they will try incessaritly to organise a band of selfless and devoted workers who will devote their be energies towards the political and social emancipation of their country. They will always remember that "the making of natins requires the self-sacrifice of thousands of obscure men and women who care more for the idea of their country, than for their own comfort or interest, their own lives or the lives of those whom they love".

(Sd.) VIJAY KUMAR,
President, Central Council,
The R. P. of India.

THE HINDUSTAN REPUBLICAN ASSOCIATION

Name:—

The name of the association shall be the Hindustan Republican Association.

Object.—

The object of the association shall be the establish a Federated Republic of the United States of India by an organised and armed revolution.

The final form of the constitution of the Republic shall be framed and declared by the representatives of the people at the time when they will be in a position to enforce their decisions.

The basic principle of the republic shall be universal suffrage and the abolition of all systems which make any king of exploitation of man by man possible.

Constitution—Governing Body:—

The governing body of the association shall be the Central Council composed the representatives every province of India. All decisions of the Central Council shall be arrived at by unanimous consent. The Central Council shall be vested with absolute powers.

The principal function of the Central Council shall be to supervise, adjust and co-ordinate the activities in the different provinces of which it shall have full knowledge.

The Central Council shall be in direct charge of the work to be carried on in countries outside India.

Provincial Organisation.—

There shall be a committee ordinarily of five (5) men representing the five (5) different departments of the association in every province which shall regulate all the activities of the association in the province.

Departments.—

Every provincial organisation shall have the following departments :—

1. Propaganda.
2. Collection of men
3. Collection of Funds and Terrorism.
4. Collection and storage of arms and ammunitions.
5. Foreign connection.

1. *Propaganda* shall be carried on:—

(*a*) by an open and a secret press,

(*b*) through private conversations,

(*c*) through public platforms,

(*d*) through a system of organised Kathas, and

(e) through magic lantern slides.

2. *Collection of men* shall be done by organisers in charge of different districts.

3. *Funds* shall be collected generally by means of voluntary subscriptions and occasionally by contributions exacted by force. In extreme cases of repressions by agent or agents of a foreign government it shall be the duty of the association to retaliate in whatever form it shall consider suitable.

4. Every effort shall be made to arm every member of the association; but all such arms shall be stored at different centres and be used according to the directions of the provincial committee only.

No arms shall be removed from any place in the district or used without the knowledge and the permission of the district organiser or the officer-in-charge of this department.

5. *Foreign connection.*—This department shall

carry on its work under the direct orders from the C.C.
District organiser—His duties.—

The district organiser shall be in sole charge of the members of his district.

He shall try to start branches of this association in every part of his district. In order to have efficient recruitment he should keep himself in touch with the different public bodies and institution in his district.

The district organisers shall be subordinate in every way to the provincial committee who shall supervise and direct all their activities.

The district organisers must sec that the members are divided into separate groups and the different groups do not know each other.

So far as possible the district organiser of any province must not know the activities of each other and if possible they must also not know each other by person or by name.

No district organiser shall leave his station without previously informing his superior.
Oualifications of a District Organiser.—

1. He must have the tact and the ability to guide and handle men of different temperaments.

2. He must have the capacity to grasp political, social and economical problems of the present day with special reference to his Moterland.

3. He must be able to grasp the spirit of the history of India, with special reference to the particular civilization which India has evolved.

4. He must have faith in the mission and the destiny of a free India, which is to bring harmony in the difficult spheres of human activities both spiritual and material.

5. He must be courageous and self-sacrificing without which all his brilliant qualities will have no real value.

Provincial Council and Centracl Council.—

P.C. and C.C. members must see that every member of this association gets full scope and ample opportunity to develop and use his individual abilities, without which the association will tend to disintegrate.

Programme

All the activities of the association shall be divided into two parts: public and private.

Public.—

1. To start associations in the forms of clubs, libraries, seva sammitis and the like.

2. To start labour and peasant organisations. Suitable men must be engaged on behalf of the association to organise and control the labourers in the different factories, the railways and in the coalfields, and instil into their minds that they are not for the revolution but that the revolution is for them.

Similarly the Kisans must also be organised.

3. To start weekly paper in every province to propagate the idea of an independent Indian Republic.

4. To publish booklets and pamphlets with a view to enlighten the public as to the course of events and the current of thoughts as prevalent in the conuntries outside India.

5. To utilise and influence the Congress and other public activities as far as possible.

Private.—

(a) To establish a secret press and through it to publish such literature which cannot easily be published openly.

(b) To circulate such literature.

(c) To establish branches of this association in every part of the country, district by district.

(d) To collect funds in as many ways as possible.

(e) To Send suitable men to foreign countries where they may get military or scientific training so that they may become military or scientific training so that they may become military or scientific experts to take charge of armies and ammunition stories at the time of open rebellion.

(f) To import arms and ammunitions and also to manufacture them, as far as possible, in the country.

(g) To remain in close touch and to co-operate with the Indian revolutionaries outside India.

(h) To get the members of the association enlisted into the pre..

(i) To enlist the sympathy of the public to our cause by occasional retaliatory measured and propaganda and thus create a band of sympathisers.

Membership

All members shall be recruited by organisers in charge of different districts in every province. every member must be ready to devote his whole time for the association and to risk his life if necessary.

He must obey the commands of the district organiser implicity.

He should develop his even initiative and remember that the success of the association depends much on the esourcefulness, the initiative and the sense of duty of its individual members.

He must behave in a manner that may not prejudice the cause for which his association stands or may not do any harm directly or indirectly to this organisation.

No member of this association shall belong to any other organisation without the consent of the district organiser.

No member shall leave his station without informing the district organiser about it.

Every member must try to avoid being suspected of revolutionary connections by the police or public.

Every member must remember that his individual behaviour and mistakes might lead to the ruin of the whole organisation.

No member shall conceal anything from the district organiser as far as his public life is concerned.

Members who well betray shall be punished either with expulsion or death.

The authority of punishment shall rest entirely with the 'P. C."

The Hindustan Socialist Republican Association

Manifesto

The Philosophy of the Bombs

Introductory

Recent events, particularly the congress resolution on the attempt to blow up the Viceregal Special on the 23rd December 1929, and Gandhi's Subsequent writings in 'Young India', clearly show that the Indian National Congress, in conjunction with Gandhi, has launched a crusade against the revolutionaries. A great amount of public criticism, both from the press and the platform, has been made against them. It is a pity that they have all along been, either deliberately or due to sheer ignorance, misrepresented and misunderstood. The revolutionaries do not shun criticism and public scrutiny of their ideals, or actions. They rather welcome these as chances of making those understand, who have a genuine desire to do so, the basic principles of the revolutionary movement and the high and noble ideals that are a perennial source of inspiration and strength to it. It is hoped that this article will help the general public to know the revolutionaries as they are and will prevent it from taking them for what interested and ignorant persons would have it believe them to be.

Violence or Non-violence

Let us, first of all, take up the question of violence and non-violence. We think that the use of these terms, in itself, is a grave injustice to either party for they express the ideals of neither of them correctly. Violence is physical force applied for committing injustice, and that is certainly not what the revolutionaries stand for. On the other hand, what generally goes by the name of non-violence is in reality the theory of soul-force, as applied to the attainment of personal and national rights through courting suffering and hoping thus to finally convert your opponent to your point of view. When a revolutionary believes certain things to be his right, he asks for them, pleads for them, argues for them, will to attain them with all the soul-force at his command, stands the greatest amount of suffering for them, is always prepared to make the highest sacrifice for their attainment, and also backs his efforts with all the physical force he is capable of. You may coin what other word you like to describe his methods but you cannot call it violence, because that would constitute an outrage on the dictionary meaning of that word. Satyagraha is insistance upon Truth. Why press, for the acceptance of Truth, by soul-force alone? Why not add physical force also to it? While the revolutionaries tand for winning independence by all the forces, physical as well as moral, at their command, the advocates of soul-force would like to ban the use of physical force. The question really, therefore, is not whether you will have violence or non-violence, but whether you will have soul-force plus physical force of soul-force alone.

Our Ideal

The revolutionaries believe that the deliverance of their country will come through Revolution. The Replution, they are constantly working and hoping for, will not only express itself in the form of an armed conflict between the foreign government and its supporters and the people, it will also usher in a New Social Order. The revolution will ring the death knell of Capitalism and class distinctions and privileges. It will bring joy and prosperity to the starving millions who are seething today under the terrible yoke of both foreign and Indian exploitation, I will bring the nation into its own. It will give birth to a new State a new social order. Above all, it will establish the Dictatorship of the Proletariat and will for ever banish social parasites from the seat of political power.

Terrorism

The revolutionaries already see the advent of the revolution in the restlessness of youth, in its desire to break free from the mental bonds, and religious superstitions that told them. As the youth will get more and more saturated with the psychology of revolution, it will come to have a clearer realisation of national bondage and a growing, intense, unquenchable thirst for freedom. It will grow, this feeling or bondage, this insatible desire for freedom, till in their righteous anger, the infuriated youth will begin to kill the oppressors. Thus has Terrorism been born in the country. It is a phase, a necessary, an inevitable phase of the revolution. Terrorism is not the complete Revolution and the Revolution is not complete without Terrorism. This thesis can be supported by an analysis of any and every revolution in history. Terrorism instils fear in the hearts of the oppressors, it brings hopes of revenge and redemption to the oppressed masses, it gives courage and self-confidence to the wavering, it, shatters the spell of the superiority of the ruling class and raises the status of the subject race in the eyes of the would, because it is the most convincing proof of a nation's hunger for

Freedom. Here in India, as in other countries in the past, Terrorism will develop into the Revolution and the Revolution into Independence, social, political and economic.

Revolutionary Methods

This then is what the revolutionaries believe in, this is what they hope to accomplish for their country. They are doing in both openly and secretly and in their own way. The experience of a century. Long and world-wide struggle, between the masses and the governing class, is their guide to their goal and the methods they are following have never been known to have failed.

The Congress and the Revolutionaries

Meanwhile, what has the congress been doing? It has changed its creed from Swaraj to Complete Independene. As a logical sequence to this, one would expect it to declare a war on the British Government. Instead, we find, it has declared war against the Revolutionaries. The first offensive of the Congress came in the form of a resolution deploring the attempt made on the 23rd December 1929, to blow up the Viceroy's special. It was drafted by Gandhi and he fought tooth and jail for it, with the result, that it was passed by a trifling majority of 81 in a house of 1,713. Was even this bare majority a result of honest political convictions? Let us quote the opinion of Sarla Devi Chaudhrani, who has been a devotee of the Congress all her life, in reply. She says, "I discovered in the course of my conversations with a good many of the Mahatma's followers that it was only their senses of personal loyalty to him that was keeping them back from an expression of the independent views and preventing them from voting against any resolution whatsoever that was fathered by Mahatmaji". As to Gandhi's arguments in favour of his proposition, we will deal with them later, when we discuss his article, "The Cult of the Bomb" which is more or less, an amplification of his speech in the congress. There is one fact about this deplorable resolution which we must not lose sight of, and that is this. Inspite of the fact, that the congress is pledged to non-violence and has been actively engaged in carrying on propaganda in its favour for the last ten years, and, inspite of the fact also, that the supporters of the resolution indulged in abuse, called the revolutionaries 'cowards' and described their actions as 'dastardly' — and one of them even threaseningly remarked, that if they wanted to be lead by Gandhi, they should pass this resolution without any opposition— inspite of all this, the resolution could only be adopted by a dangerously narrow majority. That demonstrates, beyond the shadow of a doubt, how solidly the country is backing the revolutionaries. In a way Gandhi deserved our thanks for having brought the question up for discussion and thus having shown to the world at large that even the congress—that stronghold of non-violence is at least as more if not much, with the revolutionaries than with him.

Gandhi on War Path

Having achieved a victory which cost him more than a defeat, Gandhi has returned to the attack in his atticle "The Cult of the Bomb". We will give it our closest attention before proceeding further. That article consists of three things, his faith, his opinion and his argumem. We will not discuss what is a matter of faith with him because reasont has little in common with faith. Let us then take such of his opinion as are by arguments and his arguments proper, against what he calls violence and discuss them one by one.

Do the Masses Believe in Non-violence?

He thinks that on the basis of his experience during his latest tour in the country, he is right in believing that the large masses of India. Humanity are yet untouched by the spirit of violence and that non-violence has come to stay as a political weapon. Let him not delude himself on the experiences of his latest tour in the country. Though it is that the average leader confines his tours to places where only the mail train can conveniently land him, while Gandhi has extended his tour limit to where a motor car can take him, the practice, of staying only with the richest people in the places visited, of spending most of his time on being complimented by his devotees in private and public and of granting Darshan, now and then, to the illiterate masses, whom he claims to understand so well, disqualities him from claiming to know the mind of the masses. No man can claim to know a peoples mind by seeing them from the public platform and giving them Darshana and Updesh. He can at the most claim to have told the masses what he thinks about things. Has Gandhi, during recent years mixed in the social life of the masses? Has he sat with the peasant round the evening fire and tried to know what he thinks? Has he passed a single evening in the company of a factory labourer and shared with him his vows? We have, and therefor we claim to know what the masses think. We assure Gandhi, that the awrage Indian, like the average human being, understands little of the fine theological niceties about 'Ahinsa' and 'loving one's enemy'. The way of the world is like this. You have a friend you love him, sometimes so much that you even die for him. You have an enemy, you shun him, you fight against him and if possible, kill him. The gospel of the revolutionaries is simple and straight. It is what it has been since the days of Adam and Eve and no man has any difficulty about understanding it. We affirm that the masses of India are solidly with us because we know it from personal experience. The day is not far off when they will flock in their thousands to work the will of the Revolution.

The Gospel of Love

Gandhi declares that his faith in the effcacy of non-violence has increased. That is to say, he believes more and more, that through his gospel of love and self-imposed suffering, he hopes someday to convert the foreign rulers to his way of thinking. Now, he has devoted his whole life to the preaching of his wonderful gospel and has practised it with unwavering constance, as few others have done, Will he let the world know how many enemies of India he has been able to turn into friends? How many O'Dwyers, Readings and Irwins has he been able to convert into friends of India? If none, how can India be expected to share his 'growing faith' that he will be able to persuade or compel Englandto agree to Indian Independence through the practice of non-violence.

What Would Have Happened.

If the bomb, that burst under the Viceroy's special, had exploded properly, one of the two things suggested by Gandhi would have surely happened. The Viceroy would have either been badly injured or killed. Under such circumstances there certainly would have been no meeting between the leaders of political parties and the Viceroy. The uncalled for the undignified attempt on the part of these individuals, to lower the national prestige by knocking at the gates of the Government House with the beggar's bowl in their hands and Dominion Status on their lips, inspite of the clear terms of the Calcutta Ultimatum, would have been checkmated and the nation would have been the better for that. If fortunately, the explosion had been powerful enough to kill the Viceroy, one more enemy of India would have met a well deserved doom. The author of the Meerut prosecutions and the Lahore and Bhusawal persecutions can appear a Friend of India only to the enemies of her Freedom. Inspite of Gandhi and the Nehrus and their claims to political sagacity and statesmanship, Irwin has succeded in shattering the unity between different political parties in the country, that had resulted from the boycott of the Simon Commission. Even the Congress today is a house divided against itself. Who else, except the Viceroy and his olive tongue, have we to thank for our grave misfortunes? And yet there exist people in our country who proclaim him a Friend of India!

The Future of the Congress

There might be those who have no regard for the Congress and hope nothing from it. If Gandhi thinks that the revolutionaries belong to that category, he wrongs them grievously. They fully realise the part played by the congress in awakenang, among the ignorant masses, a keen desire for freedom. They expect freat things of it in the future. Though they hold firudy to their opinion, that so long as persons like Sen Gupta, whose wonderful intelligence compels him to dicern the hand of the C.I.D. in the late attempt to blow up the Viceroy's Special, and persons like Ansari, who think abuse the better part of argument and know so little of politics as to make the ridiculous and fallacious assertion that no nation had achieved freedom by the Bomb, have a datermining voice in the affairs of the congress, the country can hope little from it, they in the affairs of the congress, the country can hope little from it, they are hopefully looking forward to the day, when the mania of non-violence would have passed away from the congress, and it would march arm in arm with the revolutionaries to their common goal of Complete Independence. This year it has accepted the ideal which the revolutionaries have preached and lived upto for more than a quarter of a century. Let us hope the next year will see it endeors their methods also.

Violence and Military Expenditure

Gandhi is of opinion that as often as violence has been practised in the country, it has resulted in an increase of military expenditure. If his reference is to revolutionary activities during the last twenty-five years we dispute the accuracy of his statement and challenge him to prove his statement with facts and figures. If, on the other hand, he had the wars that have taken place in India since the British came here in mind, our reply is that even his modest experiment in Ahinsa and Satyagrah which had little to compare in it with the wars for independence, produced its effect on the finances of the Bureaucracy. Mass action, whether violent or non-violent, whether successful or unsuccessful, is bound to produce the same kind of repercussions on the finances of a esate.

The Reforms

Why should Gandhi mix up the revolutionaries with various constitutional reforms granted by the government? They never cared or worked for the Morley-Minto Reforms, Montague Reforms and the like. These the British Government threw before the constitutionalist agitators to lure them away from the right path. This was the bribe paid to them for their support to the government in its policy of crushing and uprooting the revolutionaries. These toys—as Gandhi calls them—were sent to India for the benefit of those, who, from time to time, raised the cry of 'Home Rule',

'Self-Government', 'Responsible', 'Full Responsible Government', 'Dominion Status' and such other constitutional names for slavery. The revolutionaries never claim the Reforms as their achievements. They raised the standard of independence long ago. They have lived for it. They have ungurdingly laid their lives down for the sake of this ideal. They claim that their sacrifices have produced a tremendous change in the mentality of the people. That their efforts have advanced the country a long way on the road to Independence, is granted by even those who do not see eye t eye with them in politics.

The Way of Progress

As to Gandhi's contention that violence impedes that march of progress and thus directly postpones the day of freedom, we can refer him to so many contemporary instances where violences has led to the social progress and political freedom of the pecple who practised it. Take the case of Russia and Turkey for example. In both countries the party for progress took over the state organisation through an armed revolution. Yet social progress and political freedom has not been impeded. Legislation, backed by force, has made the mases go 'double march' on the road of progress. The solitary example of Afghanistan cannot establish a political formula. It is rather the exception that proves the rule.

Failure of Non-Co-operation

Gandhi is of opinion that the great awakening in the people, during the days of non-co-operation, was a result of the preaching of non-violence. It is wrong to assign to non-violence the widespread awakening of the masses which, in fact, is manifested where ever a programme of direct action is adopted. In Russia, for instance, there came about widespread awakening the peasants and workers, when the communist launched forth their great programme of Militant Mass Action, though nobody preached non-violence to them. We will even go further and state that it iwas mainly the mania for non-violence Gandhi compromise mentality that brought about the disruption of the forces that had come together as the call of Mass Action. It is claimed that non-violence can be used as a weapon for righting political wrongs. To say the least, it is a novel idea, yet untried. It failed to achieve what were considered to be the just rights of Indians in sough Africa. It failed to bring 'Swaraj within a year' to the Indian masses inspite of the untiring labours of an army of national workers and one and a quarter crores of rupees. More recently, it failed to win for the Bardoli peasants what the leaders of the Satyagraha movement had promised them—the famous irreducible minimum of Gandhi and Patel. We know of no other trains non-violence had had on a country-wide scale. Up to this time non-violence has been blessed with one result—Failure. Little wonder, then, that the country refuses to give it another trial. In fact Satyagraha as preached by Gandhi is a form of agitation—a protest, leading up invariably, as has already been seen, to a compromise. It can hardly be of any use to a nation striving for national independence which can never come as the result of a compromise. The sooner we recognise, that there can be no compromise between independence and slavery, the better.

It is a New Era?

'We are entering upon a new era' thinks Gandhi. The mere act of defining swaraj as Complete Independence, this technical change in the congress constitution, can hardly constitute a new era. It will be a great day indeed when the congress will decide upon a countrywide programme of Mass Action, based on well recognised revolutionary principles. Till then the unfurling of the flag of Independence is a mockery and we concur with the following remarks of Sarla Devi Chaudharani, which she recently made, in a press interview.

"The unfurling of the Flag of Independence", she says "at just one minute after midnight of the 31st December 1929 was too stagy for words—just as the G.O.C. and the assistant G.O.C. and others in gaudy uniforms were card board Grand Officers Commanding."

"The fact that the unfurling of the flag of Independence lay hanging in the balance till midnight of that date, and that the scales might have been turned at even the eleventh hour fifty ninth minute had a message from the Viceroy or the Secretary of State come to the Congress granting Dominion Status, proves that Independence is not a heart hunger of the leaders but that the declaration of it is only like a petulant child's retort. It would have been a worthy action of the Indian National Congress if Independence was achieved first and declared afterwards." It is true that the congress orators will henceforth harangue the masses on Complete Independence instead of Dominion Status. They will call upon the people to propare for a struggle in which one party is to deliver blows and the other is simply to receive them, till beaten and demoralised beyond hope of recovery! Can such a thing be named a struggle and can it ever lead the country to Complete Independence? It is all very well to hold fast to the highest ideal worthy of a nation, but it is none the less necessary to adopt the best, the most efficacious and tried means, to achieve it ere you became the laughing stock of the whole world.

No Bullying please

Gandhi has called upon all those who are not past reason to withdraw their support from the revolutionaries and condemn their actions so that 'our deluded patriots may, for want of nourishment to their violent spirit, realise the futility of violence and the great harm that violent activities have every time done'. How easy and convenient it is to call people deluded, to declare them to be past reason, to call upon the public to withdraw its support and condemn them so that they may get isolated and be forced to suspend their activities, specially when a man holds the confidence of an influential section of the public! It is a pity that Gandhi does not and will not understand revolutionary psychology inspite of his life-long experience of public life. Life is a precious thing. It is dear to every one. If a man becomes a revolutionary, if he goes about with his life in the hollow of his half read to sacrifice it at any moment, he does not do so merely for the fun of it. He does not risk his life merely because sometimes, when the crowd is in a sympathetic mood, it cries 'Bravo' in appreciation. He does it because his reason forces him to take that course, because his conscience forces him to take that course, because his conscience dictates it. A revolutionary believes in reason more than anything. It is to reason, and reason alone, that he bows. No amount of abuse and condemnation, even if it eminats from the highest, of the high, can turnt him from his set purpose. To think, that a revolutionary will give up his ideals if public support and appreciation is with drawn from him, is the highest folly. Many a revolutionary has, ere now stepped on to the scaffold and laid his life down for the cause, regardless of the curses that the constitutionalist agitators rained plentifully upon him. If you will have the revolutionaries suspend their activities, reason with them squarely. That is the one and the only way. for the rest let their be no doubt in anybody mind. a revolutionary is the last person on earth to submit to bullying.

An Appeal

We take this opportunity to appeal to our countrymen—to the youth, to the workers and peasants, to the revolutionary intelligentsia—to come forward an join us in carrying aloft the banner of freedom. Let us establish a new order of society in which political and economic exploitation will be an impossibility. In the name of those gallant men and women, who willingly accepted death so that we, their descendants, may lead a happier life, who toiled ceaselessly and perished for the poor, the famished, and exploited millions of India, we call upon every patriot to take up the fight in all seriousness. Let nobody toy with the nation's freedom, which is her very life, by making psychological experiments in non-violence and such other novelties. Our slavery is our shame. When shall we have courage and wisdom enough to be able to shake ourselves free of it? What is our great heritage of civilisation and culture worth if we have not enough self-respect left in us to prevent us from bowing surveillance to the commands of foreignes and paying homage to their flag and king?

Victory or Death

There is no crime that Britain has not committed in India. Deliberate misrule has reduced us to paupers, has 'bled us white'. As a race and a people we stand dishonoured and outraged. Do people still expect us to forget and to forgive? We shall have our revenge—a people's righteous revenge on the Tyrant. Let cowards fall back and cringe for compromise and peace. We ask not for mercy and we give no quarter. Ours is a war to the end—to Victory or Death.

Long live revolution
Kartar Singh
President
Hindustan Socialist Republic Association

The Hindustan Socialist Republican Association Manifesto

"The food on which the tender plan of liberty thrives is the Blood of the Martyr."

For decades this life blood to the Plnt of India's liberty is being supplied by revolutionaries. There are few to question the magnanimty of the noble ideals they cherish and the grand sacrifices they have offered, but their normal activities being mostly secret the country is in dark as to their present policy and intentions. This has necessitated the Hindustan Socialist Republican Association to issue this manifesto.

This association stands for Revolution in India in order to liberate her from foreign domination by means of organised armed rebellion. Open rebellion by a subject people must always in the nature of things be preceded by secret propaganda and secret preparations. Once a country enters that phase task of an alien Government becomes impossible. It might linger on for a number of years but its fate is sealed. Human nature, with all its prejudices and conservatism, has a sort of instinctive dread for Revolution. Upheavals have always been a terror to holders of power and previlege. Revolution is asphenomenon which nature loves and without which there can be no progress either in nature or in human affairs. Revolution is certainly not unthinking, brutal campaign of murder and incendiarism; it is not a few bombs thrown here and a few shots fired there: neither it is a movement to destroy all remnant of civilization and blow to pieces time-honoured principles of Justice and Equity. Revolution is not a philosophy of despair or a creed of desperadoes. Revolution may be *anti*-God but is certainly not *anti*-Man. It is a vital, living force which is indicative of eternal conflict between the Old and the New, between Life and Living Death, between Light and Darkness. There is no concord, no symphony, no rhythm without revolution. 'The music of the spheres' of which poets have sung, would remin an unreality if a ceaseless Revolution were to be eliminited from the space. Revolution is Law, Revolution is Order and Revolution is the Truth.

The youths of our Nation have realized this Truth. They have learnt painfully the lesson that without Revolution there is no possibility of enthroning Order, Law and Love in place of chaos and Legal Vandalism and Hatred which are reigning supreme today. Let no one, in this blessed land of ours, run with the idea that the youths are irresponsible. They know where they stand. None knows better, than their own selves, that their path is not in with roses. From time to time they have paid a fairly decent price for their Ideals. It does not, therefore, lie in the mouth of anybody to say that youthful impetuosity has feasted upon platitudes. It is no good to hurl denunciatory epithets at our Idealogy. It is enough to know that our Ideas are sufficienctly active and powerful to drive us on aye, even to gallows.

It has become a fashion these days to indulge in wild and meaningless talk of non-violence. Mahatma Gandhi is great and we mean no disrepect to him if we express our emphatic disapproval of the methods adocated by him for our country' emanicipation. We would be ungrateful to him if we do not salute him for the immense awakening that has been brought about by his non-coperation movement in the country. But to us the Mahatma is an impossible visionary. Non-violence may be a noble Ideal, but it is a thing of the morrow. We can, situated as we are never hope, to win our freedom by mere non-violence. The world is armed to the very teeth. And the world is too much with us. All talk of peace may be sincere, but we, of the slave Nation, cannot, and must not, be led away by such false Idealogy. What Logic, we ask, is there in asking the country to traverse a non-violent path when the world atmosphere is surcharged with violence and exploitation of the weak? We declared with all the emphasis we can command that the youths of the Nation cannot be lured by such mid-summernight's dream.

We believe in violence, not as an end in itself but as a means to a Noble End. And the votaries of non-violence, as also the advocates of Caution and circumspection will readily grant this much at least that we know how to suffer for, and to act upto, our convictions. Shall we here recount all those sacrifices which our comrades have offered at the alter of our common Mother? Many a heartrending and soul-stirring scene has been enacted inside the four walls of His Majesty's Prison: We have been taken to task for our Terroristic Policy. Our answer is that terrorism is never the object of revolutionaries, nor do they believe that terrorism alone can bring independence. No doubt the revolutionaries think, and rightly, that it is only by resorting to terrorism alone that they can find a most effective means of retaliation. The British Government exists, because the Britishers have been successful in terrorising the whole of India. How are we to meet this official terrorism? Only counter-terrorism on the part of revolutionaries can checkmate effectively this bureaucratic bullying. A feeling of utter helplessness pervades society. How can we overcome this fatal despondency? It is only by infusing a real spirit of sacrifice that that lost self-confidence can be restored.

Terrorism has its Inter-national aspect also. England's enemies, which are many, are drawn towards us by effective demonstration of our strength. That in itself is a great advantage.

India is writhing under the yoke of imperialism. Her teeming millions are today a helpless prey to proverty and ignorance. Foreign domination and economic exploitation have unmanned the vast majority of the people who constitute the workers and peasants of India. The position of the Indian Proletariat is, today, extremely critical. It has a double danger to face. It has to bear the onslaught of Foreign Capitalism in one hand and the treacherous attack of Indian Capital on the other. The latter is showing a progressive tendency to join forces with the former. The leaning of certain politicians in favour of Dominion Status shows clearly which way the wind blows. Indian Capital is preparing to betray the masses into the hands of Foreign Capitalism and receive as a price of this betrayal, a little share in the Government of the country. The hope of the proletariat is, therefore, now centred in Socialism which alone can lead to the establishment of Complete Independence and the removal of all social distinction and privileges.

The future of India rests with the youths. They are the salt of the earth. Their promptness to suffer, their daring courage and their radiant sacrifice prove that India's future in their hands is perfectly safe. In a moment of realization the late Deshbandhu Dass said, "The youths are at once the hope and glory of the Motherland. Theirs is the inspiration behind the movement. Their is the sacrifice. Their is the victory. They are torch-bearers on the road to Freedom. They are the pilgrims on the road to Liberty."

Youths-ye-soldiers of the Indian Republic, fall in! Do not stand easy, do not let kness tremble. Shake off the paralysing effects of long lethargy. Yours is a noble Mission. Go out into every nook and cornor of the country and prepare the ground for future Revolution which is sure to come. Respond to the clarion call of duty. Do not vegetate. Grow ! Every minute of your life you must think of devising means so that this your ancient land may arise with flaming eyes and fierce yawn! Sow the seeds of disgust and hatred against British Imperialism in the fertile minds of your fellow youths. And the seeds shall sprout and there shall grow a jungle of sturdy trees, because you shall water the seeds with your warm blood. Then a grim and terrible earthquake having a univerfally destructive potentiality shall inevitably come along with portentous rumblings, an this edifice of Imperialism will crash and crumble to dust, and great shall be the fall thereof. And then and not till then, a new Indian Nation shall arise and surprise humanity with the splendom and glory all its own. The wise and the mighty shall be bewildered by the simple and the weak.

Individual liberty shall be safe. The sovereignty of the proletariat shall be recognised. We court the advent of such Revolution. Long live Revolution!!!

Kartar Singh
President
Printed at the Republican Press, Erehwon, India

Copy of the notice found pasted on the gate of St. Johns College, Agra Long Live Revolution

"Without libery life is not worth living."

Youths ye are the source of liberty, the hope of the country, nay the saviour of the motherland. Loyalty to this tyranny and exploitation makes you traitor to your country by summarily disposing off and launching many of your brothers to eternity.

Make India another Ireland and the reins of

Government are in your hands. Without the least agitation you should meet the scaffold even as a yogi enters the samadhi. The appetite for revolution is apt to grow with what it feeds on.

Remember the words of an Englishmen who says "we have the power of life in our hands and I assure you we spare not...."

Atrocities were committed in the burning of villages and massacre of innocent inhabitants at which Mohammad Tughlak himself would have stood ashamed. They have sewed Mohammedans in pig skin and smeared them with pork fat before execution during the mutiny and then burning their bodies and they have forced Hindus to defile themselves. It is plain enough from Russels diary. They did not deliberately hang Indians but burnt them in their villages. The Englishmen did not hesitate to boast that they had spared no one and that peppering away at niggers was pleasant past time enjoyed amazingly.

An Englishman is almost suffocated with indignation when he reads that Chambers of Miss Jernnings was hacked to death by a dusky ruffian but in native history or legends and tradition in may be recorded against our people that mothers, wives and children with less familiar names fell miserable victims to the first swoop of English vengeance.

Our C.I.D. friends must remember the report of Montgomery Martin:

"All the city people were bayonated on the spot when our army entered Delhi, the number was considerable when I tell you that in some houses 40 or 50 persons were hiding, they were not mutineers but residents of city who trusted to our **Well Known Mild Rule of Pardon,** I am glad to say that they were disappointed."

Further they warned that they stake their lives if

they come in our way. British officials should take long furloughs and go home. We hold humanity sacred but Government out enemy.

We thank the Principal, Agra College and the Warden, Medical School for the loyalty they have shown to the Government. The students should condemn the action of that boy who took the Manifesto to the Principal. A social boycott is sufficient for such a traitor.

Get yourself enlisted soon. More you will find next week at this very place.

Long Live Revolution

Branch Office: Kailash Singh
Naudub, Budaon. *President*

Typed at the branch office of Hindustan Republican Association

Erehwon, India

Notes 1. The antiques are in red in the original.

2. The Poster appeared in Agra in January 1930.

Copy of a leaflet found in the Mcehuobazar Street, search (December 1929).

The Youths of Bengal

"From the seeming stillness of the sea of Indian humanity a veritable storm is about to break out."

The critical moment for the fire-worshipping youthful sons (anarchists) of Bengal to bring the truth into reality has come. It has become necessary to stem the tide of the hideous oppressions that are being practised on the men and women of this country by the powerpuffed and appressive foreign rulers in the name of law and order. Since the beginning of the 20th century and up till now many youths of the country sacrificed completely their youthful qualities in order to stop the tide, some by welcomeing hangman's rope, some by receiving bullet wounds, some by courting imprisonment in solitary cells and some by welcoming transporation in distant islands. That midnight dawned with the self-sacrifice of the revolutionary hero, Khudiram, Rudra violence worshipper, Kanialal and the bloody revolutionary Satyen. Then slowly as the light of day began to be scorching the fertile soil of Bengal was reddened with the hot blood of the many revolutionary heroes maddened with the joy of shedding blood. The Bengali youths with great pains have not been able to forget up till now the offering of Jatin Mukherji and Nalini Bagchi of that age. Then, when the political sky of India became surcharged with the vilification of the anarchists consequent on the agitation of non-violent non-co-operation, and when Mohandas Gandhi, the inaugurator of non-co-operation, and who is confident in English co-operation himself, smelt nothing but blunder in this extraordinary self-sacrifice, the embracing of death by dreadful soldier Gopinath by breaking the stillness, explained to the confounded Rudra worshippers (anarchists) of Bengal which was the road to freedom. In search of that path many youths ran recklessly, and in their attempt to destroy the blood-sucking of the covetous ruler, they, according to the custom of a dependent country, sacrificed themselves as a bloody offering in that fearful oblation with fire. But unfortunately, in spite of it ithe stillness of the country did not break. The inanimateness o the nation remained unmovingly fixed like a heavy chain and the helpless nation sank down in dolefulness. The matter of regret is that if anyone ever wants to draw a ray of light in this great night of New Moon, then there will rise from all quarters an uproar of incantation of "non-violence" or there will come out a false hoax of something very great. If any one ever giving our owing to mortal anguish and says "No, I shall never bear silently this sort of wron\gdoing by the foreigner. Anyhow I shall try to make a campaign with my little power againt it"—

it will at once be proclaimed by the self-sufficient leaders that this is the work of a spy. In this way the so-called grandiloquent leaders want to pulverise the movement of a nation's life; because it strikes at the root of their proficiency—hurts their leadership.

The extreme proof of barbarism of the fiendish English people is the murder of Jatindranath in the Lahore Prison House. Bengali Youths! Will it not drag you now towards a bloody campaign? Will the fascination of untruth keep you as imbecile even now? Young Bengalis? Will not your revolutionary spirit stir up to play with fire at the self-sacrifice of Jatin? Will it not blossom like a red lotus? Will not the proof of convetousness of the English Government the merciless oppressions on all quarters and the harrowing persecutions teach you to think seriously where your path lies? Do not select a wrong path being stupefied by the old leaders of Bengal. Stand on your legs. You will find that your strength is irresistible and unlimited. You will be in a position to crumble everything. What is you fear? What is you anxiety? This is how a nation awakes. Flare up with the fire of vengeance for the annihilation of foreigd enemies. You will find that the victory is yours. History bears testimony to this. Read and learn the history of Pearce—the gem of young Ireland and you will find how noble is his sacrifice; how he stimulated new animation in the nation, being mad over independence. When everybody was reluctant to die he alone proclaimed loudly—"I cannot live. Even if I am alone I shall have to come to the field of activity with the banner of an armed revolution in order to bring vigour in the life of this inanimate nation. With my death a hundred heroes will spring up who will triumph over death, who with their fresh blood prepare the steps to Independence of Young Ireland in the next era". Pearse died and by so dying he roused in the heart of the nation an indomitable desire for armed revolution. Who will deny this truth? That lion of a hero did not tremble owing to the inferiority of his number—that revolutionary was not moved at the request of the old man. This is his peculiarity. Oh, the party of men deprived of everything—open your eyes and see where your position is. So, the all to break the bondage has come today and you will have to respond to that call. You will have to make the place of the enchained Bharat Mata in the world glorious, and it would be a matter of pride if you will have to stand alone at the outset against the despotism of the blood-thirsty English.

No fear there is no fear.
He who will give his life completely
will sustain no loss.

Extract from pages 244-245. Volume I, of the Proceeding of the Court of Special Tribunal, Chittagong.

The Indian Republican Army, Chittagong Branch hereby declares today the lives of all Englishmen and white-skinned Anglo-Indians who are prejudicial to the interest of Indian freedom, forfeited to it. It also entreats all the members of **The Indian Republican Army** and the people of Chittagong to begin a vigorous campaign of murdering these people wherever found to avenge the murders of their forefathers and thus to relieve the country of the pernicious exploitations which they are doing in this land of OURS.

The Indian Republican Army further declares that any person who will be able to produce any Englishman, woman or child of any age to its headquarters, dead or alieve, will be amply rewarded.

By order,
President in Council,
Indian Republican Army,
Chittagong Branch.
(Terrorism in India– 1917–1936).

The Kakori Conspiracy

The Kakori conspiracy is the natural sequel to the resumed revolutionary activities which followed the withdrawal of the Non-cooperation Movement in 1922. Emissaries from Bengal came to organise branches of the revolutionary party in Benaras. On the other hand, Sachindra Nath Sanyal, an old revolutionary of the Benaras Conspiracy case, revived his secret society. Sachindra Sanyal was given transportation for life in the Benaras Conspiracy Case but was released in February 1920 in the amnesty that followed the British victory in the First World War. Many other frustrated non-cooperators like Chandra Shekhar Azad, Manmathnath Gupta, Vishnu Saran Dublish and Ram Dulare Trivedi were also very keen on the revival of the revolutionary activities.

Chandra Shekhar Azad had already gained some fame as a non-cooperator in Benaras where he was studying in the Sanskrit Pathshala. He was arrested while picketting at the Sanskrit college when he was only fifteen years of age in 1921. The trying Magistrate asked Chandra Shekhar certain questions which are interesting to cite. The following is the text of the conversation that followed:

"What is your name?"

"Azad."

"What is your father's name?"

"Swadhin (Independent)."

"Where is your residence?"

"My residence is in prison."

Chandra Shekhar was awarded fifteen stripes as punishment. At each stroke he shouted "Mahatma Gandhi ki Jai". He was badly wounded as a result of flogging. But after the incident, he was hailed as a "young hero" in Benaras and was accorded a warm reception at a public meeting. His photograph was published in the newspaper *Maryada* with the caption "Veer Balak Azad" (young hero Azad). The editor of this newspaper was Sampoornanand, an eminent Congressman, and its publisher was the prominent Congress leader Shiv Prasad Gupta of Benaras. Since then Chandra Shekhar came to be known as Azad.

After the withdrawal of the Non-Cooperation movement Chandra Shekhar Azad joined the Kashi Vidyapeeth, founded by Mahatma Gandhi in 1921. Manmathnath Gupta and Pranavesh Chatterji–who were already members of the revolutionary group–were his class-fellows. Pranavesh Chatterji inducted Azad into the revolutionary party where he came in contact with Jogesh Chandra Chatterji.

Ram Prasad Bismil and Roshan Singh also joined the revolutionary group. Through the efforts of Sachindra Sanyal, all these revolutionary groups merged together and formed the Hindustan Republican Association in early 1924. Sachindra Sanyal became the overall leader of the party.

Sachindra Sanyal had been in the revolutionary party since 1907 in Calcutta. He was an intellectual, a writer and an orator. A man of his calibre could easily set up an organisation. He was the brain behind all the intellectual activities of the party. His book *Bandi Jiwan* (Prison Life) had inspired many a youngmen. It contained a thrilling account of the attempt at revolt by the revolutionaries at the time of the First World War. The author described the story of Benaras, Lahore and Bengal Conspiracy Cases, in continuity; sacrifice of his colleagues, their hangings, long imprisonments and other sufferings. A British official once said of this book; "It is one of the best known gems of terrorist literature," and another official commented: "The author has sent more youngen to the gallows or to prison for terrorism than any man who has lived in India." Sachindra Sanyal gave the newly formed party a constitution and a revolutionary status.

Besides Sachindra Sanyal, Ram Prasad Bismil, Jogesh Chandra Chatterji and Suresh Chandra Bhattacharya also worked hard for the organisation of the party. The constitution of the party was called the "Yellow Paper" as it was printed on six yellow sheets of paper, and did not bear mark of any printing press. The party aimed at the establishment of a Federated Republic of India by an organised and armed revolution. It envisaged a system of society in which the exploitation of man by man would not be possible. The party was to have five departments dealing with—(1) Propaganda; (2) Collection of men; (3) Collection of funds, and terrorism; (4) Collection and storage of arms and ammunition; and (5) Foreign connection. Propaganda of party ideology was to be carried on through private conversations and by means of an open and secret press. Other means of propaganda such as the use of public platforms and magic lantern slides, were also contemplated. The party was in favour of collecting funds generally by means of voluntary subscriptions, but it did not rule out the possibility of extracting contributions by force if the occasion demanded so. Through its department of foreign connection, the party had a plan to send suitable men to foreign countries in order to get military and scientific training so that they could become military or scientific experts to take charge of army and ammunition factories at the time of open rebellion. It was also to be the endeavour of the party to remain in close touch and to cooperate with the Indian revolutionaries outside India.

The overall governing body of the association was to be Central Council composed of the representatives of every province of India. The association did not rule out the use of terrorism as a means to retaliate the extreme repression by the British government in India. The party was to work as a secret organisation, but open platforms in the forms of clubs and libraries were also planned, and party members were entrusted with the work of organising labour movements in factories, railways and the coal-fields. Similarly, the *kisans* were to be organised for the sake of a revolution. The party though in terms of influencing the Congress and other public activities as far as possible. The recruitment of new person to the party was the duty of the district organiser. The qualifications and the duties of the district organiser are given in some detail in the party constitution as he was supposed to be an important person responsible for giving the party a well organised shape in terms of man and material. Consequently, it was impressed upon in the constitution itself that the district organiser must be a well-informed person about the current political, social and economic affairs of the country, and he must be a courageous and self-sacrificing person. He was expected to have comprehensive information of his district in various fields.

The party, generally, drew its recruits from young congressmen and students. Only patriotic, courageous and trustworthy persons were picked up by the party, but there was always the possibility of somebody turning an approver. So the party took certain precautions. Even before recruitment, the trend of mind of the persons was judged by the District Organiser, and if it was found to be patriotic and revolutionary, the persons were gradually initiated into the movement. They were given revolutionary literature such as Sachindra Sanyal' *Bandi Jiwan, Life of Garibaldi and Mazzini,* Savarkar's *History of the First War of Independence* and a copy of the *Rowlatt Act.* They were told the stories of bravery of Barindra Ghosh, Khudiram Bose, Rash Behari Bose, Kanailal Dutt, Sachindra Sanyal and other revolutionaries, specially the martyrs of the Hardinge Bomb Case. This created a wave of patriotism among these youngmen. Then began a free and frank talk followed by enrolment. The enrolment meant only a mental note and not a written pledge. However, it was mentioned in the party constitution that if a member betrayed the party, he would be punished either with expulsion or with death.

Sometime after the publication of "Yellow Paper" a four-page pamphlet entitled *The Revolutionary* prepared, by Sachindra Sanyal was published and secretly distributed, by hand and by post, in many parts of the country. The wide circulation was meant to give the impression to the public and the police that the HRA had a big organisation. The pamphlet began with the quotation: "Chaos is necessary to the birth of a new star." It stated the ideals and their means of achievement by the party. The association intended to pursue the policy of coopertion when possible and dissociation were necessary with the Congress. But it viewed all constitutional agitations with contempt and ridicule. In the opinion of the party, it was a mockery to say that India's salvation can be achieved through constitutional means, where no constitution existed; it was self-deception to say that India's political liberty can be attained through peaceful and legitimate means when the enemy was determined to break the peace at his own convenience. At the same time, the party said that the revolutionaries were neither terrorists nor anarchists. They never aimed at spreading anarchy in the land, and terrorism was never their object. They never believed that terrorism alone could bring independence although they did not rule out this method as an effective means of retaliation. The Indians helped the British simply because they were terrorised. On the other hand, the fear of the British prevented the Indians from helping the revolutionaries. The revolutionaries, therefore, wanted to retaliate official terrorism by counter-terrorism.

The revolutionaries thought that acts of terrorism would get them sympathy and publicity in foreign lands from the enemies of England, and thus expedite the attainment of India's freedom. As the party had been waiting to deliver the final blow to the enemy, it did not indulge into terrorist campaign. But at the time of need, the party planned to enter into a desperate campaign of terrorism when the life of every Englishman and his Indian lackey in India would be made in possible.

The Revolutionary expressed the party's sintention to "follow the footsteps of the great Indian *Rishis* of the glorious past and of Bolshevik Russia in the modern age." But at that time, the ideas of socialism prevailing in the Soviet Union were not clear to the Indian revolutionaries. The manifesto bracketted the ancient saints of India with Bolshevik Russia as if their ideas and ideals had been translated into action in Russia. But this did not look preposterous at that time. Sachindra Sanyal who had a major hand in formulating the ideology and constitution of the party was a sincere believer in spiritual values as preached by Indian saints and seers. Morever, it should not be forgotten that this constitution was prepared when in India neither a Communist party nor any of the socialist parties had come into being. So far as the young revolutionaries were concerned, they were simply thrilled by the introduction of new ideas, and were happy that such new ideas were readily accepted by the rank and file of the party. Soon after distribution of *The Revolutionary* another pamphlet written in Bengali by Sachindra Sanyal was circulated. It was titled *Deshbashir Prati Nivedan* that is, "An Appeal to the Countrymen." The contents of all these pamphlets revealed that the HRA was slowly deviating from the old ideology of Lokmanya Tilak and Aurobindo Ghosh which was based on religious nationalism, but under the leadership of Sachindra Sanyal, it could not make much progress in this direction. At the same time Sachindra Sanyal was able to see that the new ideas of Russia were influencing the younger revolutionaries. But he fondly liked to believe that these new ideas and much more was contained in the philosophy of the ancient Indian seers. He was nearer to Vivekanand and Aurobindo than to Marx and Lenin.

Sachindranath Sanyal had some correspondence with Gandhiji early in 1925. Earlier in 1924, at the Ahmedabad Congress Session, Gandhiji was disappointed to find some of his dearest and closest followers voting against the resolution condemning the revolutionary Gopi Mohan Saha for his terrorist act. Gopi Mohan Saha had made an attempt on the life of the Police Commissioner Sir Charles Tegart in Calcutta in 1924. But he mistook another European Mr. Day for Tegart and killed him. Saha was later hanged for this terrorist act. At the time of adoption of the resolution, Gandhiji wept in public. The tension at the AICC session was more due to the fact that at the Dinajpore (Bengal) Provincial Conference of the Congress a much stronger resolution had been passed praising Gopi Mohan Saha's selfless sacrifice and patriotism. The Dinajpore resolution was too much for Gandhiji and he openly denounced the revolutionaries. Then Sachindra Sanyal wrote a letter anonymously to Gandhiji, Gandhiji published the letter as well as his reply in the *Young India* of 12 February 1925. In this letter, the writer said that the revolutionaries had promised to remain silent only for a year to enable Gandhiji to carry out his experiment of non-cooperation. And now as the experiment was over, they were free to resume their activities. Further, the revolutionaries did not want to develop contact with the masses till they became sure of their own strength. But they believed that the masses of northern India were ready for any emergency. Towards the end of the letter, the writer requested Gandhiji to be at least tolerant towards the revolutionaries if he could not help them.

Sachindra Sanyal made considerable progress in furthering the organisation and activities of the HRA. In 1924, he went into hiding in Bengal having passed in the work of organisation to Jogesh Chandra Chatterji who extended the party work to Allahabad, Kanpur and other districts of the UP. After completing his organisational work in the UP, Jogesh Chandra returned to Calcutta where he was interned under the Bengal Ordinance on 18 October 1924 as a suspicious character. At the time of his arrest, a paper was found on him which gave the party strength as 100, and also the future programme of the party regarding propaganda and publicity. After Jogesh Chandra Chatterji's arrest, Ram Prasad Bismil came to the forefront as the leader of the military department of the party. Bismil belonged to Shahjahanpur in the UP. He was an Arya Samajist. He was fond of hunting and was a good marksman. In 1916, at the time of the Congress Session in Lucknow Bismil went there as he was keen to see and hear Bal Gangadhar Tilk. There he joined the band of those youngmen who wanted to give a rousing reception to Tilak at the railway station, and then take him in a grand procession through the streets of Lucknow. The moderates among the Congressmen did not subscribe to this idea as they were afraid that such a reception to Tilak would be in effect giving him more importance than the Congress President himself. But ultimately, the group of youngmen was successful in carrying out their plan of giving a grand reception to Tilak at the railway station, and subsequently they took him out in a grand crowded procession through the main thorough fares of Lucknow. Bismil participated in the reception and procession of Tilak with great enthusiasm. It was a great sentimental experience for him. He came in contact of the revolutionaries during the Lucknow Congress.

Bismil was a singularly handsome person with a strong physique. He was an old revolutionary, and an absconder of the Mainpuri Conspiracy Case. He remained disguised as a peasant for a long time, and reappeared in public only when he was included in the First World War Victory amnesty. Ram Prasad Bismil was a brave man. He was also a poet of some distinction. But he lacked organisation capacity. He was a bit reckless and cared little for party rules. Gradually the militant section of the party became its most important department, and its leader Ram Prasad Bismil, the most important man in the party.

The revolutionaries tried to procure arms and ammunitions from different sources. Under the leadership of Ram Prasad, arms were procured from the Indian States, specially from Gwalior. Arms were also bought from armymen, and from other places and people like international smugglers at exhorbitant prices. As there was no war going on, the revolutionaries could not expect donations of arms from foreign powers, as they got from German agents during the First World War.

Apart from the purchase of arms and ammunition, the party needed money for carrying on its various propaganda and organisational activities. Some party members had to depend entirely on the party for their upkeep. The party often used messangers for important communications because of the fear of government censorship. A lot of money was spent by the party on buying books and publishing pamphlets. Some members paid subscriptions to the utmost of their capacity, but most of them were students and belonged to the lower middle class, and so they could not contribute much to the party. The party received money from its sympathisers who were well-off but not many. For instance, Babu Shiv Prasad Gupta of Benares, a staunch and devout Congressman used to contribute an amont of rupees five hundred now and then, when approached by Sachindra Sanyal. Another sympathiser of the party, famous Congress leader Ganesh Shankar Vidyarthi of Kanpur, provided work and employment to revolutionaries like Suresh Chandra Bhattacharya in his newspaper *Pratap*. Vidhyarthi was also a personal friend of Sachindra Sanyal. But all these resources put together were very insufficient to carry on the activities of the party.

The monetary needs of the party were so pressing and urgent that its members were always on the look out of new avenues for the collection of money. Once Chandra Shekhar Azad was made the disciple and heir of a wealthy Mahant in the hope that the party would get the huge wealth of the old Mahant after his death. But the plan did not work out as Azad felt that the old Mahant was physically too stout to oblige them, and so Azad ran away from his palace. After such misadventures, the revolutionaries proposed to use the method of "forced contribution" or dacoities in the jargon of the Irish and previous Indian revolutionaries. These Indian revolutionaries during the First World War justified dacoities on the plea that the political dacoit was aiming at the good of the society as a whole by trying to expel the British.

By the end of 1924, the organisation of the party had made sufficient progress in the UP. Then, the party embarked upon a programme of village dacoities in order to raise funds. They thought the method was in full accord with the principle and tradition of the revolutionaries. Without recourse to political dacoities, the only other alternative before the party was the suspension of their activities for which the revolutionaries were not prepared at any cost. Even in the HRA the department responsible for committing dacoities was considered to be a necessary evil. The party committed several dacoities in the villages and in each case Ram Prasad Bismil was the leader. The story of one village hold-up from another did not differ materially. The *modus operandi* was similar in each case. Some armed revolutionaries trekking to the village by night, then stopping in a grove near the village, took the villagers by surprise and decamped with the booty.

One of the first armed dacoities was committed by the party on 25 December 1924 in Bamrauli, a large village in Pilibhit district of the U.P. In this dacoity, the revolutionaries looted about Rs. 4,000 and shot dead one villager who challenged them. The money was used for publishing the pamphlet *The Revolutionary*. Another dacoity was committed on 9 March 1925 in Bichpuri, district Pilibhit. It was the only occassion on which professional dacoits were called upon by Ram Prasad Bismil to collaborate with the revolutionaries, though a party member, Thakur Roshan Singh was in the habit of committing dacoities before he joined the revolutionary party. The professional dacoits were included in the gang because Ram Prasad thought that the young revolutionaries of his gang were not experienced enough for the commission of dacoities. The professionals had come on a share basis. A person was shot dead in this dacoity too, and the party had to return without any booty.

On 24 May 1925, a dacoity was committed by the party at Dwarkapur in Pratapgarh district. This expedition was an unmitigated disaster from begninning to the end. In order to escape from the villagers, the revolutionaries shot at, and wounded some of the villagers. They lost a revolver which was a very valuable thing for them. The incident compelled the party to think over the matter of village hold-ups. Ram Prasad said that he was tired of shooting at the brave villagers. Many other members of the party were also not happy with the commission of village dacoities and considered it the most heinous crime. Moreover, the village hold-ups were not much of a success from the monetary point of view also. But at that time the police could not trace and connect these dacoities with revolutionaries' terrorist activities. After long deliberations, the Provincial Committee of the HRA decided that village dacoities should be discontinued, and only banks and other Government property should be looted. The party took such a decision because it felt that Ram Prasad Bismil would continue to be misled by informers if village hold-ups continued.

Ashfaqullah was opposed to the new policy of looting government money. He felt that the party was not yet strong enough to challenge the government directly. But most of the revolutionaries favoured the new policy and the majority view prevailed. The party was in urgent need of money to purchase arms and ammunition that had arrived by a ship from Germany. So the party decided to loot railway cash. It was decided to hold-up the 8 down train that collected the day's earnings from various railway stations between Saharanpur and Lucknow. Some young revolutionaries wanted to add to it the killing of the engine driver or guard if they happened to be Englishmen. But the leader Ram Prasad Bismil was against this and extracted a promise from the members that they would not kill anybody.

After elaborate planning under the leadership of Ram Prasad Bismil, the train dacoity was committed near Kakori, a small station in the vicinity of Lucknow, on 9th August, 1925. In all ten revolutionaries took part in this dacoity. According to their plan, three of them, Ashfaqullah Khan, Rajendra Lahiri and Sachindranath Bakshi boarded the second class compartment. Others travelling third class were Ram Prasad Bismil, Chandra Shekhar Azad, Mukandilal, Murarilal, Kundanlal, Banwarilal and Manmathnath Gupta. They were spread over the whole train. When the train left Kakori at about quarter past seven in the evening, and had moved over a mile towards Lucknow, the revolutionaries in the second class pulled the communication chord and stopped the train. The other revolutionaries came out of the third class compartments. They overpowered the guard, and pushed out the iron safe containing the money from his compartment. Two revolutionaries on each side of the railway line stood guard with Mauser pistols in their hands. Cries were raised by the revolutionaries in Hindustani that their object was not to injure or harm private persons but they were only after government property. The men on guard were regularly firing to keep the passengers inside the compartments. Ashfaqullah Khan, the strongest man among the revolutionaires with the possible exception of Ram Prasad Bismil, broke open the iron safe with the help of a hammer. The money bags were taken out from the iron safe, and the revolutionaries disappeared with the booty—estimated about Rs. 10,000. In the firing during the hold-up, one man was killed and two were wounded. The man in spite of warnings from the revolutionaries had come out of his compartment to see if his newly wed wife was safe, and was killed by the flying bullets. The revolutionaries escaped to Lucknow, taking advantage of the darkness of the night and passed the night in the city. In the early hours of the morning, they left to safer places.

The Kakori train hold-up was of a character unusual in India. It created a sensation in the press and public. *The Indian Daily Telegraph* of Lucknow, and *The Tribune* of Lahore, published sensational stories about the hold-up. *The Tribune* in its first report gave the news that in the daring train dacoity about twenty armed dacoits took part. Four of them held the guard at the point of revolver, pulled the communication chord and stopped the train. They were then joined by about sixteen of their confederates who rifled the brake van and decamped with three cash chests and some parcels. While four or five dacoits were busy in the guard's van, a number of their confederates jumped into every passenger compartment and kept watch on the movement of the passengers. The dacoits found one Gurkha passenger arming himself with a rifle, and the Gurkha was shot dead at once; a Mohammadan gentleman who peeped out of the window to see what the matter was, was shot dead as well. A European passenger who had a rifle, attempted to come out of his compartment, and was shot in the leg. The report also said that the dacoits wore masks and were armed with revolvers. But it subsequently corrected the news that only one person was killed. The money collected in the raid was utilised by the party in the work of organisation, and the purchase of arms and ammunition.

The train hold-up, especially the announcement by the revolutionaries that they did not want to loot passengers but only government property, alerted the government. A letter in the handwriting of Ram Prasad Bismil regarding the party-meeting on 13 September 1925 at Meerut at the residence of the District Organiser Vishnu Saran Dublish, fell in the hands of the police which was later produced as prosecution evidence in the trial of this case. The meeting was attended by many important members of the party except Sachindra Sanyal and Jogesh Chatterji who were then in jail. The purpose of the meeting was to take stock of things that had already taken place and to chalk out future programme of the party. As fire-arms could be procured only in a limited quantity, it was decided by the party that more and more members should learn to make bombs. With this purpose in view, Rajendra Lahiri left for Bengal from Benaras where he was the District Organiser.

The government announced a reward of Rs. 5,000 to persons giving the clue leading to the arrest of the culprits in the train hold-up. Posters of this announcement were pasted on the notice boards of all the railway stations as well as all police stations. The police then swooped on the revolutionary suspects without sufficient evidence against them. But in the process, it recovered documents and other articles from the suspects which showed their involvement in revolutionary activities. When Govind Charan Kar was arrested in Lucknow, the "Yellow Paper" showing the party's constitution was recovered in the search of his hostel room. Many arrests were simultaneously made on 26 September 1925 throughout the UP and even outside it. Houses of suspects were quietly surrourndned and searched by the police in the night. When Manmathnath Gupta was arrested in Benaras and his house was searched, a typewritten extract from the *Revolutionary* was found in his possession. Ram Prasad Bismil was arrested at Shajahanpur, his home town, but Ashfaq gave the slip to the police and could not be arrested at that time. In Kanpur, the offices of the Congress Committee were searched along with the houses of the revolutionaries Virbhadra Tiwari, Office Suprintendent of the Congress Reception Committee.

Suresh Chandra Bhattacharya, Assistant Editor of the *Pratap*. In all some fifty arrests were made. The arrests were reported in the press at great length. The *Partap* edited by Ganesh Shankar Vidyarthi, a top Congressman, came out with the headline *Desi Ke Nava Ratna Giraftar* that it, "Jewels of the Country in Custody."

Rajendranath Lahiri who could not be apprehended on 26 September, was, however, arrested in Calcutta, on 10 November 1925 in a house known as Dakashineshwar House, where he had gone for learning bomb-making. During a search of the house, a live-bomb, gun powder and explosive chemicals were found. Ashfaqullah Khan was arrested in Delhi while trying to go to Afghanistan. Before his arrest, Ashfaqullah had make up his mind to go to Russia, and for that purpose, he wanted first to reach Kabul. He had gone to Delhi for making the necessary arrangements for the purpose but he was arrested there.

Sayed Ainuddin, the Committing Magistrate, escorted Ashfaqullah from Delhi to Lucknow in a second class railway compartement. His object was to prevail upon Ashfaqullah as a Muslim and get all information from him. So was the motive of Khan Bahadur—Tassaduqi Hussain, Dy. SP of CID who tried his utmost to inject communalism in mind of the resolute revolutionary. He told him that Ram Prasad was a Hindu and wanted to establish Hindu Raj in place of the British one. But Ashfaqullah remained unmoved. Sachindranath Bakshi was arrested at Bhagalpur in a very indifferent state of health. Kundanlal and Chandra Shekhar Azad were declared absconders. A reward of Rs. 2,000 was declared by the government for the arrest of Azad. But Azad was determined not to be arrested any more, and he often told his revolutionary comrades that nobody would be able to arrest him alive and he would live as

"Azad" (a freeman). As an absconder, he was constantly hunted by the police. But Azad was an alert person and strictly followed the party rule of secrecy. Whenever, any of his associates was arrested, he made it a point to change his place of residence, and he never indulged in correspondence with anyone.

The police then started collecting evidence against the arrested revolutionaries in order to try them in the Kakori Conspiracy Case. "The police in British India was a past-master in concocting evidence and manufacturing eye-witnesses." They needed just a skeleton of truth to prop up the inert mass of false evidence, and they got it from the two arrested revolutionaries Benarasilal and Indu Bhushan Mitra who turned approvers under pressure. The police terrorism that followed the train dacoity, imprisonment of most of the leaders, general round-ups, searches and harassment of suspects—had a very adverse effect on the revolutionaries. The situation was later described by one of the revolutionaires thus; "Men who had professed sympathy with our cause would now avoid us. Boys who had talked tall began now to leave the gymnasium we had started in Kanpur for physical culture and as a recruiting centre. The whole province was in the grip of panic."

The trial of the accused, came to be known as the Kakori Conspiracy Case, was conducted in the Sessions Court, Lucknow A Defence Committee was formed to defend the accused, and it consisted of eminent Congress leaders like Pandit Motilal Nehru, Ganesh Shankar Vidharthi, Govind Ballabh Pant and Mohanlal Saxena. Barrister B.K. Chaudhary was engaged as Defence Counsel at a fee of Rs. 500 per month. Kripa Shankar Hajela, Harkaran Nath Misra and Chandra Bhanu Gupta were also among the defence counsels. The Defence Committee raised a fund to meet defence expenses. The case of the Kakori prisoners became a *causecelebre.* Motilal Nehru and Lala Lajpat Rai openly expressed sympathy with the accused. Prominent Congressmen like Babu Shri Prakash and Acharya Narendra Dev went to the prison to interview some of the revolutionaries but the later was, however, not allowed to see them.

The government appointed Jagat Narain Mulla as Prosecution Counsel at a fabulous fee. During the trial period, the Kakori prisoners used to sing national songs while going to the court from the jail, and also in the court They raised revolutionary slogans. The patriotic songs were reproduced in the local English and Urdu dailies. The revolutionaries got publicity in the public by the court reports published in the newspapers.

Sachindranath Sanyal who had been undergoing his sentence of two-year rigorous imprisonment for sedition, was brought from Bengal to stand trial at Lucknow as an originator and leader of the Kakori Conspiracy. Rajendra Lahiri was brought from another prison in Bengal. Jogesh Chandra Chatterji was also made an accused in the Kakori case. But another accused, Virbhadra Tiwari of Kanpur was released while under trial, though he was also a member of the Provincial Committee of the HRA. At the time of his release, a revolutionary Manmath Nath Gupta told the party leaders in jail that Virbhadra Tiwari had bartered the party's secrets for this release. But the leaders thought he had been released on account of legal flaws and technicalities. Afterwards, it transpired that he was a double dealer.

In the legal files of the government, the Kakori case was known as "King Emperor versus Ram Prasad Bismil and others." It was branded as a "Revolutionary Conspiracy Case." The Kakori conspirators were charged with the crimes of dacoity and waging war against the King Emperor. But they were not being treated as political prisoners. The food supplied to them was of poor quality. The European and Anglo-Indian criminals were getting far better treatment than the revolutionaries. So the Kakori prisoners started hunger-strike in the Lucknow jail with the twin objects of getting treatment as political prisoners, and publicising their revolutionary ideals outside the prison. On the eleventh day of the hunger-strike the provincial government issued a communique. It said that the revolutionaries could not be considered political prisoners as they had been accused of heinous crimes, and so the question of special treatment did not arise. But the pitch of the press propaganda was mounting every day. Ganesh Shanker Vidyarthi and his famous Hindi paper *Pratap* took up the revolutionaries' case. After all, the Superintendent of the prison became ready to give special treatment to the prisoners as was given to the European prisoners, but this was to be done not on political but on medical grounds. The revolutionaries were not happy with the medical ground clause. However, considering it as the first ever victory of the revolutionary prisoners, they accepted the terms and called off the strike.

While living in the Lucknow jail as under-trials, the revolutionaries prepared a plan of escape with the help of the absconders Chandra Shekar Azad and Mukandilal who were contacted for the purpose. The plan was to intercept the vans when the prisoners were being escorted to court or back to prison and then to rescue them by forcibly overpowering the guards. But somehow the police got hint of the plan and the number of guards was increased. Many spies who could recognise Azad and other comrades, were deputed throughout the city of Lucknow for the purpose of apprehending them. Thus the plan was abandoned.

After nearly 18 months of court proceedings, the judgement in the main Kakori Conspiracy Case was delivered by the Sessions Court, Lucknow, on 6th April 1927. On the day of the judgement, the revolutionaries started singing patriotic songs as soon as they boarded the police vans for going to the court. They sang songs of Rabindranath Tagore, Kazi Nazrul Islam and Ram Prasad Bismil. They raised slogans, especially the one "Bharatiya Prajatantra ki Jai" that is, "Hail the Republic of India." There was not a big crowd outside the court. The public of Lucknow had remained more or less apathetic to the case, although people like the famous Hindi novelist Munshi Prem Chand and many others made it a point to attend the court whenever they were on a visit to Lucknow. When the revolutionaries faced the crowd before the court-room, they started singing the Urdu song of Ram Prasad Bismil, that since become a classic:

सर फरोशी की तमन्ना अब हमारे दिल में है।
देखाना है ज़ोर कितना बाजू-ए-क़ातिल में है।।

* * *

ऐ शहीद-ए-मुल्को मिल्लत, मैं तेरे ऊपर निसार।
इक तेरी हिम्मत का चर्चा गैर की महफ़िल मे है।।

(Presently there is one supreme longing in our hearts—the longing to sacrifice ourselves. We wish to see how mighty the hands of the executioner are...O martyr for the creed and the country, I am simply enamoured of thee. Even in the camp of the enemy, they are paying tributes to your valour). Only after singing the whole song, did the revolutionaries enter the court.

Of the 22 accused, Ram Prasad Bismil, Roshan Singh and Rajendra Lahiri were sentenced to be hanged and, others were given long terms of imprisonment. In the supplementry case, Ashfaqullah was sentenced to be hanged and Sachindranath Bakshi was awarded transportation for life. But subsequently on appeals of the Chief Court of Oudh in the UP by the revolutionaries, the four death sentences were confirmed and other sentences were enhanced in many cases. Thus, finally, Sachindra Sanyal, Jogesh Chatterji, Sachindranath Bakshi, Mukandilal and Govind Charan Kar were given transportation for life. Manmathnath Gupta got 14 years' rigorous imprisonment. Vishnu Saran Dublish, Suresh Bhattacharya, Raj Kumar Sinha and Ram Kishan Khatri were awarded 10 years' rigorous imprisonment each. Ram Dulare Trivedi, Prem Kishan Khanna, Bhupendranath Sanyal and Banwarilal got five years' RI each. Pranavesh Kumar Chatterji was awarded 4 years' RI and Ram Nath Pande got 3 years' RI. The two approvers Benarasilal and Indu Bhushan Mitra were given pardon.

Many of the revolutionaries did not hope that their punishments would be enhanced as a result of their appeals. But it was not surprising as the Magistrates in British India were mostly puppets in the hands of the police and danced to its dictates. The political trials conducted by the police during the First World War were also not based on complete truth. The police concocted false stories and trapped many innocent people in most of the cases of which the Benaras Conspiracy Case is the glaring example. The Kakori trial was also not conducted on the basis of justice and fairplay. The Judges and Magistrates involved in it were all biased people. The CID which conducted the case was guided by government, and it influenced the judges. Except the evidence of the approvers the witnesses produced by the prosecution were mostly false. Raj Kumar Sinha was nowhere near the Kakori train hold-up, yet the evidence as prepared and processed by the police against him proved convincing. Similarly, Govind Charan Kar did not take part in the Kakori dacoity, yet he was falsely implicated in it and given transportation for life. Thus, many people in this case were convicted of charges that were false.

After the judgement of the Chief Court of Oudh in the appeals of the Kakori revolutionaries, an appeal was filed on their behalf in the Privy Council, London. But it was also rejected, and the four hangings appeared to be a certainty. However, an agitation to get the sentences commuted was going on in the country. In spite of this, a day in October 1927 was fixed, but the hangings did not actually take place on that day. Soon after, another date in the same month was fixed. But on this day too the executions were not carried out. Meanwhile, the condemned prisoners were transferred to different jails. During his last days in the prison, Ram Prasad Bismil became a frustrated person. He wrote his autobiography in Hindi and smuggled it out of the prison page by page. It was published by Ganesh Shankar Vidyarthi after some editing. The book amounts to a condemnation of the revolutionary movement and was written in a repentant mood. It is full of invectives against the leader, Sachindra Sanyal. Bismil even tried to attribute all this to some sort of provincialism. He expressed his wish for the rejuvenation of the society and the country by improving the condition of the farmers, the labourers and women. He wanted that the labourers and peasants should be organised in the country.

On the day of his hanging in the Gorakhpur jail, Ram Prasad Bismil's mother went to see him for the last time. A young revolutionary Shiv Verma accompanied her as Bismil's younger brother. He wanted to know from Bismil about the arms and ammunition of the revolutionary party. During the course of his interview, Ram Prasad told his mother that he was fully satisfied with his approacing death. He was hanged on 19 December 1927. His last words were: "I wish the downfall of the British Empire." After his death, his deadbody was taken in a procession throughout the city by the people of Gorakhpur. The huge procession consisted of Hindus as well as Muslims.

Ashfaqullah Khan who was a personal friend of Ram Prasad Bismil, and also belonged to Shahjahanpur, was hanged in the Faizabad jail on 19th December 1927. He was also a poet and wrote some verses under the pen-name of "Hasrat Warsi." Among his last verses was the couplet:

वतन हमेशा रहे शाद कायम और आज़ाद।
हमारा क्या है? हम अगर रहें रहे न रहें।।

(May our country always remain prosperous and free. What of us, whether we remain here or not). Ashfaq had written a letter to Benarasilal from Bhopal in which he expressed his love of freedom more than anything else in life. In his last letter written to his countrymen from the jail, Ashfaq appealed for helping his brothers, and wanted this appeal to be distributed among the public through Ganesh Shankar Vidyarthi's *Pratap* in the form of leaflets in the Congress session. Ashfaq stepped to the gallows with a copy of the *Koran* tied round his neck. He kissed the ropes and said: "My hands are not smeared with human blood. The accusation against me is false. I shall get justice at the hands of God."

The revolutionaries did not expect death penalty for Roshan Singh. When the judgement was delivered, Roshan Singh got a mild shock for a moment but soon he recovered and showed great composure and calmness. On 13 December 1927, a few days before his execution Roshan Singh wrote to one of his friends not to grieve on his death as he was dying for a good cause. He wrote a couplet in the letter:

ज़िन्दगी ज़िन्दा दिली को जान ऐ रोशन,
वरना कितने मरे और पैदा होते जाते हैं।

(Life full of activity and boldness is the real life; otherwise so many people die and take birth everyday).

Roshan Singh was hanged in the Malaka jail of Allahabad on 19 December 1927. He held the *Bhagavada Gita* in his hand at the time of mounting the gallows, and "Bande Mataram" and "Om" on his lips.

Rajendra Lahiri was hanged on 17 December 1927, two days before the other three revolutionaries. According to the revolutionary, Man Mohan Gupta, some revolutionary comrades of Rajendra Lahiri had planned to break into the Gonda prison and rescue Lahiri on the night of 18th December. The authorities somehow got the information, and decided to hang Lahiri on the 17th December. Lahiri had not submitted any mercy petition to the government after his conviction. Before his execution, he wrote a letter to one of his friends from the prison. In this letter he said that the country needed the blood of the martyrs, and expressed the hope that their sacrifice would not go waste.

The Kakori hangings created quite a furore in the country. The Benaras daily *Aaj,* commenting on the hangings in its issue of December 23, 1927, lamented on the helplessness of the country at the execution of the four youngmen. The celebrated Hindi magazine *Chand* of Allahabad brought out a special "*Phansi* number" in which tributes were paid to the departed martyrs. A special resolution was passed by the Congress deploring the callousness of the government in not commuting the brutal sentences passed in the Kakori case in spite of the powerful public indignation aroused by the vindictive sentences. The Congress offered its heartfelt sympathy to the families of the victim.

The Kakori Conspiracy Case was closely linked up

with the entire secret revolutionary activities in the whole of northern India in the period between 1923 to 1931. The Deoghar Conspiracy in East Bihar was part of the Kakori Conspiracy and its leading accused belonged to the U.P. Shailendra Chakravarty of Allahabad was a member of the HRA. He was arrested in connection with the Deoghar Conspiracy, and was found in possession of some arms and a copy of the rules and regulations of the Hindustan Republican Association. He was sentenced to 7 years' RI. Jogendra Sukul a recruit of the HRA at Benaras, became prominent in more than one case in Bihar, and was ultimately transported to the Andamans.

Though Bhagat Singh and Jatindranath Das, who later attained martyrdom, were not declared absconders in the Kakori Conspiracy Case, the police were in search of them. Bhagat Singh was being sought as Balwant Singh, the name Jogesh Chatterji gave him at Kanpur. Jatindranath Das whose name came in connection with the Kakori Case, was being sought as a Kali Babu and Kamini Kaka. The police had taken Banwarilal to Calcutta for the identification of Jatin Das, but he failed to identify the latter. Rajendra Lahiri who was a leader of the Kakori Conspiracy Case, was also a leader of the Dakshineshwar Bomb Case, and was awarded the maximum punishment among those involved in it. Chandra Shekar Azad who later became the Commander-in-Chief of the Hindustan Socialist Republican Army, was declared an absconder in the Kakori, Lahore and Delhi Conspiracy Cases.

Though the Kakori Case started with the incident of a train hold-up action, the government realised that the real motive behind the train holdup was a very serious one. It was an armed challenge to the sovereignty of the King Emperor over British India by an armed revolution. The Kakori train dacoity was only one of the incidents for the furtherance of the conspiracy to overthrow the foreign government and thereby to make India free.

After the Kakori Conspiracy Case, there was a feeling of despondency among the absconding revolutionaries and their sympathisers. But the Kakori hangings had not remained unnoticed among the general public who were filled with horror and anger at the callousness of the British Imperialism in India. The UP branch of the revolutionary party was left considerably weakened, but the party was by no means dead.

(Courtesy: Dr. (Smt.) Kaushalya Devi Dublisb—Revolutionaries and their Activities in Northern India—B.R. Publishing Corporation, Delhi, 1982)

Kakori Train Outrage (1925-1927)

Of the many revolutionary activities in the United Provinces, the Kakori train outrage comes out pre-eminently to be the most important particularly in respect of sacrifice of four, valuable lives over one particular incident.

Young men hailing from different districts of the U.P. and also from Bengal came together by a common bond of love of their Motherland to discuss ways and means for driving out the foreigners from the country. Ramprasad Bismil of Shahjehanpur declared that nothing would come out of non-violent struggle and the country must adopt other means for its emancipation.

Almost all the members of the present conspiracy met at Ramprasad's house early in 1924, to chalk out a programme of work and in a subsequent meeting the course of action was decided upon amongst themselves. Each of them assumed a separate name to be used amongst the members of the Society such as, 'Nawab', 'Gangaram', 'Quick-silver', and so on and so forth. The leader, Ramprasad had four such names. And Ashfaqulla was known as 'Kunwarji' and used to put on Hindu dress on occasions.

The party under Ramprasad in conjunction with those charged in the Mainpuri Conspiracy Case, where Gendalal Dikshit figured prominently, were alleged to have been involved in several actions taking place in Sherganj, Bichpuri, Mainpuri, etc.

On August 9, 1925, a passenger train,was stopped by the pulling of the alarm chain between Kakori amd Alamnagar within fourteen miles of Lucknow Junction. The first information report was lodged with the police on the same day at about 8-30 p.m.

It transpired that when the train had left Kakori for Lucknow at quarter past seven at night four men had previously entered the brake van of the moving train and asked the guard to stop it as they had left their luggage behind at the railway station at Kakori. The guard refused to do so and two raiders instantly overawed him with open revolvers and pulled the communication chord. As the train stopped about sixteen men entered the brake van and removed the chests carrying cash from the guard's van. A number of them kept watch over the passengers.

A Gurkha passenger who tried to take up his rifle was shot dead by one of the raiders and another passenger who leaned out of the window was wounded by a revolver shot. A European who was armed with a rifle was wounded on the leg as he was about to alight from the train to attack the strangers.

The raid had been going on when the arrival of the Dehra Mail near the standing train forced the raiders to take to their heels.

The chests that had been removed from the brake van were emptied at a place not very far from the scene of occurrence the next day.

Searches were conducted at every suspected area

in the U.P. and other places and the most of the suspects were arrested on September 25, 1925, from various places in the U.P. No attempt was left untried to establish connection with the revolutionaries of Bengal, Singapore and elsewhere.

A case was started with twenty-five accused including Ramprasad Bismil, Rajendra Nath Lahiri and Raushan Singh in December, 1925. After the preliminary judicial enquiry the case was sentup to the Sessions on April 16, 1926 which started sitting at Lucknow from May 1, 1926, with twenty, five accused having been discharged. Some had been absconding and the trial proceeded *in absentia.* Besides Kakori, the accused were held resposnsible for Bamrauli Dacoity, Bichpuri (Pilibhit dist.) Dacoity (Mar, 9, 1925) and Dwarakapur Dacoity (committed on May 24, 1925).

After a protracted trial which was held up for a long time due to hunger-strike of the accused three youngmen, Ramprasad Bismil, Raushan Singh and Rajendra Nath Lahiri were condemned to death and others to various terms of imprisonment under Secs. 121-A, 120-B, 396 and 302 of the Indian Penal Code on April 6, 1927. In the meantime Ashfaqulla was arrested with a few others and a separate case on the same charges was started against him. The trial at the sessions was started on March 24, 1927. The judgement awarded extreme penalty of the law for the accused. The prisoners were separated from one another and Ramprasad was lodged in the Gorakhpur Jail, Rajen Lahiri in the Gonda, Roshan Singh in Allahabad and Ashfaqulla in the Fyzabad Jail.

A petition for mercy to the Viceroy was rejected on October 10, 1927, and the prisoners were informed of the date of execution fixed for October 12, 1927.

The execution was to be stayed as the prisoners appealed to the Privy Council which was admitted in the last week of Novemeber, 1927. It was rejected on December 12, and the respective jailors were informed about the result of the appeal.

(i) Rajendra Nath Lahiri was executed in the Gonda Jail on December 17, 1927. (ii) Ashfaqulla and (iii) Ramprasad Bismil on December 19, 1927, in the Fyzabad and the Gorakhpur Jail, respectively. In the Naini Jail on December 21, 1927, (iv) Roshan Singh, the last of the comrades, lost his life on the scaffold.

Each of the young men showed exemplary courage in the face of death. The statements and communications are worthy of preservation for the future generations who would be called upon to safeguard the freedom of their Motherland.

From the Gonda Jail wrote Rajen Lahiri on December 13, 1927:

"The Superintendent informed this morning that my appeal to the Privy Council had been rejected....My death will be a glorious one and none need be sorry for it....All of you should pray to God so that I may be born again and may devote my life for the good of the Motherland."

Rajen did not forget to offer his hearty thanks to his fellow countrymen who had helped them in all possible ways in their defence.

A brother of Rajendra Nath who had seen him on the day of his execution informed the public that he (Rajen) looked so cheerful.

"as if he was simply changing his material body for a fresh and more dignified one. He faced the punishment quite boldly and there was something divine on his face. He engaged himself in the *bhajan* songs throughout the previous night and was citing hymns from the Gita and Upanishads until it was 6-15 in the morning.

"He withbold steps and smiling face followed the warders and stood erect on his feet on the platform of the gallows and faced the eternity in a cheerful mood."

Ramprasad with all his courage and resourcefulness in the field of action was moved by the sight of his mother who had come to bid adieu to him before execution. It was a case of transferred grief, of the thought that the mother might feel deeply for the loss of her son.

At the sight of her weeping son and mistaking it to be one of fear for execution, she said that she had not expected to see him so moved at a time when he should face death with the greatest joy and utmost courage. She was at once corrected of her mistake and forthwith her countenance changed from one of sorrow to that of pride.

Ramprasad consoled his father by saying that it did not behove a man, and further of Ramprasad at that, to weep when a lady had overcome her feelings of grief at the loss of her dear son.

Roshan Singh, the report goes, "remained notably composed till his end and the last word which escaped his lips was *Bande Mataram.*"

Ashfaqulla showed a remarkably cool courage and love for his Motherland. The lawyer defending him in the Sessions Court has given a picture of his client which holds him in lofty relief even amongst the revolutionaries. He spurned an attempt on the part of the Government to make a statement relating to his association with the comrades and his own part in the Kakori drama and buy his release.

The outcome of the trial was a foregone conclusion. Three had been condemned to death; further evidence had been adduced to prove his guilt and there was nothing to inspire any hope of escape with his neck. In this background Ashfaqualla appeared in the court-room on the day when the judgment was to be delivered in a very jovial mood clad in a light yellow coloured attire.

His mien, his stature and his denouncement on that occassion displayed the inner strength of his soul.

Ashfaqualla was awarded two capital punishments for his participation in the Kakori and also in Bichpuri outrages; and given long terms of imprisonment for other offences.

Friends and relations were overwhelmed with emotion on the pronuouncement of the judgment. On the other hand Ashfaqulla said there was nothing to give oneself up to grief. There was one matter over which he was not feeling happy. The jailor had said that the prisoner had gained considerably in weight; so much so that he had broken all previous records except of one who had exceeded Ashfaqulla's by another six pounds. He assured the jailor that he would not allow his record to be broken. But alas! he would be prevented from securing that exalted position because he would be put in the condemned cell after the delivery of the judgment. Had he been allowed to receive the 'B Class prisoners' treatment as he had been enjoying as an undertrial, during the remaining few days of his life, he would certainly have been able to beat all records of all times in this respect.

At the last interview with a friend, his brother and nephews who were allowed to see him in the Fyzabad Jail for the last time, he calmly told his sobbing relations that the least sorrow should not mar the solemn occasion of great rejoicing; they should behave in a different way. He felt himself honoured to find him as a representative of his countrymen on whom had devolved the noble task of struggling for the freedom of the Motherland. They ought to be glad to find that one of their near relations, a brother and an uncle, had been sacrificing his life for the country. They ought to remember that there had been such high-souled men like Kanai and Khudiram in the Hindu community and it was an additional privilege for him because most probably he happened to be the first Mahomedan to follow the footsteps of martyrs of undying fame. It is a great pity that the halo of glory that these young lads had wrapped around them should be bedimmed by their countrymen in a most flagrant way.

Kakori Case

Offences

1. Conspiracy.
2. Bamrauli dacoity.
3. Bichpuri dacoity.
4. Dwarkapur dacoity.
5. Kakori train dacoity.

Accused

Name	*District*	*Province*	*Sentence*
Ram Prasad Bismil	Shahjahanpur	U. P.	Hanged.
Ashfaqullah Khan	Shahjahanpur	U. P.	Hanged.
Rajendra Nath Lahiri	Benares and Pabna	U. P. and Bengal	Hanged.
Roshan Singh	Shahjahanpur	U. P.	Hanged.
Jogesh Chandra Chatterji	Dacca	Bengal	Transportation for life
Sachindra Nath Bakhshi	Benares and Jhansi	U. P.	Transportation for life
Sachindra Nath Sanyal	Benares and Allahabad	U. P.	Transportation for life
Makundi Lal	Etawah	U. P.	Transportation for life
Govind Charan Kar *alias* D.N. Chaudhuri	Dacca	Bengal	Transportation for life
Manmotho Nath Gupta	Benares	U. P.	14 years' R.I.
Raj Kumar Sinha	Cownpure	U. P.	10 years' R.I.
Ram Kishan Khattri	Chanda	C. P.	10 years' R.I.
Suresh Chandra Bhattachariya	Cawnpure and Benares	U. P.	10 years' R.I.
Vishnu Saran Dublis	Meerut	U. P.	10 years' R.I.
Banwari Lal	Rae Bareli	U. P.	5 years' R.I.
Bhupendra Nath Sanyal	Benares and Allahabad	U. P.	5 years' R.I.
Prem Kishan Khanna	Shahjahanpur	U. P.	5 years' R.I.
Ram Dulare Trivedi	Cawnpure	U. P.	5 years' R.I.
Parnawesh Kumar Chatterji	Jubbulpore	C. P.	4 years' R.I.
Ram Nath Pande	Benares	U. P.	3 years' R.I.
	Approvers		
Banarsi Lal	Shahjahanpur	U. P.	
Indu Bishan Mitra	Shahjahanpur	U. P.	
	Absconding		
Chandra Shekhar Azad	Benares	U. P.	

Kanpur Conspiracy Case

The government's main purpose in launching this conspiracy case was to damn the Communist International, to do vicious and poisonous propaganda against communists showing them up as 'foreign' or 'Moscow' agents and the danger from their existence to the law and order and property thus winning over the propertied classes and terrifying the ignorants and the petty-bourgeois nationalist to have no truck or contact with the communists.

Muzaffar Ahmad was arrested in Calcutta on 19 May 1923 and Ghulam Hussain in Lahore about the same time. Ten Days earlier Shaukat Usmani had been taken into custody. So three communists—Shaukat Usmani, Muzaffar Ahmad and Ghulam Hussain were already in government custody. The government of India asked the provincial governments of Madras and Bombay to arrest Singaravelu and Dange and detain them 'under the respective regulation'. Legal advisers had told the government that "it would be absolutely futile to stage a trial against these five under Section 121-A in Bombay, Calcutta or Madras." The remedy they suggested was to detain them under regulation 3 of 1818. The conspiracy trial could not be successful "in places where there was a jury and so detention without trial was the only remedy till conspiracy was properly cooked and held in a place where there was no jury."

Then Ghulam Hussain funked in July and apologised. The Bombay government objected to the use of Bombay Regulation against Dange. The action against Singaravelu was also postponed for similar reasons. Hence Dange and Singaravelu were not arrested.

On 20 December 1923 Nalini Gupta was arrested and he made a long statement showing that he had links with the Communist International and the emergent communist groups in India. After securing information from Nalini Gupta and Ghulam Hussain, the India government consulted the secretary of state in London about the starting of a conspiracy case including Dange and Singaravelu in it.

The government took the decision to launch the conspiracy case on 20 February 1924 under Section 121-A against the eight accused. They were—(1) M.N. Roy, (2) Muzaffar Ahmad, (3) Shaukat Usmani, (4) S. A. Dange, (5) Ghulam Hussain, (6) Nalini Gupta, (7) Singaravelu and (8) R.C. L. Sharma. Of these, M.N. Roy was in Germany, Sharma in Pondichery and Ghulam Hussain was never brought to Kanpur. Singaravelu was released on bail on 7 March 1924 and allowed to remain in his house. The Bolshevik Conspiracy Case began on 17 March against the remaining four accused, viz. Muzaffar Ahmad, Shaukat Usmani, S.A. Dange and Nalini Gupta.

The burden of the charges was that the above mentioned communists had established relations with the Communist International and were determined to set up its branch in India the object of which is to deprive the king-emperor of his sovereignty in India. In pursuance of this aim M.N. Roy and others had communicated secretly and openly with each other. They also attempted to make use of an association of workers and peasants or a people's party under their leadership. Their association wanted to overthrow his majesty's government with the support and guidance of the Communist International which would be used as an instrument for securing "the complete separation of India from imperialistic Britain", by a "violent revolution". Hence conspiracy to overthrow the king, etc. And further, for the achievement of their objective 'the accused as well as others' circulated in British India newspapers circular and pamphlets of a revolutionary character.

It was truly a prosecution of communist ideology. The charge of deprival of the king-emperor of his throne was merely a subterfuge to hoodwink the politically-unconscious people. The prisoners had committed no overt action to deprive the king-emperor of his sovereignty. They were fighting for national freedom in the same way as other nationalists were doing and organising the workers and peasants for that purpose. Love of freedom was their crime.

It was a foregone conclusion as matters stood that the so-called accused would be convicted and given heavy sentences. They were given four years rigorous imprisonment each by the session judge on 29 March 1924. Thus did the curtain drop on the Kanpur Conspiracy Case trial.

But did these heavy sentences prove deterrent to the spread of the communist movement? No, not at all. On the contrary, they spurred the working class leaders already working outside as well the petty-bourgeois intellectuals and other pro-revolutionary and revolutionary forces in the country to accept this imperialist challenge by continuing the work begun by the imprisoned comrades, by organising on a firm footing powerful organisation of the workers' and parties throughout India, coordinating their activities and peasants' establishing a real working class Communist Party of India with international links.

The trial played a part in the spread of revolutionary ideas among fairly wide circles of the working class and intelligentsia. It focused their attention on socialism. The proof of this is that soon after the sentences were pronounced an Indian Communist Defence Committee was formed in Bombay, which published an appeal to the Indian public and the CPGB to open a fund for the purpose of fighting to get the sentences annulled in the court of appeals and recognition of the right for Indians to form a communist party.

So new communist and pro-communist forces arose among the working class and petty-bourgeois intellectuals who defiant the terror unleashed by British rulers boldly went ahead to carry on their revolutionary work without caring a damn for the consequences. The imprisoned comrades had done their duty by the working class to the Indian revolution well. Now it was the duty of the others to step into their shoes, shoulder the responsibility and take the country forward.

But before we proceed further, some observations have to be made with regard to the two Bolshevik conspiracy cases—Peshawar and Kanpur. At the time of the Peshawar Conspiracy Case there was hardly any communist or revolutionary movement in the country. There was no defence committee worth the name to defend them. They had to depend mostly on their friends and relations for defence. The anti-bolshevik propaganda unleashed by the British press and the rulers had frightened the intelligentsia much. The prisoners were hardly befriended by anybody in the region ridden with big landlords who were out and out loyal to the British rulers.

But at the time of the Kanpur Conspiracy Case trial, local patriots under the leadership of Shri Ganesh Shanker Vidyarthi had set up a defence committee to look after the defence of the accused in the case. V. H. Joshi from Bombay and Abdul Halim from Calcutta were also contributing to the Defence Committee and helping the accused comrades in accordance with Dange's and Muzaffar Ahmad's advice.

Before their arrests the communist movement had advanced a little. Strikes had taken place in the textile mills of Bombay, Calcutta and Kanpur. The arrests of communists had created a feeling of resentment against the British rulers.

The Bolshevik Conspiracy Case did not overawe

the communist prisoners. They stood their ground and showed their mettle in the trying and sessions courts.

The conspiracy case was meant to deny the communists the democratic right of political propaganda and association that is to say, the right to organise the workers and peasants and to form the Communist Party of India. The Communist Party of Great Britain was legal and could utilise civil liberties. But here in India, the communist party was illegal and imperialist dictatorship was ruling the roost.

The accused in the Meerut Conspiracy Case challenged and bearded the British imperialist lion in its own den and made communist ideology ring throughout India—as we shall see anon.

On 27 March 1924 the *International Press Correspon-dence* (Inprecor) published an open letter from the CPI signed by M.N. Roy to the Prime Minister of Great Britain Ramsay MacDonald and other highups, in which Roy said:

"It is not we eight accused who are on trial in Cawnpore. It is the entire Indian working class and the idea of political agitation and organisation of the working class which awaits the verdict of the court. The time-honoured charge of conspiracy is to damn the working-class movement for social, economic and political emancipation as illegal." This is "to throttle the constitutional right of agitation, organisation and association which exists unchallenged in every part of the British empire." In this long letter M.N. Roy at the end asserted that if bolshevik propaganda is not illegal in Britain, why is it so in India? and if the CPGB is not illegal in Britain, why is it so in India?

And we can add that if the CPGB in Britain could publish papers, the communists had the same right to start newspapers to defend the interests of the working people in India.

Communist Party of India Formed

The Kanpur Communist Conspiracy Case could not hinder the growth of communist thought and movement in the country. In the five years from March 1924 to March 1929 communist ideas and movement spread continuously under one cover organisation's name or another. We will trace and place before the readers the story of the growth of the communist movement in the next five years.

There was discussion among the Kanpur Conspiracy Case accused as to whether an open Communist Party of India be set up or not and whether it would be allowed to function. Dange was for setting it up. But while they were discussing the matter a person named Satyabhakta took the initiative and sent letters to whatever known communist groups were there to attend an open Communist Conference which was going to be held in Kanpur in the last week of December 1925.

The conference was held on the appointed dates. S.V. Ghate took part in it and was elected one of the general secre-taries. He records about that Communist Conference as follows:

"We in Bombay decided to attend the conference. J.P. Bagerhatta, who was in touch with M.N. Roy, was in Bombay and we together decided to attend the conference." Ghate further said that "the resolutions committed at the conference consisted of Satyabhakta, Joglekar, Bagerhatta, S. Hassan (Lahore), Krishnas-wamy (Madras) and Ghate himself, Satyabhakta objected to the name Communist Party of India as he smelt bolshevik flavour and wanted the name to be Indian Communist Party. Ultimately our suggestion was accepted. The resolutions were placed before the open session on the third day. President, M. Singaravelu Chettiyar, two joint secretaries, Bagerhatta and myself and an Executive Committee were elected."

Ghate further adds: "Within four days Satyabhakta announced the formation of a new National Communist Party and left the organisation in the formation of which he himself was a party. When he was approached to hand over the minutes and documents of the conference, he refused to pass them on since he had established his own party."

It was decided that the headquarters of the Communist Party of India were to be at Bombay. Ghate further says: "We set to work in 1926. I remember we issued a manifesto in the name of the Communist Party of India against hindu-muslim riots and for communal unity."

The other Joint Secretary Bagerhatta was expelled from the party in 1927 as a police agent. Then Ghate became the General Secretary of the party. Ghate held this position till his arrest in the Meerut Communist Conspiracy Case on 20 March 1929.

Muzaffar Ahmad wrote an article on the Communist Conference in which he said: "Uniting the communists of various places we constitute for the first time the Central Committee of the Communist Party of India in Kanpur itself. The conference was openly held and, therefore, the committee was also constituted openly." On this he commented, "we had to face plenty of criticism, we deserve this criticism, but there was no other way either. Had we not joined the conference at Kanpur, the communist party of Satyabhakta would have hindered us considerably in the future."

The Communist Conference received wide publicity in the press—both progressive and pro-imperialist. Reactionary papers voicing capitalist viewpoint poked fun at the conference. The progressive nationalist press took note of the fact cautiously. But a new phenomenon had emerged on the Indian scene—a phenomenon which heralded the left-wing politics in the country aspiring and desiring to unite the left and nationalist forces.

It was in Kanpur that the first all-India communist centre was formed. The Central Executive Committee was elected and a constitution was adopted. The conference brought together and united four communist groups of Bombay, Calcutta, Madras and Lahore under one banner—the red flag. They were represented in the Central Executive Committee duly. However, the CPI was still in the developing process. But it was noted that the Gordian knot had been cut and a beginning made.

There were drawbacks, no doubt. The CPI's attitude towards the Communist International was vague. A genuine communist party could not be organised openly, exposing all its leaders to imperialists enemies to be arrested whenever they liked. But weaknesses apart, it was a step forward—a basis which in course of time could help bring into being the genuine Communist Party of India.

The ultimate goal of the party was the establishment of a workers' and peasants' republic of India and the immediate object was the securing of a living wage for the workers and peasants through the nationalisation of land, mines, factories, etc. And to attain the above objective the party was going to organise the workers' and peasants' unions.

From 1927 onwards communist activities spread still further. May Day, Soviet Revolution Day and Lenin Day—international features of the communist movement—began to be observed in different parts of the country. Articles appeared in progressive journals on the 10th anniversary of the Russian revolution.

The Peshawar Conspiracy cases, the Kanpur Communist Conspiracy Case and the anti-bolshevik propaganda carried on by the British rulers created great interest among the youth and intelligentsia and they wanted to find out what bolshevism or communism really stood for, about which so much ado was being made by the British rulers of India. Foreign journals entering into India were to great help in securing some balanced information in this regard

The Communist Party of India was as yet confined to small groups in a few industrially developed provinces of India. To become a real all-India communist party, it had yet to travel a long way and do hard and difficult spade work. Its hammer and sickle banner had been unfurled only in a few provinces where trade-union activities had begun purging the TUs of opportunist and pro-capitalist leaders who had captured them. The movement was still suffering teething troubles.

Soon Punjab came into the picture. Santokh Singh had attended the Kanpur Conference of communist workers. He started the Punjabi monthly *Kirti* (Worker) in February 1926, began propagating communist ideas in a very guarded way. He was one of the leaders of the Hindustan Ghadr Party movement in San Francisco, USA he had gone to Soviet Russia, attended the Congresses of the 4th International and Red Trade Unions and had met some of the Soviet communist leaders. He had come to India to continue the national-freedom struggle by organising the workers and peasants of India.

Santokh Singh was a great revolutionary who had proved his mettle and bonafides in the San Francisco Conspiracy Case in America. He had studied communism in Moscow. He wrote about the Kanpur Communist Conference in the first issue of the *Kirti*. Unfortunately, he was fatally taken ill and died on 19 May 1927.

The death of Santokh Singh, according to a government report, caused a definite setback to the activities of the party in Punjab. In him they lost a capable organiser, a tireless worker whose pioneering work laid the foundation on which the movement had built ambitious schemes.

On his selection and advice Sohan Singh Josh became the editor in-charge of the *Kirti* in January 1927. The *Kirti* was the organ of the Hindustan Ghadr Party which had become communist-oriented after the defeat of its armed struggle in 1914-15. The new editor had some experience of building an organisation.

In the first issue of the *Kirti* Santokh Singh wrote an editorial note under the heading, "Why did *Kirti Appear*? in which he said: "Charkha and Khadi were not the panacea for Swaraj. Mahatma Gandhi could not win Swaraj within a year as he had claimed. Khadi has not harmed the British capitalists nor has it overawed them in any way.

"The call of the *Kirti* is this that Hindustan will have to pay for its freedom the same price as history proves other countries have paid for their freedom and as a free country has always to pay for the preservation of its freedom."

And he further added that India should not remain isolated from the world. "We are a colonial country, we should not see the oppressed pepples of the world as the oppressors do." The programme of India's freedom should not only be based on conditions obtaining in India but also be based on the situation prevailing in the world. "In present times a country cannot came into its own unless its working class stands on its own feet" and so on he wrote.

Workers' & Peasant' Parties

Communists had understood the compromising nature of the Indian National Congress. The quintessence of the whole programme of Mahatma Gandhi included compromising with British imperialists. Compromise with the British rulers was an inherent component of Mahatma Gandhi's political policy. Non-violent struggles were launched to create conditions for a compromise now on home rule, now on dominion status. The communists had learnt well the lessons of the Chauri Chaura debacle of 1918-1922 movement.

Marxism had taught the communists that the working class and peasantry were the principal and decisive forces in the struggle for national liberation. They decided to organise the workers' and peasants' parties in the country. Bengal comrades were the first in the fields to do so. They organised the workers' and peasants' party in 1926. They were formerly organising the Labour Swaraj Party. They changed the latter into the Workers' and Peasants' Party.

Idea behind this organisation was that the legal communist party could not be used as a mass anti-imperialist organisation. Only the Workers' and Peasants' Party could fulfil that role. The organisation was the result of growing dissatisfaction of the broad masses with the compromising policy of the National Congress leaders. Freedom could not be won without organising the more or less 80 per cent of the working population.

Bengal comrades held the first conference of the workers and peasants in February 1926 in Krishnanagar (Nadia) where they changed the name of the Labour Swaraj Party into the Peasants' and Workers' Party. Later, understanding the key role of the working class, they changed the order into Workers' and Peasants' Party. Trade union work at that time in Bengal was weaker than in Bombay. But all the unions which existed in Bengal accepted the leadership of the Worker's and Peasants' Party.

The party published its own journal in Bengali

Ganavani. It appeared on 12 August 1926 under the editorship of Muzaffar Ahmad. The journal's main emphasis was that national liberation could not be achieved without the organised mass struggles of the workers and peasants.

The second conference of the Bengal Workers' and Peasants' Party took place in February 1927 and it adopted the party's immediate and ultimate aims document.

The programme declared that it was vitally necessary to create a political party of the working class, the peasantry and the lower sections of the middle class and that the Workers' and Peasants' Party met this necessity. It stressed that the chief aim of the Workers' and Peasants' Party was the establishment of a federal republic where the means of production, distribution and exchange would be in the hands of the people and will be used in the interests of the society.

The programme further advanced a number of immediate political, economic and social measures to improve the condition of the working people.

It also stressed that the main condition required to achieve these demands was that the country should become independent and freed from British imperialism and that to realise this aim, the party was prepared to work with other political parties in the country.

The programme criticised the Indian National Congress for ignoring the interests of the working people. It pointed out that the Workers' and Peasants' Party would work to get the Indian National Congress devote its attention to the demands of the working class, the peasantry and the lower section of the middle class.

Thus, the programme, despite its drawbacks, put forward the task of fighting for complete independence and proceeded from necessity of uniting for this purpose the working class, the peasantry and the urban petty bourgeoisie. The programme did not set the Workers' and Peasants' Party in opposition to the Indian National Congress but at the same time it did not define clearly its attitude towards the Indian National Congress.

The Workers' and Peasants' Party in Bombay was founded in March 1927 with S.S. Mirajkar as its secretary on the basis of a Congress labour group which existed there since 1925. The party published its own organ, the Kranti a weekly in Marathi. The party had a fairly strong workers' section and it is natural that the communists had the greatest influence in it.

The Bombay Workers' and Peasants' Party launched its activities by publishing a comprehensive resolution which it had already put forward at a meeting of the All India Congress Committee in May 1927. The resolution expressed the party's point of view on the current tasks of the national freedom movement. A brief summary of the programme is as follows:

(a) The Indian National Congress and its leaders as at present constituted represent the interests of the Indian propertied classes. The bulk of the Indian population are not in sympathy with the work of the Congress.

(b) In the interests of the revolutionary majority of the people it is necessary to liberate the Congress from the fetters of class interests and to set before it the task of winning national liberation. The achievement of this aim will be the first step on the road to complete liberation of the masses from exploitation and oppression.

(c) The aim of the Indian National Congress should be complete national independence and the establishment of swaraj based on universal suffrage.

(d) The Congress should affirm that civil disobedience and 'direct action' are the only effective weapons with which the Indian people will put an end to their state of subjugation.

(e) 'Direct action' and 'civil disobedience' can be successfully used only if there is a general broad awakening of the masses.

(f) To ensure the earliest awakening of the masses, the Congress should immediately adopt a programme of action aimed at improving the condition of the working people.

The Bombay Workers' and Peasants' Party's stand with regard to the Indian National Congress was more definite and mature than the other provincial ones. The Bombay party did not set itself in opposition to the Congress as the above programme shows but the party wanted to make the Congress more democratic and it wanted to transform it into an all India organ of struggle for complete independence.

The party demanded that the Congress adopts a programme which accords with the interests of the working masses but it did not put forward the demand for abolition of landlordism. The Punjab Workers' and Peasants' Party was taking a left sectarism mistaken stand with regard to the Indian National Congress.

The third province was the Punjab where the Workers' and Peasants' Party was formed on the initiative of the Amritsar Kirti comrades on 12 August 1928. The Lahore comrades', group joined the party later. That shows the political backwardness of Punjab. The need of this party had been felt as early as April 1927 but it did not materialise then.

In September 1927 the Kirti group had convened a Labour Conference at Hoshiarpur with Sohan Singh Josh in the chair. A cable from the workers of Berlin conveying the greetings to the League Against Imperialism and asking the conference to affiliate itself with the league was received at the conference.

Resolutions passed at the meeting, according to government reports, clearly indicated that the Kirti group stood for a socialist republic and was starting a new agrarian movement based on revolutionary methods.

Two factors helped the formation of the Workers' and Peasants' Party. One was the betrayal by the Indian National Congress of the interests of the peasantry as indicated in the Bardoli resolution and its pro-capitalist class policy vis-a-vis the working class. Second was that the patriotic youth and intelligentsia were disgusted with communal riots which were engineered and instigated by the British rulers in order to keep their stranglehold over India. The Kirti group which ran the *Kirti* magazine played a big role in founding the Workers' and Peasants' Party in the Punjab on secular and revolutionary democratic lines.

The second conference of the Workers' and Peasants' Party was held in Lyalpur on 29 September 1928. Comrades from Bombay and Calcutta were sent letters to come and attend the conference but none came. The reason for holding the conference at Lyalpur was to undermine the influence of the Zamindara League there and to release the peasantry from the influence of the landlords and big zamindars by exposing the true class character of the Zamindara League Leadership. The conference in a certain measure did achieve its objective.

We held the conference in the open near the pandal of the Punjab Provincial Political Conference whose leaders had refused to permit the use of the pandal to us. The result was that after a short time of the starting of our conference the Congress pandal became empty because the peasants left that pandal and came to the open conference. Many resolutions were passed in the conference emphasising the need for overthrowing

British imperialism, for establishing complete national freedom and setting up a workers' and peasants' republic in India. In the speeches the gains of the Russian revolution for the working people were explained; nationalisation of wealth and removal of the British army from India were advocated.

The third conference was held at Rohtak on 10 March 1929. Sohan Singh Josh spoke against the philosophy of predestination and empha-sised the fact that man as an individual as well as a class is the architect of his own fate. Broadly speaking, there were two main classes, the rich and poor and their interests were antagonistic to each other. The workers and peasants wanted to work for setting up their own government. The main problem was the land hunger of the peasantry. Unless that problem is solved, no improvement in their conditions could take place. Resolutions demanding reduction of the debt burden to the sahukars, rent burden to the landlords and heavy taxes of the government were passed.

The party celebrated the Friends of Russia Week in the Punjab and many processions were taken out in the province under the leadership of the party demanding betterment of the condition of the workers. The party organised the press workers' union, motor-drivers' union and some other small unions of the workers.

The Workers' and Peasants' Party was formed much later in UP than the three provinces mentioned above. A Conference was called in Meerut in October 1928 by the provincial peasant and trade union leaders for this purpose. Muzaffar Ahmad and Spratt from Calcutta and M.A. Majid, Sohan Singh Josh and Kedarnath Sehgal from Punjab were called to address it. the organisers were mostly reformist congressmen but the secretary elected was P.C. Joshi who came into prominence later as the general secretary of the CPI and who later did much to put the CPI on a firm footing.

It must be noted that coordination of work was far off. British surveillance, lack of funds and communication difficulties stood in the way. The British government had a fool-proof machinery of censorship. Hence the organisational principles of the workers' and peasants' parties were not always the same.

Communists were as yet inexperienced and theoretically immature in Marxist science and it was they who determined their policy and practical work. But the idealistic passion with which they worked spread the movement. Had they concentrated on building the working class party alone, the results would have been much more fruitful and profitable.

In the conditions prevailing in India at that time, the organisation of workers' and peasants' parties was of utmost political significance. "The slogan of struggle for real independence. One of the basic programme slogans of the workers' and peasants' parties, began to win more and more recognition among the broad masses both outside and inside the Congress, and this was the tremendous service rendered by the Indian communists and the workers' and peasants' parties. The workers' and peasants' parties organised the masses in their active struggle against imperialism and in the fight for the class demands of the working class and the peasantry. All this had its effect on the development of the national-liberation movement." This is how *A Contemporary History of India* has summed up the situation up to the first half of the year 1928.

(Courtesy: Peoples Publishing House and Sohan Singh Josh. The great Attack—Meerut Conspiracy Case. PPH. N.Delhi, 1979).

Kasur Case (1919)

On April 12, 1919 at Kasur a mob excited by speeches delivered by national leaders on that day invaded and wrecked the Railway Station, attacked the incoming train, killed two warrant officers, infuriated two officers, assaulted Mrs. and Mr. Sherbourne of the Railway Department, burnt the Post Office and Munsif's Court, attacked the Tehsil and was finally dispersed by fire from the police. About 15 persons were held out of which 11 were sentenced to death and three for transportation for life.

Kasur Supplementary Case (1919)

On April 12, 1919 at Kasur a mob inspired and excited by speeches delivered by national leaders that day, invaded and wrecked the Railway Station, attacked the incoming trains, murdered two warrant officers, Mrs. Gunner Mallet and Conductor Selby, assaulted and injured two officers Captain Libiby, R.E. and Lieut Munno of the XVII Loyal Regiment and Corporate Battron and Gringlam of the Queen's Regiment, assaulted Mr. and Mrs. Sherbourne of the Railway Department, all of whom were travelling in the train, burnt the Post Office and Munsif's Court, endeavoured to free prisoners in the lock up and in the Thana, attacked the Tehsil and was finally dispersed by fire from the police. In this case, about 49 persons were charged out of which eleven persons were sentenced to death and 14 to transportation for life. In each case, the property belonging to the convicts was forfeited.

Khulna Gang Case

Twenty persons suspected of complicity in the Nandanpur and Soleganti (Khulna) and Dhulgram and Mahisa (Jessore) dacoities and for incidents at other places were haulted up before the District Magistrate,

Khulna, on October 21, 1910. The accused numbering 18 were convicted by the trying Magistrate under Section 400 I.P.C. for being members of a gang of dacoits and awarded various terms of imprisonment. The convicted preferred an appeal to the High Court which was heard on April 2, 1911. All the prisoners pleaded guilty. At the instance of the prosecution, the High Court took a lenient view of the case and all the accused were bound down to be of good behaviour and in case of lapses to surrender and serve the sentence passed by the Magistrate. One was acquitted by their Lordships. Two absconders were subsequently apprehended and sentenced to long terms of rigorous imprisonment in a separate case.

Lahore Conspiracy Case No. I

Nine batches of conspirators were tried by Special Tribunals constituted under the Defence of India Act, 1914. The first batch of 61 persons was tried in the Lahore Conspiracy Case No. I and the trial began on 26th April, 1915. They were accused of waging war against the Crown, or conspiring to do so in and out of India, seducing troops, villagers and students to that end, committing dacoities, abetting murder, attempting murder, abetting mutiny of troops, manufacturing and collecting arms and bombs, attacking railways, bridges, ports, arsenals and projecting a general rising. Some were charged with offence under the Explosives Act. In view of the nature of the conspiracy, extraordinary precautuons were taken to ensure the safety of the jail during this and the subsequent trials. In addition to the ordinary guard, a strong military guard was posted at the jail. The public was denied access to the hearings. The judgement in the case was declared on 13th September, 1915. Four persons were acquitted, 24 sentenced to death (the sentence of 17 of these was changed into life imprisonment by the Viceroy), 27 sentenced to transportation for life and forfeiture of property, and six were sentenced to lesser terms.

Lahore Conspiracy Trial (1909-1915)

The most extensive preparations next to Burma for the overthrow of the Government was made in Punjab, the idea having taken root in 1909 and developed during the early years of the World War I.

To get a picture, however imperfect of the conspiracy it is necessary to take into account, related elsewhere, the events happening abroad in U.S.A., Canada, Malay and other Far Eastern countries including Burma. The *Ghadr*, the *Komagata Maru* and the Budge-Budge Riot, San Francisco Trial, Revolt of the 5th Native Light Infantry and the Malay State Guides, Mandalay Conspiracy and other cases on charges of waging war against the King, tempering with the army are some of the incidents. They are closely related to the Punjab Conspiracy Trials of 1915 and after.

The movement in sulky Punjab received a great momentum with the arrival of the emigrants from U.S.A., Canada, Shanghai and other countries in the Far East. With large and varied experience abroad and with a mind fully prepared for any eventuality they added strength and ingenuity to the organisations that had already been functioning in the area. A large quantity of arms and ammunition, obtained in America and Canada or secured *en route,* were smuggled into India. A fairly good number of the returned men were interned as soon as they set their feet on Indian soil. Some of them as were not arrested or released after a close scrutiny came to Punjab and proceeded to infuse revolutionary ideas in the minds of troops and the villagers.

It was rather plain to the revolutionists that the preparation for the attainment of the objective lay through ways and alleys beset with grim danger yet they were not deterred. The principal programme was seduction of Indian soldiers from their allegiance to the King and to induce them to join the rebellion; to secure arms and ammunition from private and other sources including Government armoury, from soldiers' barracks and smuggling from outside. Money was to be obtained by raids on Government treasury or looting of private property. It was deemed a part of the programme of action to assassinate police and other officials and all civil Europeans who might come forward to help the authorities. The movement of troop and supplies to the affected areas were to be stopped by wrecking of trains and railway bridges; communications to other stations to be dislocated by cutting off telegraph wires, etc., etc.

It could not be safe or sufficient to depend on supplies of arms and ammunitions from doubtful sources. Measures were, therefore, adopted to purchase relevant chemicals for the purpose of manufacturing bombs and other explosives. The principal centres for such purpose were at Jhabewal, Ludhiana District, at Lohatbodi in the Nabha State and elsewhere.

The idea of forging a revolution in Punjab was advanced by a member of the party organised as early as 1909 (who was awarded a death sentence but later commuted to transportation for life) through *Tarkhind* (History of India), a highly seditious literature and through clandestine writings bearing on a mass rebellion. A manual on bombs was also published at the time. A person was deputed to Peshawar in 1914 to collect arms in the manner as best as possible.

Acting upon the suggestions of the *Ghadr*, attempts were made for the seduction of troops *en route* to India at Shanghai, Hong Kong, Singapore, Penang, Rangoon and other places and efforts were also made in India in this direction at Mian Mir, Jullundur, Bannu and Kohat, Nowshera, Rawalpindi, Kapurthala, Ferozepore, Meerut, Agra, Cawnpore, Allahabad, Benares, Fyzabad, Lucknow, Ambala, etc. To facilitate the work of the party maps prepared showing the centres at which the work would be continued. One Vishnu Ganesh Pingley, visited sepoys in the barracks at Meerut and was arrested on March 23, 1915, with high explosive bombs in his possession. Pingley was assisted by Kartar Singh and Harnam Singh who approached soldiers' barracks to join them in the coming insurrection by distributing to reading *Ghadr* amongst them.

The most outstanding figure in the whole conspiracy was Rash Behari Bose, Satinder Chander or "Fat Babu", the name by which he was known to his comrades-in-arms in Punjab.

The entire details were worked out by him and he would be moving from place to place like a whirlwind. His tact and presence of mind would seldom forsake him. While scores of men were arrested, put into prison or lost their lives on the gallows, Rash Behari could never be arrested throughout the whole of his startling political career.

Returned emigrants were approached on their arrival in Punjab and those who were found to have any inclination for *Ghadr* work, were placed in the different sections of the organisation according to their taste and capability. It was not desirable that everyone should know the business or movement of any other member of the party whereas one may require a particular information of the party whereas one may require a particular information about a matter or a person. It was, therefore, necessary to arrange for some agency to act as "Post Offices" and for this purpose persons were selected who were for some reasons or other could not be entrusted with work involving grave risks.

Foreign help was sought for according to plan and indications pointing to some understanding about assistance from the Germans, especially individual Germans, were very frequent.

Having equipped themselves, however inadequately, the party engaged themselves into serious work. It was arranged that on November 26, 1914, there should be an armed military array at Jhar Sahib which was to be joined by mutineers from the 23rd Cavalry and which was to march on Sarahli Patti and Tarn Taran. The mutineers in Lahore got themselves armed but for some reasons or other did note move out.

An armed military group assembled at Jhar Sahib and Khairon and marched on Sarahli and then quitely dispersed. Some others made an armed demonstration on November 25, 1914, at Lahore Cantonment and then moved to Ferozepore with the intention of assaulting the treasury and arsenal at Moga on November 30, 1914. The men proceeding for the purpose clashed with a police party at Ferozepore (Ferozeshar) on November 27, which resulted in the death of a Sub-Inspector and a *Zaildar*. Two of the group of revolutionaries were killed at the place of occurrence in mutual exchange of fire with the police and seven others were subsequently tried and hanged.

Looting of private properties occurred at Sannewal and Mansuran (Ludhiana District on January 23 and 27, respectively), at Jhaner (in Malerkotla State on January 29), at Chabba (Amritsar on February 2), at Rabhon (Ludhiana District on February 3, 1915), and also at other places.

Individual acts of resistance and skirmishes were not infrequent. A Head Constable and a Sub-Inspector of Police were killed by a revolutionary at Anarkali Bazar on February 20, 1915, for which he was hanged.

One armed gang met on June 5, 1915, to attack the Kapurthala Magazine to secure arms and then to attack the Lahore and Montgomery Jails. The action was postponed to the 12th June as the party was considered insufficient for the purpose, a section having been despatched to attack the Valla Bridge military picket stationed there. On June 12, the guards were attacked in the course of which four persons were killed and four of the attackers were tried and hanged.

The Valla Bridge raid was a part of the activities for disrupting railway communications which formed a part of the programme of the revolutionaries. Another plan for attack on Darha Railway bridge on February, 1915, had to be abandoned at the last moment.

There were contacts between the disaffected persons in the Mandi State and the revolutionists in Punjab. It was resolved to collect bombs and arms in the State, bring up men from Punjab to murder the Wazir and the representative of the Government of India and take possession of the State. The idea was to use Mandi as a vantage point for extensive operations around. In a separate trial as Mandi Conspiracy Case five persons were convicted, one being sentenced to transportation for life and others receiving various terms of imprisonment.

There were men of outstanding ability, courage and resourcefulness. Decision was taken at Lahore on February 12, 1915, for effecting a mass rising on February 21, 1915, and emissaries were sent to several cantonments to announce the coming event. The infected troops were to rise throughout Punjab on receipt of news of an outbreak at Mian Mir.

Arrangements were made for collecting groups of villagers in Lahore to participate in the insurrection. Bombs were manufactured; arms got together to be given to men responsible for serious actions. To complete the arrangement, instruments for cutting telegraph wires and destroying centres of communications were collected on a large scale. Flags representing Free India were prepared which were to be hoisted in proper quarters after the revolution had succeeded. In a word, everything was put hastily in the line for the general rising.

Almost at the last stage of preparation it came to be known that the police had got scent of the affair through a spy and steps had been taken to prevent the occurrence by all means. Guards were placed at important centres and troops having sympathy or promising support to the organisers of the revolt, were transferred to different places overnight.

Confronted with this contingency the leaders hurriedly advanced the date to February 19 so that efforts of long months might not go in vain. But the time was rather too short to reach the changed date to the various centres not very close to one another. The result was disastrous for the organisers; before anything could be done, the grand project ended in a dismal failure.

There were mass arrests of the members of the revolutionary party in Punjab. Houses were searched frantically for every bit of paper and other articles furnishing any clue to the conspiracy. On February 19, a search at Mochi Gate, Lahore, resulted in the find of complete bombs, and other materials for the manufacture of bombs, a revolver, and a dogger. On February 20, revolver cartridges of various bores, percussion caps, files, duplicators, a sword stick, flags and seditious literatures were recovered. Searches conducted on February 24, 1915 at a house at Gumti Bazar and another at Wachhwali, Lahore, discovered four Bengal bombs, a pistol, cartridges of various bores, a bottle containing a solution called “Greek Fire” and chemicals for bombs.

A conspiracy case of unprecedented magnitude was started in the Lahore Central Jail on April 27, 1915, before a Special Tribunal constituted for the purpose with sixty-two accused rising eventually to eighty of whom sixteen were found to be absconders.

The accused were charged in a wholesale fashion under Sections 121, 121A, 122, 122-109, 123, 124A, 124A-107, 131, 132, 302, 303/109/120B, 395, 395-397, 396, 412, 414 I.P.C., Sections 3, 4, 5, and 6 of the Explosive Substances Act (Act VI of 1908).

Judgement was delivered on September 13, 1915, in a case which was unique in its origin, motive, time, character and ramifications, the number of men involved and the area covered by their activities.

Twenty-four men were condemned to death and twenty-six to transportation for life. Others received varying terms of imprisonment, only a few being acquitted.

On November 14, 1915, the Governor General-in-Council commuted the death sentences of seventeen leaving the seven others to die. They were:

(i) Bakshish Singh,
(ii) Bishnu Ganesh Pingley,
(iii) Surain Singh, son of Ishar Singh,
(iv) Surain Singh, son of Bur Singh,
(v) Harnam Singh of Sialkot,
(vi) Jaggat Singh, and
(vii) Kartar Singh (Saraba).

All of these fighters for India's freedom who had worked long years and suffered privation and sacrificed everything that man runs after, were executed in the Lahore Central Jail on November 17, 1915.

In the Court room as also standing before the gallows the condemned men refused to accept their endeavour to be termed a 'conspiracy'. They contended that it was an open challenge to the foreigners who charged the patriots sacrificing everything for the freedom of their Motherland with the offence of sedition, of waging war against the King.

Kartar Singh was not at all sorry for what they had done; rather he felt proud for enjoying the privilege of throwing out the challenge at the face of a lot of usurpers. He was really sorry over the outcome of their efforts. He averred that every slave had a right to revolt and it could never be a crime to rise in defence of the primary rights of the sons of the very soil.

When asked to appeal he restorted, "Why should I? If I had more lives than one, it would have been a great honour to me to sacrifice each of them for my country."

Lahore Conspiracy (1st Supplementary) Trial (1915-1916)

The heroes of Punjab were given no rest. With the conclusion of the comprehensive Lahore Conspiracy Case of supplementary trial of a larger number of accused persons was started on October 29, 1915, before the same Tribunal.

The evidence adduced by the prosecution in the most part was almost the same as in the first case relating to preparations in U.S.A., receiving aid from the enemy country, stirrings in the Far East, return of the emigrants to India and forthwith entering into a conspiracy to wage war against the King, etc., etc.

The incidents of Ferozepore, Anarkali Bazar, plan for assaulting the Moga Treasury and all others in their train were recapitulated and revived for bringing about a conviction of the accused. The First Supplementary Conspiracy Trial was started with no less than 102 accused of whom nine were absconders, cases of six were withdrawn and accused discharged, one turned approver and granted pardon, another ten were discharged by the Court leaving a total of seventy-six accused to stand the trial.

The accused comprised absconders in the original case against whom proceedings were taken under Section 512 Cr. P.C. and some of whom had since been arrested; alleged associates of those convicted in the previous case and those who were accused of having committed fresh offences since the last trial.

On March 30, 1916, judgement was delivered in which six were awarded the highest penalty of the law, forty-five to undergo transportation for life, eight received imprisonment for various terms and fifteen were acquitted.

Of the six condemned men sentence of one was changed to transportation for life. The other five were:

(i) Bir Singh Bahoowal, Hoshiarpur, found to have taken part in Sannewal and Chabba dacoities and to have been present in the Kapurthala rising;

(ii) Isahr Singh, *alias* Suran Singh of Bhudike, Moga, Ferozepore, was present at the Ferozepore Raid and the attack on the Doraha Bridge and to have been the foremost in the Kapurthala Raid;

(iii) Ranga Singh *alias* Roda Singh of Khurdapur, Kartarpur, Jullundur, was in close touch with Dhundike revolutionists and was present at the Kapurthala meeting and selected to form one of the Valla Bridge attacking party;

(iv) Rur Singh of Talwandi, Dusanj, Moga, Ferozepore, one of the Dhundike revolutionists, assisted in the initial assault on the Valla Bridge;

(v) Uttam Singh of Hansi Jograon, Ludhiana, early got into touch with the Lohatbadi revolutionists in procuring arms and ammunitions in Lohatbadi and in making bombs and taking part in the Ferozepore district raid. He was also present at the Kapurthala gathering on June 5, 1915, when the Valla Bridge attack was planned. He also absconded to Faridkot State to evade arrest.

On June 12, 1916, the five comrades were hanged in the Lahore Jail.

Lahore Conspiracy Case II or Lahore First Supplementary Conspiracy Case

The second case was started on 29th October, 1915 and was conducted by a Special Tribunal. To begin with, 102 accused were involved; some remained absconders and some were released before trial, and finally 74 were actually tried. In this case, the number of prosecution and defence witnesses was 365 and 1042, respectively. Judgement was delivered on 30th March, 1916. Six were sentenced to death (five of whom were actually executed), forty-five to transportation for life and eight given sentences ranging from 6 months to 3 years. The rest were acquitted.

Lahore Conspiracy (2nd Supplementary) Trial (1916)

On the same charges and on the same evidence as in the first two Lahore Conspiracy Trials, a large number of men were hauled up before the same Tribunal (the Second Supplementary) and trial commenced on November 8, 1916. It was a comparatively short trial inasmuch as evidence was concluded on December 14, 1916. By this time prosecution witnesses had been well trained and got used to say whatever the police would like them to adduce and the accused persons also got accustomed with the nature of evidence and the fate that awaited them.

On January 5, 1917, six persons were sentenced to death. In a review of the case the Government commuted the punishment of one to one of transportation for life.

(i) Babu Ram,
(ii) Balwant Singh,
(iii) Safiz Abdulla,
(iv) Rur Singh, and
(v) Naina

added themselves to the list of martyrs who had sanctified the gallows of the Lahore Central Jail on March 29, 1917.

Of the other accused no details are available in spite of a diligent search. About Balwant Singh it is known that unquestionably he was one of the most prominent and influential men in the revolutionary movement in Canada. He visited U.K. early in 1913 and saw a number of men having extreme political views. In the August of the same year he visited Lahore and made eloquent speeches on *Ghadr* and the movements supporting India's struggle for independence outside India.

In 1914 he returned to Canada arriving at the same time when the *Komagata Maru* affair had been agitating the Sikh community there and took a prominent part in the agitation arising out of the vessel's voyage. He was the most ardent advocate of the plan for returning to India for revolutionary purposes and in December 1914, he left Canada and stopped for some time in San Francisco where he was in touch with the headquarters of the *Ghadr* Party. He was next heard of as having reached Siam in July and arrested in Bangkok in August, 1915.

He was deported to Singapore and brought to India under custody to stand his trial in the omnibus conspiracy cases the fever of which had engrossed the attention of the authorities who found it a handy instrument to teach the sturdy daring Punjabis a lesson in loyalty and good citizenship.

Lahore Leaders' Case (1919)

Some prominent leaders of Lahore such as Lala Harkishan Lal, Pandit Rambhaj Dutt, Lala Duni Chand, Lala Dharam Das Suri, Dr. Gokul Chand Narang, Lala Mathura Prasad, Mr. Habbibullah Khan, Karam Chand Hateshi, M. Allah Din and Mota Singh held a protest meeting on February 4, 1919, in Lahore and they announced a general strike on April 11, 1919. On April 11, nationalists paraded the city of Lahore and inflammatory notices were pasted throughout the city. A mob assembled at the Badshahi Mosque and held a meeting in which resolutions against the repressive policy of the Government of India were passed. After this meeting the agitated nationalists walked through the city shouting national slogans, destroying portraits of the King and the Queen. On April 12, 1919, the mob re-assembled near the Fort. All the above named leaders were arrested and tried under Sections 120-B, and 121-A I.P.C. Lala Harkishan Lal, Rambhaj Dutt, Duni Chand, Allah Din and Mota Singh were sentenced to transportation for life and forfeiture of their property.

Lahore Conspiracy Case III or Lahore Second Supplementary Conspiracy Case

The trial case was heard at Lahore by a Special Tribunal consisting of three Commissioners. There were 17 accused in this case and the trial started on 8th November, 1916. The prosecution and defence witnesses numbered 86 and 44, respectively. Judgement was pronounced on 4th January, 1917. Six were sentenced to death (the sentence of one was later changed to transportation for life and forfeiture of property) and one was sentenced to two years' rigorous imprisonment. The remaining fiver were acquitted.

(*Courtesy:* Role of Honour—Kali Charan Ghosh)

The Lahore Conspiracy Case and Its Repercussions

The bomb-throwing in the Assembly was followed by the discovery of a bomb factory on the Mcleod Road, Lahore by the Punjab CID, on 15 April, 1929. The factory was situated in a house rented by Bhagwati Charan Vohara. Three young revolutionaries—Sukhdev, who had a loaded revolver in his possession, Jai Gopal and Kishori Lal—were arrested in the raid. A live bomb, eight bomb-shells, a large quantity of chemicals together with notebook containing bomb-formulae and a photograph of B.K. Dutt were recovered in the raid. Jai Gopal turned an approver and told everything in his knowledge about the activities of the party to the police. Another revolutionary Hansraj Vohra was arrested on 2 May 1929. He too turned an approver. These two approvers divulged many party secrets, and on the basis of their disclosures many revolutionaries were arrested.

The Saharanpur centre of the party was raided on the morning of 13 May 1929, when the two revolutionaries Shiv Verma and Jaidev Kapoor were arrested. Six live bombs, three bomb-shells and three revolvers and cartridges were recovered. Many blank letters-heads of the Hindustan Socialist Republican Army and books including *Manufacture and Use of Explosives* and *Bandi Jiwan* and a large quantity of chemicals and apparatus were recovered. Negatives of photographs of Bhagat Singh and B.K. Dutt were also found by the police in this raid. A third revolutionary, Gaya Prasad who returned to the Saharanpur Centre on the morning of 14 May, was also arrested by the police. Within a few weeks almost all the leaders of the Hindustan Socialist Republican Association and a large number of members were arrested, and government instituted the Lahore Conspiracy Case against them in 1929. Bhagat Singh who was sentenced to transportation for life in connection with the throwing of bombs in the

Assembly Hall, was also an accused in this case and was brought to the Lahore jail.

In the Lahore Conspiracy Case, the revolutionaries were charged with the crime of waging war against the King, while Bhagat Singh, Sukhdev and Rajguru were also charged with the murder of Saunders in Lahore. When Bhagat Singh was brought to Lahore in connection wth the Lahore Conspiracy Case, he wanted that the revolutionaries should be treated as political prisoners. But these prisoners were being treated as ordinary criminals and were suffering torture. The Kakori prisoners earlier had also fought and gone on hunger-strike for their demand of being treated as political prisoners but the government had not acceded to their demand. Though, ordinary European and Anglo-India criminals were getting far better treatment than the revolutionary prisoners. A Member of British Parliament, J.M Kenworthy who visited India in 1930, drew the attention of the Secretary of State for India towards the condition of the political workers in Indian jails. He was told by the active and sincere members of the Congress party that in the Indian jails people convicted for political were treated worse than criminals convicted of very heinous offences. *The Daily Worker of* New York in its report of 26 March 1930, described the conditions in Indian jails as abominable where the political prisoners were tortured for their crime of fighting for the freedom of their country.

Bhagat Singh and his comrades claimed the status of political prisoners as the British Government was trying them for waging war against the King and for cherishing political ideas. They demanded better food, clothes, newspapers and facilities for study as political prisoners. They threatened to go on an indefinite hunger-strike if the government failed to accept their demand. By resorting to hunger-strike, the revolutionaries had in mind the twin objectives of securing better facilities as political prisoners, and to propagate their revolutionary ideals by getting publicity for their hunger-strike.

Bhagat Singh and B.K. Dutt started their hunger-strike in the middle of June 1929. The other undertrial prisoners of the Lahore Conspiracy Case and many other prisoners in the lock-ups of the police stations in Lahore observed one-day token hunger-strike on 30 June 1929 in sympathy of Bhagat Singh and B.K. Dutt. The proceedings of the Lahore Conspiracy Case commenced before the Magistrate on 11 July 1929. The other Lahore Conspiracy Case prisoners joined Bhagat Singh and B.K. Dutt in the hunger-strike on 13 July. On the 14 July, Bhagat Singh sent a special petition to the Home Member of the Government requesting him to concede the revolutionaries' demands for better facilities in jail. The government, however, refused to extend the same facilities to Indian prisoners as were extended to European prisoners. Pandit Madan Mohan Malaviya reminded the government that the treatment of the Lahore Conspiracy Case prisoners was attracting the attention of the whole country, and that the whole country wanted the matter to be settled early in a fair and humane way.

As the hunger-strike continued, the condition of the revolutionary prisoners kept on deteriorating. The condition of Jatindranath Das became critical on 28 July. He was inspired by the feeling of self-sacrifice. Many Congress leaders including Dr. Gopi Chand, Lala Duni Chand and Ganesh Shankar Vidyarthi met Jatin Das in the jail and tried to pursuade him to give up his hunger-strike but he remained steadfast on his decision of fasting unto death till the demands were fully met. Jawaharlal Nehru met Jatin Das, Bhagat Singh and a few other hunger-strikers in the Lahore jail. He found them all very weak and bedridden, and it was hardly possible to talk to them much. He was impressed by the intellectual and calm appearance of Bhagat Singh, and the gentle looks of Jatin Das, though the latter was in considerable pain at that time.

Meanwhile the Jail Enquiry Committee appointed by the Punjab government, recommended some facilities for the revolutionary prisoners. But Bhagat Singh and B.K. Dutt insisted that Jatin Das should be released unconditionally before the revolutionaries suspended hunger-strike. The members of the Jail Enquiry Committee unanimously accepted this condition. But the Punjab government did not release Jatin Das unconditionally. Consequently, Bhagat Singh, B.K. Dutt and other revolutionaries resolved to continue the hunger-strike as the only course left to them. Their long sufferings did not bear any fruit and in the meanwhile Jatin Das died on 13 September 1929 on the 63rd day of his fasting. His death created a sensation all over the country, and brought the question of the treatment of political prisoners to the front.

Next day, on the 14 September, speaking on an adjournment motion on the action and policy of government regarding the under-trial accused in the Lahore Conspiracy Case, Motilal Nehru observed:

For days and days the news came that his (Jatin Das's) life was ebbing away, that at any moment he might breath his last, the news came that there were other hunger-strikers who were in a very precarious condition, and what was the Government doing all this time? It is said, Sir, that Nero fiddled while Rome was burning. Our benign Government has gone one better than Nero. It is fiddling on the death-beds of these youngmen, misguided they may be, but patriots they are all the same.

Pandit Madan Mohan Malaviya described the

Lahore Conspiracy Case prisoners as "men of high ideals, possessed of a high sense of national self-respect." He said:

"They are not ordinary criminals. They are persons who however much one may condemn any act of violence of which they might be proved to be guilty—they are persons who are not prompted by any sordid selfish motive. They are, everyone of them, persons who are inspired by a high sense of patriotism and a burning desire for the freedom of their country.

Amarnath Dutt, MLA from Burdwan division, charged the government with the murder of Jatin Das, and commended the courage of the young revolutionaries. He warned the government in the words of a British poet, thus:

'England shall perish, write that word in the
blood she has spilt,
Perish hopeless and abhorred
Deep in ruin as in guilt.'

The Home Secretary, Mr. H.W. Emerson admitted in the Legislative Assembly that Jatin Das did sacrifice his life for cause which he believed to be just.

The deadbody of Jatin Das was taken in a huge procession in Lahore. The large crowd was bare-headed, solemn and sad. Prominent Congressmen were supporting the bier. Jatin's body was buried under a pile of flowers. The deep silence was intermittently broken by the thundering cries of "Long Live Revolution" and "Down with Imperialism". The procession resolved itself into a meeting in the garden opposite the *Zamindar* office. The flower laden bier of Jatin Das was placed on an elevated platform. Pointing to the bier, Dr. Alam, Congress MLC said: "Cowards die many a time before their death, but brave men die only once." Then, Dr. Alam and another Congress leader Dr. Gopi Chand, both announced their resignations from the Council as a homage to Jatin's memory.

As Jatin's body was taken from Lahore to Calcutta for cremation, people assembled in very large numbers at every station to pay their homage to the martyr, and his martyrdom acted as a profound inspiration to the youth of India. The parting words of Jatin Das were: "I do not want that my obsequies should be performed at the Kali Bari in the orthodox Bengali fashion. I am not a Bengali, I am an Indian." There were mourning processions and hartals in many cities of the country. Among the many condolence messages that were received on the occasion was a message from the family of Terence McSwiney, the Lord Mayor of Cork, who had died a martyr under similar conditions in Ireland. The message ran thus: "Family of Terence McSwiney have heard with grief and pride of the death of Jatin Das. Freedom will come."

After the death of Jatin Das, the revolutionaries decided to suspend their hunger-strike on the request made to this effect in an AICC resolution. They accepted the recommen-dations of the Jail Enquiry Committee in the interest of the political prisoners, including the Kakori prisoners, all over the country.

The process was however delayed and on 28 January 1930, Bhagat Singh. B.K. Dutt and other Lahore Conspiracy Case prisoners sent a petition to the Government of India, complaining about their treatment in jails. They reminded the Government that they had suspended the hunger-strike on the assurance given by the members of the Punjab Jails Enquiry Committee that the question of the treatment of political prisoners was going to be finally settled to their satisfaction within a very short period. The same assurance was given by Sir James Crerar in the Legislative Assembly when the matter was taken up there after the death of Jatin Das. In the petition they mentioned that the Lahore

Conspiracy Case under trials were assaulted brutally on 23 and 24 October 1929 by orders of high police officials. They felt grieved at the continued vindictive treatment of political prisoners.

The Jail Enquiry Committee formulated new jail rules, creating three classes of prisoners according to their social status. No special class of political prisoners was created. The principle of 'Divide and Rule' was thus extended to the do main of prison administration. The practice of classifying certain prisoners as 'European' who used to get better food, clothing and accommodation than Indians of the highest ranks, was abolished. In practice, however, the position remained unchanged. These new rules, which seemed to promise a change for the better, in reality, made little difference and the position remained highly unsatisfactory.

In the Lahore Conspiracy Case, 24 persons were arrested but five persons evaded arrest. These five revolutionaries–Chandra Shekhar Azad, Bhagwati Charan Vohra, Yashpal, Kailashpati and Satgurudayal Avasthi—were declared absconders. Kailashpati and Satgurudayal Avasthi were arrested later. While the revolutionaries inside the jail were continuing their struggle through hunger-strikes, their comrades outside were busy in reorganising the party. Their main activity was directed towards the murder of the Viceroy, Lord Irwin, by way of revenge for the Lahore Conspiracy Case. The revolutionaries were not against Lord Irwin as an individual. But the Viceroy was the representative of the British Imperialism in India, and by killing him, the revolutionaries wanted to express their protest against the policies of the British rulers in India.

Yashpal and Bhagwati Charan prepared a plan to blow up the Viceregal train, and it was approved by Chandra Shekhar Azad, the Commander-in-Chief of the HSRA. The plan was to blow up the Viceregal train with a bomb which was to exploded by electricity from a distance. The whole scheme was carefully planned by Yashpal and Bhagwati Charan, and was to be executed with the active help of Inderpal, Bhag Ram, Hans Raj and Lekh Ram. The battery for producing electricity was prepared by Hans Raj.

It was originally intended to blow up the Viceregal train on its arrival from Bombay on 27 October 1929, at a spot some 9 miles from Delhi on the Delhi-Mathura road. In order to make preparations without arousing suspicion, Inderpal was deputed by Yashpal and Bhagwati Charan to live at the spot in the guise of a Sadhu and gain the confidence of the villagers. The plan was abandoned as the Viceroy did not return from Bombay on the expected date. Later it was decided to blow up the special train on its departure for Kolhapur from Delhi on November 15, but this plan had to be abandoned because the requisite materials could not be procured in time.

Finally, a spot about 2½ miles from New Delhi Railway Station and opposite the 'Purana Qila' was chosen for the blast. Over 300 years of flexible electric wire was buried under the earth by Yashpal, Bhagwati Charan, Inderpal and Lekh Ram on the night of December 21. The connections were tested by Bhagwati Charan and Inderpal on the night of December 22 with the battery, and bombs were then buried under the track.

A meeting of the revolutionaries was held in Delhi on 22 December at the Hindu College Hostel, residence of a party member Nand Kishore Nigam who was a Lecturer in Hindu College, and Superintendent of its hostels. The meeting was convened at the instance of Yashpal, and was attended by Chandra Shekhar Azad, Bhagwati Charan, Virbhadra Tiwari and Yashpal. It discussed the plan for blowing the Viceregal train next morning for which all preparations had been completed. Chandra Shekhar Azad, Virbhadra Tiwari and Bhagwati Charan wanted the action to be postponed because of the likely meeting of Lord Irwin with Gandhiji and other leaders on 23 December. But Yashpal was adamant and wanted to carry out the action at any cost. He left the meeting without the deliberations reaching at a final decision.

At that time Yashpal and Bhagwati Charan had been living, ostensibly as Insurance agents, in a room of a house situated in the Naya Bazar of Delhi, which served as a rendezvous for members of the revolutionary party. In the early morning of 23, December, Yashpal, who was dressed in Khaki military uniform, set out with Bhag Ram on a motor bicycle. The morning was very cold and a dense fog prevailed all round the countryside. When the train arrived at the spot where the bombs were buried, Yashpal fired the mine. But he was not able to see the train clearly on account of the heavy fog, and he passed the switch of the battery when he thought that the Viceroy's compartment was over the buried bombs. The bombs exploded with a loud sound which was within the hearing of the New Delhi Railway Station. The Restaurant Car, under which the bombs exploded, was almost completely wrecked. Its floor was blown upwards and an attendant was injured and suffered from the shock.

The Viceregal Coach was just at a distance of two other small apartments from the damaged restaurant car. In spite of the bomb explosion, the Viceregal special was not derailed, and it arrived at the New Delhi Station punctually, and the Viceroy escaped unhurt. Reporting the incident, *The Times of India* reminded the people:

It is recalled that exactly this day seventeen years ago when Lord Hardinge made his State enrty into Delhi, a bomb outrage occurred. Today on the first entry of the

Viceroy into his new house on the ridge overlooking Humaun's old fort, a similar outrage took place.

After the action, Yashpal left all his accessories on the spot and wanted to run away from there with Bhag Ram on the motor-bicycle. But its engine had jammed due to cold and it could not be started. They both had to push it towards the city. The motor bicycle was then left at the shop of a mechanic for repairs in Darya Ganj. Yashpal then straight went to the Railway Station from where he left for Ghaziabad. There he met Bhagwati Charan, and they both left for Calcutta.

The motor bicycle was then brought by the revolutionaries to the hostel of Nand Kishore Nigam. It was dismantled there. The police later recovered the parts of the motor bicycle from the shop of a mechanic in the Red Fort of Delhi. The engine of the motor bicycle was recovered from the river Harnad at Nalagarha in Bulandshahr district of the UP. The Nalagarha dairy farm was a frequent resort for members of the revolutionary party, including Chandra Shekhar Azad, where sometimes they used to have shooting practice. The proprietor of the farm was a friend of the revolutionary Vimal Prasad Jain, and it was through him that arrangements were made to store the engine of the motor-bicycle in the farm.

The bombing of the Viceregal train was widely condemned by various Congress leaders throughout the country as unfortunate incident. But it had the desired effect of creating a sensation from, the revolutionaries' point of view. The incident shocked London, and persons like Sir John Simon, Mr. Wedgwood Benn and Mr. Baldwin expressed horror at the outrage. A special meeting of the British Cabinet was summoned on 23 December 1929 to discuss the incident. *The Evening Standard* of London in an editorial emphasised that the British policy in India would not be deflected in the slightest by deeds of violence.

The Congress session at Lahore passed a resolution on 27 December 1929 which condemned the bomb outrage and congratulated the Viceroy and Lady Irwin on their narrow escape. But the sympathisers of the revolutionaries in the Congress seriously challenged Gandhiji's creed of non-violence in the AICC meeting. They were beaten after two hours of exciting debate, but the extent of the support must have been a sharp eye-opener to Gandhiji, if not to Motilal Nehru. Commenting on the resolution *The Times of India* said:

It was Mr. Gandhi's superior strategy and his moving appeal rather than reason that won the day for him. He has, however, no reason of be overjoyed. The fight is to be renewed at the open session of the Congress and it will not be surprising in the least if the wildmen carry the day and proclaim to the world that the cult of the bomb has the approval of the Congress.

The Bombay delegate to the AICC Mr. Rajah described the motion as in effect a loyalty resolution. As a result of the Lahore Congress deliberations, the government also came to the conclusion that there was some measure of sympathy in the Congress for the revolutionaries and some disposition to encourage them.

The revolutionaries circulated a pamphlet at the Lahore Congress Session in December 1929. It was purported to be a manifesto of the Hindustan Socialist Republican Army, and began with the words: "The food on which the tender plant of liberty thrives is the blood of the martyr." The party felt the necessity of circulating this manifesto because its activities were mostly secret and the country was in dark about their present policies and intentions.

The party reiterated its goal of Revoluation and liberty by means of an armed rebellion. The revolutionaries paid tributes to the greatness of

Mahatma Gandhi but condemned his method of non-violence. They emphasised that terrorism was never their object but it was only an effective means of retaliation against the British repression. They had adopted socialism as their goal as socialism alone could lead to the establishment of Complete Independence. The pamphlet exhorted the youth of the country to shake off the paralysing effects of long lethargy was distributed just after the Viceregal train-blowing incident, it created a new enthusiasm among the youth in the Congress session. The Complete Independence resolution was passed by the Congress under the leadership of the youth leader Jawaharalal Nehru in spite of severe opposition from certain sections of the Congress.

After the Viceregal train-blowing incident and the Congress resolution condemning the action, Gandhiji wrote an article "The Cult of the Bomb" in his weekly newspaper *Young India*, wherein he condemned the revolutionaries and called them cowards and misguided persons. The revolutionaries decided to reply the criticism by Gandhiji in the form of a pamphlet titled *The Philosophy of the Bomb*. The pamphlet was prepared by the two revolutionaries Yashpal and Bhagwati Charan, and Chandra Shekhar Azad arranged for its printing at a press near Kanpur.

The revolutionaries declared that they stood for winning independence by means of all the forces, physical as well as moral, at their command as against the use of only moral force by the advocates of non-violence. They hoped that a new Social Order could be brought about in the country through the Revolution which would ring the death-knell of capitalism and class distinctions and privileges. It would bring joy and prosperity to the starving millions and free them from foreign and Indian exploitation.

The revolutionaries described terrorism is a

necessary phase of Revolution. They hoped that in India, as in other countries in the past, terrorism would develop into the Revolution and the Revolution into Independence—social, political and economic. Jawaharlal Nehru agreed that terrorism usually represented the infancy of a revolutionary urge in the country. But in his opinion India had passed that stage while the revolutionaries believed that India was passing through that stage.

The revolutionary party felt that the British oppressors could not be converted into friends of India by preaching the gospel of love and non-violence. The revolutionaries paid tribute to the work done by the Congress in awakening, among the ignorant masses, a keen desire for freedom. But they claimed that their sacrifices had produced a tremendous change in the mentality of the people. They cited the examples of Russia and Turkey in support of thier plan of an armed revolution. In the end, the revolutionaries pledged to have their revenge on the tyrannical British Government and to continue their war to the end—to Victory or Death.

A copy of the pamphlet was also sent to Gandhiji. He praised it in the *Young India* and admitted that he had not done justice to the revolutionaries in his previous article. In his next article, Mahatma Gandhi praised the courage of the revolutionaries though he still condemned their method of violence. The pamphlet *Philosophy of the Bomb* was distributed throughout the country on the eve of the "Independence Day", 26 January 1930. It gave an impression to the people that the revolutionary party had a wide organisation in the country.

The revolutionaries now concentrated on a plan to rescue Bhagat Singh and B.K. Dutt, who as convicts, used to be taken from the Lahore Central jail to the court in the Borstel jail in a separate van. The plan was prepared under the guidance and leadership of Chandra Shekhar Azad and Bhagwati Charan. For this purpose a party armed with revolvers and bombs was arranged, and its headquarters were established in a house on Bahawalpur road in Lahore. About this time, on May 1930 Bhagwati Charan, Sukhdev Raj and Vishwanath Vaishampayan took some bombs out into the waste-land near river Ravi in order to test them. One bomb exploded prematurely in the hands of Bhagwati Charan. He was killed and Sukhdev Raj received injuries in the left foot. The deadbody of Bhagwati Charan was buried under the earth.

On 1 June 1930, the revolutionaries did make an attempt to rescue Bhagat Singh and B.K. Dutt. They reached the Borstel jail gate when Bhagat Singh and B.K. Dutt were coming out of the jail in a van. But as pre-arranged, they had to return without committing the action. Later on, one revolutionaries gathered that Bhagat Singh had left the idea of being rescued after the death of Bhagwati Charan and had made up his mind to make the supreme sacrifice. Thus, the rescue plan was finally abandoned. The party members dispersed from Lahore when two bombs exploded at their residence at Bahawalpur Road on the night of 2 June 1930. But when the police was informed of the explosion by the neighbours, and the house was searched, the revolutionaries had already left it with their belongings. The police, however, could make out that the house was occupied by the revolutionaries because of the two books and pieces of a letter left by them in a hurry.

The death of Bhagwati Charan, and the arrest and trial of the main leaders of the revolutionary party in the Punjab and the UP weakened the movement considerably and removed some of the best organisers, but the revolutionary spirit had been widely spread in whole of northern India. There were still left many revolutionary enthusiasts and sympathisers to keep the activities going on. Hans Raj 'Wireless' and Inderpal changed the name of the party to "Aatishi Chakkar" or "Fire Ring Party" in the Punjab, in order that it should not be identified with the HSRA.

Hans Raj conceived a plan of exploding bombs simultaneously in various towns of the Punjab. Houses and rooms were hired in various cities of the Punjab. In the morning of 19 June 1930, small decoy bombs were exploded by means of candle fuses. The police, who rushed to the spot, found a neat black box fitted with handle resting on the top of obviously revolutionary literature. The box was a powerful 'booby trap' bomb designed to explode when lifted. These traps were arranged at Lahore, Amritsar, Gujranwala, Sheikhupura, Layallpur and Rawalpindi. As a result of these explosions, a Sub-Inspector of Police and a Head Constable were killed and several others were injured. On the night of 18 June 1930, the "Aatishi Chakkar" party distributed its manifesto in Urdu, in which it condemned the British tyranny in India, and declared its determination to carry on the fight against the British rule to the finish. On 26 August 1930, the Lahore police made a number of arrests in connection with the simultaneous bomb-explosions of 19 June 1930. Inderpal was also arrested, and he made a statement to the police disclosing many activities of the revolutionaries including the Viceregal train-blowing attempt on 23 December 1929. Many other revolutionaries who were arrested in connection with the 'booby-trap' bomb explosions, included Gulab Singh, Jahangirilal, Rup Chand, Kundanlal, Krishan Gopal and Dayanat Rai.

In November 1930, the trial of the Second Lahore Conspiracy Case opened, as the outcome of the simultaneous bomb explosions of 19 June 1930 in the

Punjab. After another lengthy trial, five of the accused—Inderpal, Rup Chand, Jahangiri Lal, Gulab Singh and Kundanlal—were sentenced to transportation for life, and eleven other were sentenced to various terms of imprisonment. Chandra Shekhar Azad, Yashpal, Hans Raj 'Wireless' and Durga Devi were among the absconders. As a matter of fact, this Second Lahore Conspiracy Case was a part of the main Lahore Conspiracy Case, as the main leaders of this case were Chandra Shekhar Azad, Bhagwati Charan and Yashpal, but Bhagwati Charan had already met with his death while testing a bomb on May 1930.

In June 1930, the revolutionary party decided to commit a dacoity as funds were low and money was urgently needed for carrying out the activities of the party. A plan was chalked out to attack the lorry which carried money from the Imperial Bank, Kashmere Gate, Delhi to the Railway Clearing Accounts Office. First July 1930 was fixed as the date for the action. But the plan was abandoned because of intensive police patrolling in the city owing to the arrest of Motilal Nehru on that day.

Chandra Shekhar Azad prepared another plan to raise money. Under his leadership, the revolutionaries committed a dacoity at the Gadodia Stores in Delhi on 6 July 1930. Chandra Shekhar Azad, Kailashpati, Dhanwantari, Lekh Ram, Kashi Ram, Vidya Bhushan and Bhawani Sahai participated in this dacoity. They carried off some Rs. 14,000 in cash in a motor car, firing in the air in the street as they left in order to discourage pursuit. The money looted in this dacoity was distributed to various centres of the revolutionary party. An amount of Rs. 4,000 was allotted to the Delhi Centre where a bomb-factory disguised as a soap-factory was opened. Another amount of Rs. 2,000 was kept to be sent to Badshah Gul, an Afridi across the frontier, for the purchase of fire-arms.

The soap factory where bombs were to be made, was named Himalaya Toilet Factory and was situated at the Qutub Road, Delhi. The revolutionaries who worked here included, among others, Vimal Prasad Jain, Yashpal, Kailashpati and Vatsyayan. Vatsyayan was the 'scientist' of the revolutionary party. Chandra Shekhar Azad often visited the factory to inspect the progress of the work. A large quantity of picric acid and gun-cotton was prepared here to be used in bomb-making. But at the end of September 1930, the factory was closed down and its materials were removed to the house of a revolutionary youth Kapur Chand in the Paharwali Gali, Delhi. It was done because of the arrests of Inder Pal and others in Lahore in August. Explosives were actually manufactured there.

Kailashpati was arrested on 28 October 1930 outside his house near Sita Ram Bazar, Delhi. The police recovered a loaded revolver from his person. The house was searched and 4 bomb shells, a Mauser pistol, large quantity of chemicals for making explosives, and a mass of revolutionary literature were recovered from the place. Kailashpati, an absconder in the Lahore Conspiracy Case, had been the incharge of the revolutionary headquarters at Delhi since the autumn 1929. He turned an approver and made important disclosures regarding the aims and activities of the revolutionary party. The immediate result was the search of the house of the revolutionary youth Kapur Chand in the Paharwali Gali, Delhi where large quantities of chemicals for manufacturing bombs and revolutionary literature were recovered.

Dhanwantari, another important leader of the HSRA, was arrested in Chandni Chowk, Delhi on 1 November 1930. He wounded a policeman with his revolver-shot before he could be overpowered by the police. Dhanwantari has become the leader of the Punjab branch of the HSRA after the death of Bhagwati Charan. But Sukhdev Raj, another revolutionary who was with Dhanwantari at the time of his arrest, escaped and could not be arrested. Other arrests followed as a result of the information given by Kailashpati to the police. Vimal Prasad Jain was arrested in Meerut on 15 November 1930. On this very day, Vatsyayan, the 'scientist' of the party, was arrested in Amritsar. Nand Kishore Nigam was arrested in Kanpur on December 4, 1930.

After a lengthy investigation, a conspiracy case was instituted in Delhi before a Special Tribunal, with Kailashpati as an approver. It was known as the Delhi Conspiracy Case. A Defence Committee was formed with Deshbandhu as President and Raghunandan Saran as Secretary. A few representatives of the Students' Union were also on the Committee. Chaudhary Zafar Ullah Khan was engaged by the government as the prosecution counsel. The accused were charged with revolutionary activities involving conspiracy and illegal possession of explosives, conspiracy to murder police officials and the illegal possession of arms. The trial dragged on for seven months, and the case was then withdrawn. Of the 14 accused, two were interned under Regulation III of 1818, four were released, and eight were charged under specific offences. Chandra Shekhar Azad and Yashpal again declared absconders.

In the main Lahore Conspiracy Case, the accused were charged with the murder of Mr. Saunders and head constable Chanan Singh in Lahore, the establishment of bomb factories at Lahore and Saharanpur, the conspiracy leading to the throwing of two bombs in the Legislative Assembly in Delhi on 8 April 1929, and various other revolutionary activities. The case had to be adjourned several times as some of the accused were found to be physically unfit to attend to the court on account of their hunger-strike. When the government did not extend facilities as demanded by the Lahore Conspiracy Case prisoners, they decided not to cooperate with the court. It was their idea to show the hollowness of the British Justice by not attending the proceedings of the court. Consequently, the government promulgated the Lahore Conspiracy Case Ordinance of 1930 to deal with obstruction by the accused. The trial of the case was entrusted to a tribunal in order to decide the case even without the presence of the accused.

The judgement in the main Lahore Conspiracy Case was delivered on 7 October 1930. Of the 24 accused, five were given pardon as approvers. Bhagat Singh, Sukhdev and Shiv Ram Rajguru were sentenced to death. Kishorilal, Jaidev, Shiv Verma, Gaya Prasad, Mahabir Singh, Vijay Kumar Sinha and Kanwal Nath Trivedi were sentenced to transportation for life. Kundanlal and Prem Dutt got seven and five years' rigorous imprisonment each respectively. Ram Saran Das and Braham Dutt who had turned approvers, were late convicted to one and a half years's RI each for perjury.

After the judgement of the Special Tribunal, the Defence Committee for the Lahore Conspiracy Case prisoners filed an appeal to the Privy Council on the ground that the Special Tribunal was not legally constituted, as the Governor General of India was not authorised to make an order constituting the special Tribunal. The revolutionaries thought that through their appeal to the Privy Council, they would be able to get publicity abroad. They wanted to tell the civilized world how inhuman treatment was given to the political prisoners in India. They also aimed at informing the enemies of England abroad that there existed a socialist revolutionary party in India too. Yet another important aim of the revolutionaries was that the hangings should take place after the public was awakened regarding the ideals and activities of the HSRA.

When the appeal to the Privy Council was rejected, an organised movement started throughout the country by the people and the national leaders for the communtation of death sentences passed of Bhagat Singh, Sukhdev and Rajguru. Public meetings were held throughout the length and breadth of the country demanding the commutation of the death sentences. On the 14 February 1931, Pandit Madan Mohan Malaviya sent a telegram to the Viceroy requesting him to commute the death sentences into those of transportation for life. He reminded the government that the action of these youngmen was not prompted by any personal or selfish consideration but by a patriotic impulse, and the execution of these youngmen would give a great shock to the public feeling in this country.

Bhagat Singh Appeal Committees were formed at many places in the Punjab. The object of these Committees was to stir the people to such a pitch of excitement that on the day of execution of Bhagat Singh and others, they would take part in offensive and possibly violent demonstrations. In Lahore and Amritsar, the Committee consisted of old members of the Naujawan Bharat Sabha. For the time being, they wanted to obtain the signatures of as many people as possible to a memorial to the Viceroy asking for the communtation of the death sentences of Bhagat Singh, Sukhdev and Rajguru to those of transportation for life. This provided an opportunity for demonstrations and violent speeches so that public attention was focused on the matter, and excitement and sympathy were aroused.

Bhagat Singh Day was observed throughout the Punjab on 17 February. In Lahore, there was partial hartal but all the colleges were affected. A procession took place in the afternoon largely attended by students, at which amongst other cries, the following words were shouted in chorus: "Destroy this old Government", "We will not rest until we have shot all high officials." This was followed by a largely attended meetings addressed by Congress leaders S. Sardul Singh, Dr. Satya Pal and Baba Sohan Singh. According to the government officials, these leaders were expected to voice the opinion of the Congress. At the meeting, they threw themselves whole-heartedly on the side of violent revolution by the praise they lavished on the condemned revolutionaries whom they described as "Martyrs", "heroes", and "immortal youngmen." Dr. Satyapal said that the execution of Bhagat Singh would be a challenge to all the lovers of the motherland, and that even Mahatma Gandhi sympathised with Bhagat Singh and considered his conviction totally unjustifiable. He told the audience that he had seen Sir Tej Bahadur Sapru and other responsible leaders; and all regarded Bhagat Singh as a national hero. He concluded by saying that if Bhagat Singh was executed, there would be no chance of peace in the future.

Meetings were held at Amritsar where the Bhagat Singh Appeal Committee was extremely active. Twelve thousand signatures had been secured there to the printed appeal to the Viceroy for clemency. The government expected that if the All India Congress Working Committee did not demand the commutations of these sentences as one of the terms of opening negotiations with the government, they would become most unpopular with the extreme wing. A leader of the Bhagat Singh Appeal Committee, Ahmad Din, said repeatedly at Amritsar that if the Congress leaders did not strive for the release of violent revolutionaries, they would received with black flags, and would be greeted with cries of "Gandhi Go Back", and "Go Back Jawaharlal."

The news of the imminent hangings of Bhagat Singh and others aroused public feelings in Delhi where people were seen procuring signatures on a public memorial praying for the commutations of the death sentence. The signatories included some of the members of the Legislative Assembly, Municipal Corporation and Local Bar. The memorialists, among other grounds, pleaded that the trial of Bhagat Singh and others was not held according to the ordinary form of law, and that the trial was conducted *ex-parte* in the absence of accused by an extraordinary court of law.

The news of Bhagat Singh's impending execution cast a gloom over the city of Bombay. A largely attended meeting was held at Azad Maidan, Bombay on 28th February where the speakers supported the move for sending a petition to the Viceroy. More than two lakhs of citizens had already signed the memorial. The petition said that the execution of the revolutionaries would be tantamount to act of political vendetta, and it would seriously impair the restoration of political peace. A meeting of the Muslims of Lahore was held on 27 February in the Sheranwala Gate mosque the Juma prayers. It was decided to send a telegraphic memorial to the Viceroy to commute the death sentences of Bhagat Singh and others. It was also decided to ask Maulana Abul Kalam Azad to prevail upon Mahatma Gandhi to get the sentence commuted by the Viceroy. Prayers were offered for the long life of Bhagat Singh. Another memorial signed by large number people was sent to the Viceroy from Benaras on 3 March, requesting him to commute the death sentences. On the same day, the Karachi Municipality sent a telegram to the Viceroy urging him to commute the death sentences of Bhagat Singh and his comrades.

A storm of indignation broke out in London and in Labour Party circles at the report from India that the

Government proposed to carry out the sentences of death pronounced of Bhagat Singh and his colleagues. A meeting was organised in London on 4 March to protest against the threat to carry out the death sentences. The meeting was addressed by several British MPs. The London branch of the Indian National Congress circulated throughout Britain a petition for submission to the British Premier, demanding the release of Bhagat Singh and his colleagues.

The popularity of Bhagat Singh and his revolutionary colleagues Sukhdev and Rajguru, and the public concern for their life was increasing with every passing day. Each town and village of the Punjab, and to a lesser extent the rest of northern India, resounded with the name of Bhagat Singh. Innumerable songs grew about him, and the popularity that the man achieved was something amazing. H. W. Hale, the then Assistant Director, Intelligence Bureau, Government of India, has recorded the position thus: "Bhagat Singh especially became a national hero, and his exploits were freely lauded in the nationalist press, so that, for a time, he bade fair to oust Mr. Gandhi as the foremost political figure of the day. His photograph was to be met within many houses, and his plaster buts found a large market.

B Pattabhi Sitarammaya, the official historian of the Congress, describes the popularity of Bhagat Singh in the following words: "It is no exaggeration to say that at that moment Bhagat Singh's name was as widely known all over India and was as popular as Gandhi's."

As a result of the signing of the Gandhi-Irwin pact on 5 March 1931, the popularity of Mahatma Gandhi had reached the high water-mark. On this occasion Mahatma Gandhi appealed to the revolutionary party to desist from its activities and give the Congress an opportunity of securing the release of all political prisoners, including those who had been sentenced to death as being guilty of murder. He cautioned the people not to raise false hopes in this regard but said that it was his own and the Congress aspiration. But after about a week at Delhi, Mahatama Gandhi got the news that the Government had decided to execute Bhagat Singh and two of his comrades. Pressure was brought to bear upon to Mahatma to try to save the lives of these youngmen. Mahatma Gandhi, in his own way, and by arguments he alone could put forward, did everything possible to save Bhagat Singh and his comrades from the gallows.

On this occasion, Subhash Chandra Bose suggested to the Mahatma that he should, if necessary, break with the Viceroy on the question, because the execution of Bhagat Singh and others was against the spirit, if not the letter, of the Gandhi-Irwin pact. But the Mahatma who did not want to identify himself with the revolutionaries, would not go so far and it naturally made a great difference when the Viceroy realised that the Mahatma would not break on that question. Mahatma Gandhi did not go to the extent of including the commutation of the death-sentences as part of pact. However, at that time, Lord Irwin told the Mahatma that he had received a largely signed petition asking for the commutation of the death sentences, and he would postpone their execution for the time being and give serious consideration to the matter, but beyond that he did not went to be pressed at the moment. The conclusion which the Mahatma and everybody else drew from this attitude of the Viceroy, was that the execution would be finally cancelled. But the expectations of the Mahatma and the nation were falsified.

The date and timings of the execution of Bhagat Singh and his two comrades were kept a closely guarded secret upto the last moment, but at the same time the government made elaborate preparation to deal with any situation and public excitement after the hangings. Processions and meetings in sympathy of the condemned prisoners were banned, and British regiments were posted in the important towns of the Punjab. It was finally decided to hang the three revolutionaries in the evening of 23 March 1931, and to make the news public on the morning of 24 March. Bhagat Singh wrote a letter to his younger brother Kultar Singh, a few days before being hanged, in which he said: "Friends of the tavern, I am here for a few fleeting moments, like the lamp in the morning about to be extinguished. But the atmosphere will be surcharged with the electricity of our ideals and thoughts." In another letter to the Punjab Government Bhagat Singh, Rajguru and Sukhdev wrote that they should be treated like prisoners of war as they had been waging war against the Crown for a long time. They should therefore, be shot dead instead of being hanged.

When the jail officials came to escort Bhagat Singh on his journey to the gallows, he was engrossed in reading a book. An officer told Bhagat Singh that they had come to lead him to the gallows. Bhagat Singh said: "Just a moment, a revolutionary is busy meeting another revolutionary." He had been reading Lenin's life. At the time of mounting the gallows, Bhagat Singh addressing the British Deputy Commissioner, who was there to witness the hangings as enjoined by law, said: "Well, Mr. Magistrate, you are fortunate to be able to see how Indian revolutionaries can embrace death with pleasure for the sake of their supreme ideal." Bhagat Singh, Sukhdev and Rajguru were hanged in the Central Jail, Lahore at 7 O'clock in the evening of 23 March, 1931.

According to the official announcement, the dead bodies of the three revolutionaries were hurriedly cremated on the bank of the river Sutlej and the remains were thrown into the same river. The relatives of the dead were not even informed. The hasty cremation and disposal of the dead bodies reflected the panic of the Government. The Government knew very well how the martyrs were honoured among their counterymen and anticipating what reactions would be produced among the people, it decided to hang them on the evening of 23rd March. The Government did not want the revolutionary fervour of the masses to mount by handing over the dead bodies of the martyrs to them.

The execution of Bhagat Singh and his comrades Sukhdev and Rajguru was the signal for a good many processions and meetings, and speeches eulogising their deeds were delivered. *Hartals* were observed throughout the length and breadth of the country. In Lahore, the military was kept ready in the fort to meet any emergency, and aeroplanes hovered over the city. The Calcutta Corporation adjourned its meetings of 25 March 'as a mark of protest against the unwise, ill-considered action of the Government in executing Bhagat Singh, Sukhdev and Rajguru in utter disregard of strong and united public opinion throughout the country." In Nagpur, there was a demonstration on 25 March as a protest against the executions. In Jabalpur, the executions increased the bitterness of the people, against the Government. Processions were taken out in the city with pictures of Bhagat Singh with the caption: "Blood be required for Blood." The news of the execution created considerable excitement in Peshawar City and Cantonment, and large processions were taken out as a mark of protest. Processions, *hartals* and holding of meeting was also reported from various other places in the county including Baroda, Indore, Satna (M.P.), Ratlam, Hyderabad and Madras. In Travancore, the processionists held black flags, wore black badges and shouted "Up Revolution."

Bhagat Singh and his co-martyrs were lavishly praised for their supreme sacrifice throughout the country. The Central Sikh League praised Bhagat Singh and his associates as great patriots and brave fighters in its meeting held at Amritsar on 8 April, 1931. In this meeting Subhash Chandra Bose also delivered a speech praising the character, patriotism and sacrifice of Bhagat Singh. Almost all the national leaders expressed their sorrow and indignation at the execution of the revolutionaries. Subhash Chandra Bose, later, wrote about the hangings:

It is impossible to understand at this distant date the poignant grief which stirred the country from one end to the other. Somehow or other, Bhagat Singh had become the symbol of the new awakening among the youth.

Jawaharlal Nehru expressed his opinion in the following words: " I have remained absolutely silent during their last days lest a word of mine may injure the prospect of commutation. I have remained silent though I felt like bursting but now all is over. Not all of us could save him who was so dear to us, and whose magnificent courage and sacrifice have been an inspiration to the youth of India. India today cannot even save her dearly loved children from the gallows. Three will be hartals and mourning processions everywhere. There will be sorrow in the land at our utter helplessness. But there will also be pride in him who is no more, and when England speaks to us and talks of settlement, there will be the corpse of Bhagat Singh between us, lest we forget.

Sardar Vallabhbhai Patel, the President of the Congress in the year 1931, described as hollow the boast of English law that no one could be convicted upon evidence untested by cross-examination. Pandit Madan

Mohan Malviya was too deeply moved by the tragedy that he found it impossible to describe his grief in words. Mahatma Gandhi, in his statement to the press on the execution of Bhagat Singh and his comrades, said: "The execution of such a youth and his comrades had given them the crown of martyrdom. Thousands feel today personally bereaved by their death." He criticised the government of losing a golden opportunity of winning over the revolutionary party of India by not commuting the sentences. In his press statement, he added: "We may accuse the Government of goondaism but we may not accuse them of a breach of these settlement. In my deliberate opinion, the grave blunder committed by the Government has increased our power for winning freedom for which Bhagat Singh and his comrades have died.

The Congress Session started at Karachi just a few days after the hangings of Bhagat Singh and his comrades. According to the official Congress historian Pattabhi Sitarammaya: "The Karachi Congress which should have met under the radiance of universal joy met really under the gloom cast by the news of the execution of the three youths, Bhagat Singh, Rajguru and Sukhdev. The ghosts of these three departed youngmen were casting a shadow over the assembly." A feeling of deep resentment prevailed on the camp. All the festivities were cancelled. The large tri-colur flag was flying half-mast, and black-flag processions marched though the Congress grounds, filling the air with cries of "Bhagat Singh Zindabad." When Mahatma Gandhi arrived in Karachi to participate in the Congress session, there was a hostile demonstration, and many youngmen received him with black flowers and black garlands and shouted slogans "Gandhi go back." Gandhiji was grieved that in spite of his efforts, he had not been able to get the sentences of Bhagat Singh and other commuted. The result was that those Congressmen who were praising Gandhi for his efforts to save Bhagat Singh, now began to show anger over the language to be adopted in regard to the resolution to be moved for the three martyrs. The feeling among a considerable section of the youth was that the Mahatma had betrayed the cause of Bhagat Singh and his comrades.

According to Pattabhi Sitarammaya: "It is really a point of doubt, even at this distance of time, as to which resolution was the more arresting one at Karachi—that relating to Bhagat Singh or that relating to the ratification of the Gandhi-Irwin agreement. *The Daily Worker* of New York published a detailed report of the tortures and execution of Bhagat Singh and his comrades, and called the execution as "one of the bloodiest deeds ever undertaken by British labour government, under the leadership of MacDonald."

At the Karachi Congress Session, the point of issue on the Bhagat Singh resolution was, whether the phrase "while dissociating itself from and disapproving of political violence in any shape or form", should be incorporated in recording the admiration of the bravery and sacrifice of Bhagat Singh and his comrades. The younger section did not want to include the phrase in the resolution. The resolution as passed by the Congress, read thus:

This Congress, while dissociating itself from and disapproving of political violence in any shape or form, places on record its admiration of the bravery and sacrifice of the late Sardar Bhagat Singh and his comrades Syts. Sukhdev and Rajguru, and mourns with the bereaved families the loss of these lives. The Congress is of opinion that this triple execution is an act of wanton vengeance and is so deliberate flouting of the unanimous demand of the Nation of commutation. This Congress is further of opinion that Government have lost the golden opportunity of promoting good-will between the two nations, admittedly held to be essential at this juncture, and own winning over to the method of peace the party which, being driven to despair, resorts of political violence.

Bhagat Singh and his two comrades Sukhdev and Rajguru had unshakeable faith in the ultimate victory of their ideals—the ultimate doom of Imperialism and Capitalism, and throughout their life, they felt proud that they had relentlessly waged war against these systems of the society.

On 28 April 1931, a meeting of some prominent citizens, including Congress leaders Dr. Satya Pal, Dr. Mohammad Alam and S. Sardul Singh was held at Lahore with the object of forming an All-India Martyrs Memorial Committee to perpetuate the memory of Bhagat Singh and others. Invitations were sent to national leaders including Gandhiji and other public workers to attend the meeting. The Committee aimed at building a worker's home, a lecture hall and a library. It also wanted to maintain a permanent fund for the purpose of relieving the suffering of political prisoners and to help their families. But the Government was determined to nip in the bud the attempts to the Memorial Committee. The project, however, remained unaccomplished as sufficient funds could not be raised for the purpose.

[Courtesy: Dr. (Smt.) Kaushalya Devi Dublish—Revolutionaries and their Activities in Northern India– B. R. Pub. Corporation–1982]

Lahore Conspiracy Case No. 1 of 1930.

Accused

Name	*District*	*Province*	*Sentence*
Bhagat Singh..	Lahore	Punjab	Hanged
Sukh Dev, *alias* Dyal, alias Swami, *alias* Villager, son of Ram Lal.	Lyallpur	Punjab	Hanged
Shivaram Rajguru *alias* "M", *alias* Ramguru *alias* Raghunath.	Benares	U.P.	Hanged
Kishori Lal Rattan, *alias* Deo Datt Rattan, *alias* Mast Ram Shastri.	Hoshiarpur	Punjab	Transportation for life.
Jai Dev *alias* Harish Chander.	Hardoi	Bengal	Transportation for life.
Sheo Varma *alias* Parbhat *alias* Harnarain *alias* Ram Narain Kapur.	Hardoi	Bengal	Transportation for life.
Gaya Parshad *alia* Dr. B. S. Nigham *alias* Ram Lal *alias* Ram Nath *alias* Desh Bhagat.	Cawnpore	U.P.	Transportation for life.
Mahabir Singh *alias* Partab of Shahpur Tehla.	Etah	U.P.	Transportation for life.
Bijoy Kumar Sinha *alias* Bachu.	Cawnpore	U.P.	Transportation for life.
Kanwal Nath Trivedi *alias* Kamal Nath Tewari.	Champaran	Bihar	Transportation for life.
Kundal Lal *alias* Partap has proved to be Bhagwan Das Mahor *alias* Gunthala arrested at Bhusawal.	Benares	U.P.	7 years' R.I.
Prem Dutt *alias* Master *alias* Amrit Lal.	Gujrat	Punjab	5 years' R.I.

Absconders

Name	*District*	*Province*	*Sentence*
Chander Shekar Azad *alias* Panditji *alias* Quicksilver	Benares	U.P.	(Shot dead in February 1931).
Kailash Patti *alias* Kali	Azamgarh	U.P.	Arrested in Delhi.

Charan.			
Bhagwati Charan *alias* B.C. Vohra	Lahore	Punjab	(died as result of bomb explosion in May 1930).
Yashpal	Dharamsala	Punjab	Arrested in U.P.)
Satgur Dayal Awasthi ..	Cawnpore	U.P.	Arrested.

Approvers

Jai Gopal *alias* Harbans Lal *alias* Gopal *alias* Kishan Chand.	Gujranwala	Punjab.	
Phoindra Nath Ghosh *alias* Dada.	Champaran	Bihar.	
Manmohan Bannerji *alias* Manohar Bannerji.	Champaran	Bihar.	
Lalit Kumar Mukarji	Allahabad	U.P.	
Hans Raj Vohra *alias* Tarlok Chand.	Lahore	Punjab	
Ram Saran Dass.	Kapurthala State.	Punjab	(Ram Saran Dass and Brahm Dutt were later convicted to 1½ years R.I. each for prejury.)
Brahm Dutta *alias* Monmohan.	Cawnpore.	U.P.	

Lahore Conspiracy Case No. 2 of 1930.

Accused

Inderpal.	Kangra	Punjab	Transportation for life.
Rup Chand.	R. Pindi	Punjab	Transportation for life.
Jahangiri Lal.	Sheikhupura	Punjab	Transportation for life.
Gulab Singh.	R. Pindi	Punjab	Transportation for life.
Kundan Lal.	Benaras	U.P.	Transportation for life.
Nathu Ram.	R. Pindi	Punjab	7 years' R.I.
Sardar Singh.	Muttra	Punjab	4 years' R.I.
Gurbaksh Singh.	Gujranwala	Punjab	4 years' R.I.
Bhim Sen.	Sheikhupura	Punjab	4 years' R.I.
Sukh Dev Raj.	Gurdaspur	Punjab	3 years' R.I.
Sita Ram..	Jhelum	Punjab	2 years' R.I.
†Kundan Lal.	Sheikhupura	Punjab	2 years' R.I.
Hari Ram.	R. Pindi	Punjab	2 years' R.I.
Gokal Chand.	Sheikhupura	Punjab	2 years' R.I.

Krishen Lal.	Jhelum	Punjab	2 years' R.I.
Harnam Singh.	R. Pindi	Punjab	2 years' R.I.
Bishen Dass.	R. Pindi	Punjab	(Died during course of trail

Absconders

Yash Pal.	Kangra	Punjab	Arrested U.P.
Hansraj (Wireless)	Lyallpur	Punjab	Arrested Sind.
Lekh Ram.	Hissar	Punjab.	
Prem Nath.	Lahore	Punjab.	
Mussumat Prakasho	Lahore	Punjab	Arrested Delhi.
‡Mussumat Durga Devi	Lahore	Punjab	Arrested Punjab.
Chandra Shekhar Azad.	Benares	U.P.	(Killed in Allahabad while offering resistance to police).
‡Mussumat Soshila.	Gujarat	Punjab.	
‡Prof. Sanpuran Singh Tandon.	Lahore	Punjab	Arrested Punjab.
‡Chailbihari.	Delhi.		

First Lahore Conspiracy Case—1930

On April 15th, a police party raided the Lahore headquarters of the party and arrested Sukhdev (who had a loaded revolver in his possession), Kishori Lal and Jai Gopal. A live bomb, eight bomb-shells and a large quantity of chemicals were recovered, together with notebooks containing formulas and numerous other books and documents. The headquarters at Saharanpur was raided on May 13, when Sheo Varma and Jai Dev were arrested, and six bombs, three shells, three loaded revolvers, ammunition, books including, 'Manufacture and use of Explosives' and a large quantity of chemicals and apparatus were recovered. Two day's later, Gaya Prasad, not knowing of the raid, returned to the Saharanpur house and was arrested. Shivram Rajguru was arrested in a garage in Poona, in possession of a revolver and ammunition, on 30th September 1929.

In all twenty-four persons were arrested in various places; five accepted tenders of pardon, three were discharged, and one, Bhagwan Das, died after a hunger-strike. After a lengthy trial characterised by the unruly behaviour of the accused in court, which ultimately necessitated the appointment of a Special Tribunal under Ordinance No. III of 1930, Sukh Dev, Bhagat Singh and Shivram Rajguru were sentenced to death, seven others to transportation for life, and two to shorter terms of imprison-ment, while there were acquitted Chandra Shekhar Azad again evaded arrest, and the other absconders were Kailash Pati *alies* Kalicharan, Bhagwati Charan, Yeshpal and Satguru Awasthi.

(Political Trouble in India–1917, 1937 by H.W. Hale– Chugh Pub., Allahabad, 1974)

Mandalay (Burma) *Conspiracy Case No. I (1916)*

The conspirator connected with the Siam-Burma were tried in two Mandalay Conspiracy Cases. The first case was tried by a tribunal of three Special Commissioners. In this case, seventeen nationalists were tried and judgement was delivered on 27th July, 1916. Seven were sentenced to death (the sentence of one of them was later changed to life imprisonment), five to transportation for life, one to seven years' rigorous imprisonment and four were acquitted.

Mandalay (Burma) *Conspiracy Case No. II (1917)*

In the second Mandalya case the revolutionaries from Siam were tried at Mandalay in 1917 in connection with the earlier conspiracy. Four stood trial in this case, three were sentenced to death and one to transportation for life. Afterwards the death sentences were commented to transportation for life and confiscation of property.

Mandalay Conspiracy (1915)

The revolutionaries of India residing in foreign lands had early conceived the idea of attacking Burma from the neighbouring countries. The idea appealed to Sohanlal, a veteran worker for the cause of freedom, and he worked heart and soul to give this idea a shape. He was in Siam in 1910, where he was held in high esteem by the Sikh residents. In early 1911, he went to Lahore and thence to U.S.A. in 1912, where he remained up to 1914. His complicity with the party becoming known to the authorities, he had to leave the place and make Siam his centre of activity with Amar Singh as his lieutenant. He came back to Siam at the end of the year and forthwith got into touch with the old friends and comrades, who were staunch supporters of the *Ghadr*.

He took upon himself the task of carrying his gospel of revolution to Burma and became the central figure of a great conspiracy. Before reaching Burma he had sent two of his confederates as forerunners to find out a suitable premises to receive '*Ghadr* pilgrims' and to continue his activities quietly and without interruption.

Sohanlal called a conference at Pakko which was attended by a large number of workers in the same line. Men were selected and commissioned with special duties. One of them, who saved himself by becoming a Crown witness in the subsequent conspiracy case, was sent by Sohanlal to proceed to Yunnan and Chipintin to meet the German officers who had been training about 200 Indians intended for invading Burma at the proper time. It was so arranged that Sohanlal, Mujtaba Hossain and Amar Singh would going advance to Burma to prepare the ground for a bigger show.

He came to Burma in the first part of 1915, and tried forthwith to establish contact with the soldiers stationed there. Out of devotion to his task and a desire for speedy results, he threw all to caution to the winds and at times would take the risk of meeting soldiers in open places and trying to convince them of the evil of British rule and the degrading position of Indians under British superior officers.

On August, 14, 1915, he met one Jemadar and three other men, Havildars, etc., all belonging to the Darajat Mountain Battery stationed at Maymyo. He exchanged solutations with one of them, asked what part of India did he come from and became friendly with him through conversations relating to India. Worming up his position slowly, he tried to explain the pitiable economic condition of India. He gave out that there were many organisations which had been working to stir up discontent amongst the people while preparing themselves for an open fight at the opportune moment. It was better for the Indian soldiers to help them in every possible way and to side with them and render passive help by not participating in any Government endeavour to quell disturbances and more directly by joining hands with the insurrectionists.

In one of his daily rounds one of the soldiers arrested him and brought him to Maymyo and placed him before the Officer-Commanding. Before Sohanlal could make any attempt to get out of the clutches of his captors he was securely held and his person was searched on the spot. He was carrying on him at the moment:

(i) two loaded Browning automatic pistols and a number of cartridges;

(ii) a small tattered book with green paper-cover written partly in Arabic, partly in Urdu and partly in Turkish entitled *Jahan-i-Islam,* printed in Constantinople;

(iii) four copies of a *fatwa* in Arabic made by a photographic process;

(iv) two pages of formulae for the manufacture of

bombs, some money, a watch and a few other articles.

Sohanlal was put on trial on December 14, 1915, in the court of the Sessions Judge, Mandalay, under Rule 2 of Section 2 of the Defence of India Act, 1915; 124, 124-A, 131 I.P.C. (spreading inflammatory reports to assist the King's enemies, sedition, attempting to seduce soldiers from the allegiance to the King). He was further accused of circulating statements with the intention of promoting feelings of enmity and hatred between different sections of His Majesty's subjects; attempting to seduce the soldiers of the Mountain Battery, Maymyo, from their duty by distribution of highly inflammatory and anti-government literature.

The accused was condemned to death on December 15, 1915. His appeal was dismissed on January 7, 1916. After the judgement was passed he was requested by one of his friends to appeal for mercy when he exclaimed: "With tyranny and injustice all on their side, it is they who should beg forgiveness and not I."

Sohanlal was executed in January, 1916, in the Mandalay Jail.

Mandalay Supplementary Trial (1915-1917)

The *Ghadr* movement in the U.S.A. spread its influence far and wide and workers were sent abroad to kick up revolution wherever possible. The Far East was deemed to be one of the most suitable regions for carrying on with their projects and ultimately to use as spring board for attack on India.

Four persons amongst the many that had gone to Burma from time to time took upon themselves to go ahead with their work connected with a rising. The leader of the group was Moolchand, *alias* Mujtaba Hussain of Jaipur; and his co-workers were Amar Singh of Ludhiana. Ram Rakka *alias* Bahle of Hoshiarpur and

Ali Ahmad Sadiq of Sahzadpur, Fyzabad district.

They maintained contact with Sohanlal and worked with the common object of driving away the British from the shores of India. Mujtaba Hussain, also known as Mohammed Jaffar, extensively travelled the Far Eastern countries.

About his peregrinations something is known from his letter written on October 30, 1915, from Singapore. From Calcutta he went to Chandernagore and on October 3, he sailed as a first-class passenger to evade police notice for Hong King travelling *via* Penang and Singapore. He left for Japan on November 3, with an American traveller meaning to go to America , to live there for three years to qualify himself for a naturalisation certificate with which he would be able to return to India safely.

But subsequent letters written from Yokahama and Nagasaki revealed that he had changed his mind and proceeded towards Manila. He become so immersed in the affairs in Burma that he could think of nothing else than to play his part in the great drama in the best way possible.

Mujtaba managed to receive *Ghadr* literature from the U.S.A. and widely circulated it among different centres in such manner as to reach the barracks occupied by Indian soldiers, particularly to those stationed in Sandakan Island between Mindanao and North Borneo.

They were successful to great extent in their aim and some sort of a mutiny occurred in the Indian army that was suppressed with utmost ruthlessness. It was remarkable that Mujtaba Hussain succeeded in persuading a Subedar of a regiment to refuse to go to the front. The Subedar was court-martialled for insubordination by the Officer-Commanding and was ordered to be shot. He met the situation with absolute unconcern and there was no expression of fear or regret on his face. Before he received the bullet in his chest, he quietly asked his comrades present there to avenge his death for a cause which should be very dear to the heart of every Indian.

The very next day the Commandant's *orderly* killed the Commandant with the inevitable consequence to the *orderly*. The Sepoys got out of control, broke the jail and released a large number of prisoners. Instances of indiscipline in the army was not frequent and this particular incident bears proof of the influence that Sohanlal, Mujtaba Hussain and his comrades wielded over those whom they were able to contact.

Amar Singh was a resident of Siam and was a naturalised Siamese subject. He made common cause with Mujtaba.

Ram Rakka engaged himself in collecting materials for the manufacture of bombs, which he had to secure from Bangkok where they were available. He was absent when the mutiny broke out but reached Singapore only a few days after the event. He believed that once the revolution had started the Germans would not be very late in coming to their aid. A resolution was taken in Rangoon to cause the uprising on the *Bakr-id* Day, 1915, which had to be abandoned at the last moment due to paucity of arms and ammunition. This was postponed to the Christmas and it never came to pass.

Acting on information gathered in connection with the first Mandalay Conspiracy Case, the police arrested the four revolutionaries at different times not very distant from one another and started the Mandalay Supplementary Conspiracy Case in 1917. The trial charged with the offence of waging war against the King, conspiracy, tampering with the allegiance of the army, etc. Evidence covered many aspects of the *Ghadr* party in U.S.A., German collaboration in the rebellion, connection with the Indian revolutionaries and the individual responsibility of the accused persons.

Judgment was delivered on July 6, 1917, and

(i) Mujtaba Hussain *alias* Moolchand *alias* Mohammed Mujtaba, *alias* Mohammed Jaffar of Jaipur,

(ii) Amar Singh of Ludhiana,

(iii) Ali Ahmed Sadiq of Sahzadpur, Fyzabad District, were condemned to death.

(iv) Ram Rakka *alias* Bahlo of Hoshiarpur was sentenced to transportation for life.

All property belonging to the accused were confiscated to the State.

The Lieutenant Governor in reviewing the case on appeal confirmed the judgement with modification regarding forfeiture of property. A Rangoon Press Note issued on December 7, 1917, announced that the death sentence of each accused had been commuted to one of transportation for life by the Governor-General-in-Council.

Ram Rakka was sent to the Andaman Cellular Jail to serve out his sentence. He came into conflict with the prison authorities for not submitting to the humiliating conditions and resisting the inhuman treatment to which the prisoners were subjected. He was mercilessly assaulted for forcing him to submission. In protest, he resorted to hunger strike. Before he succumbed, he had been vomiting blood but nothing could be forced down his throat to make him live. He expired in 1919.

Strictly speaking the particular incident does not come under the purview of the book, all the accused having escaped death. But omission of such an important chapter in the history of rebellion in the Far East was likely to be more inexcusable than the exception that has been resorted to as a very special case.

In this connection it may be mentioned that the most significant reprieve that was granted by a Viceroy concerned the accused in the Lahore Conspiracy Case (Main). Twenty-four persons were condemned to death on September 13, 1915. The Viceroy was approached and it was announced on November 14, that excepting seven the capital punishment of the rest seventeen, viz., (i) Balwants Singh, (ii) Harnam Singh II, (iii) Jaggat Ram, Hoshiarpur, (iv) Hirda Ram, (v) Kala Singh, Amritsar, (vi) Keshar Singh, Amritsar, (vii) Khusal Singh, Chuga, (viii) Nand Singh, Ludhiana, (ix) Nidhan Singh, Ferozepore, (x) Prithi Singh, Ambala, (xi) Parmanand, (xii) Ram Saran Das, (xiii) Rula Singh, Bhakna, (xiv) Sawan Singh, Amritsar, (xv) Waswas Singh, (xvi) Bhai Parmanand, Jahansi, (xvii) Sohan Singh, Amritsar, was reduced to one of transportation for life.

Mainpuri Conspiracy Case

Accused

Name	*District*	*Province*	*Sentence*
Gopi Nath	Jasrana	U.P.	7 years.
Karhori Lal	Bowar	U.P.	3 years.
Sidh Gopal	Chandrika	U.P.	5 years.
Prabhakar	Alipur	U.P.	5 years.
Chandradhar	Mainpuri	U.P.	5 years.
Dammi Lal	Alipur	U.P.	7 years.
Raja Ram	Deokali	U.P.	3 years.
Kali Charan	Shahjahanpur	U.P.	Acquitted.
Sheo Charan lal	Etah	U.P.	5 years.
Fateh Singh	Cawnpore	U.P.	5 years.
Makundi	Etawah	U.P.	3 years.

Approvers

Somdeo Sharma	Fyzabad	U.P.
Dalpat Singh	Mainpuri	U.P.

Mindon Rebellion

Insurrection at Mindon was one of the series of many such that occurred almost everywhere during the long series of turmoil that formed part of the Tharrawaddy Rebellion of the thirties. From the enormity of the sentence it can be guessed, details being absolutely lacking, that it was something more than that of any common occurrence. On September 27, 1932, the High Court disposed of the appeal of several accused charged with the offence of waging war against the King, conspiracy and some other crimes in its train and of the sentences of thirty passed by the Special Judge, it confirmed that of twenty-four had commuted to transportation of life of the rest.

Munshigunge Conspiracy Case

With 17 persons as conspirators the Munshigunge Conspiracy Case was started in Dacca on November 12, 1910. All the accused except three were discharged in the course of the trial. A case was started against the three accused before the Session Court on March 2, 1911. One was sentenced to ten years' rigorous imprisonment under Section (4) (b) of the Explosive Substances Act on April 10, 1911. An appeal to the High Court proved infructuous.

Meerut Communist Conspiracy Case

The political and economic struggles that took place in India against British rule for freedom and the struggles of the working class against exploitation by the capitalists—British or Indian, up to 20 March 1929, We have seen that since the Kanpur Bolshevik Conspiracy Case, the British policy of repression and suppression in this period could not halt, or check the growing radical movement against the enslavers. Under the impact of the Russian revolution, Marxist-Leninist ideas were continuously spreading in the country; political and class consciousness was steadily growing in the working class and sections of the intelligentsia a proof of which lay in the furious struggles fought by the workers in the textile mills, in the railway workshops and on the railway lines, in the jute mills, etc., against retrenchment, dismissal and increase in workload, for winning better wages, recognition of the right to form their unions and the right of living a human life.

To sum up: the British ruling class was terrifically alarmed, at the rapid growth of communist influence in the industrial workers; at the rising curve of struggles in the British and Indian owned industries by the workers under the influence of the communists; at the growth of trade-union movement and the steady increase of communist influence in it, resulting in continuous fall in the influence of the right reformist procapitalist trade union leadership; at the growing organisation and role of the communist-dominated workers' and peasants' parties and youth leagues; at the role the communists and the working class played in exposing and running down the Simon Commission for its anti-democratic character and its anti-self-determination mandate; at its fight against the anti-communist Public Safety Bill, the anti-labour Trade Disputes Bill and the Whitley Commission designed to shackle the working class still further; at the visit of Saklatvala who undauntedly preached communism in India and helped in strengthening the movement; at members of the CPGB—Ben F. Bradely, Philip Spratt and later Lester Hutchinson coming to India, staying with known communists and helping the building of the communist and trade union movement; at the class conscious working class becoming an independent political force and a factor in radicalising the national freedom movement; at the links bring established between the political force of the class conscious working class and the national freedom movement; at the impact of the national liberationist struggles being waged by the Chinese people and Indian people's support to it against the British imperialists; at the establishment of relations with the League Against Imperialism at Brussels and aid given to the striking workers by the Workers' Welfare League, London, the Soviet trade unions and the Red International Labour Unions; and at the decline of the influence of the British Labour Party as a pro-imperialist which stood against the interests of the Indian working class and India's freedom.

In order to fully understand the political and economic significance of the above appraisal, two things must be properly borne in mind:

One, the emergence of the first socialist state in the world was a warning signal sounding the death-knell of the colonial system and heralding an upsurge in the national-liberation movements. It was the beginning of the end of the capitalist-imperialist system. British imperialists considered and wrote it in their reports that the Soviet state was their deadliest enemy. Overthrow of the tsar's vast colonial empire showed to the colonial peoples that imperialism was not invincible and the British imperialists were afraid of a similar revolution being repeated in India—the biggest colony of the British empire.

Further the example set by the Russian revolution by setting free the colonies in the tsar's empire and calling upon the people to exercise their right of self-determination, abolition of landlordism and taking over of industries were great rousing revolutionary factors for the people of the colonies to fight fearlessly for their freedom. The growing influence and impact of the Russian revolution was worrying and frightening the

British imperialists out of their wits, impelling them to find ways to throttle the communists and the mass movements started and dominated by them.

Two, in January 1928-33, the worldwide overproduction crisis came with a bang in the conditions of the general crisis of capitalism. The crisis enveloped the entire capitalist world, shaking its system of world economic relations. The imperialists began shifting the burdens of the crisis on to the dependent and colonial countries resulting in intensification of the exploitation of the people.

In India, the impact of the world overproduction crisis was intensified by its own agrarian crisis resulting in still further deterioration of its economy affecting greatly their livelihood and causing impoverishment of the mass of the peasantry. The workers, peasants and the rural poor had no alternative but either to submit and die a slow agonising death through hunger or disease or to fight back and face bullets. The working people generally speaking choose the latter path.

This was the political and economic background which led the British rulers of India to strike at the growing communist movement and arrest communist, trade union and peasant leaders in the Meerut Communist Conspiracy Case on 20 March 1929. Now we shall proceed briefly to evaluate what happened in the long-drawn-out case lasting four years and a half.

The communist movement had become a great headache to the British Indian government. There is a lot of correspondence between the provincial governors and the viceroy on the one hand and the viceroy and the secretary of state for India on this matter on the other. They were worried as to how to lay to rest this ghost. All kinds of suggestions were being made for curbing the communist movement. There was also the threat of a general strike on the railways in the air.

F. Isemonger on 29 August 1928 wrote, "The feasibility of a general prosecution for conspiracy might be examined provided that trial on such a charge was not held in Bengal for success would be improbable." The Punjab government's view was that "power might be taken to direct by executive order that a communist should not leave the limits of his own province or district and should not make any speech at any public meeting..."

"The most important of these suggestions relate to the control of the press...reintroduce some measures of control over the press...the present law affords no effective means of checking sedition and revolutionary propaganda in the press."

The summing up was, 'Bombay and the Punjab attach special importance to the development of propaganda by government to make clear the public the real aims of the communists and to enlist the support of the classes whom the communists' programme threatens. UP and Bengal attach special importance to cutting of supplies of money that may reach the communists from outside."

In taking action against the communists, the government wanted to do it in such a way as to keep the extreme nationalists and the communists divided. The government cautioned, "communism contains grave dangers for the very classes who support the extreme national movement and our aim should be to do nothing which will produce an artificial union between the two movements..."

The Bombay Chamber of Commerce and the Bombay Indian Merchants Association were asking the government of India "to introduce immediately an emergency ordinance to deal with the strike leaders...the agitators were mainly communists."

The Secret Files' Revelations

The British Indian government was contemplating the launching of the Meerut Conspiracy Case for very long. The viceroy of India had communicated to the secretary of state for India in this regard several times. On 25 September 1928, he had sent a telegram to the secretary of state, in which he said "We might be able to proceed against Broadly and Spratt in a general conspiracy case, prospects of which are now under investigation."

H.G. Haig on 3 October 1928 wrote that his excellency was considering "the institution of a conspiracy case against communists in India... it will include Spratt and Bradely. Such a case can be built around the activities of Spratt."

"The (Public Safety) Bill to have power to intercept remittance from abroad." I(rwin) 6-10-28.

"It would be easy to point to the great harm done by Spratt and Broadly before the law was able to touch them and to the necessity for arming ourselves with power to stop such activities at the very outset." (Viceroy to S/S dated 13 November 1928).

Earlier Mr. Harton and D. Petrie had recommended to the government of India, *"Put it forthwith into a court with every hope of securing conviction"* (15 January 1929). Material shown to Langford James, practically convinced him that there will be a good case. But *"We could not, however, take the chance of submitting the case to a jury. However good the case, there could be no assurance that a jury would convict and we cannot put the case into court unless we are convinced that it will result in conviction* (emphasis added).

"The two principal centres of the activities of conspiracy have been Bombay and Calcutta. In both these places the case would be tried by the High Court with a jury and neither Mr. Langford James nor the home department are prepared to recommend this."

"It is proposed, therefore, that the case should be tried at Meerut... good reasons, quite apart from the point about a jury, for such a decision."

Reasons given were—(1) *Clearly undesirable to have the trial at either Bombay or Calcutta due to the "present dangerous atmosphere prevailing among the labouring population."* (2) A branch of the Workers' and Peasants' Party at Meerut... place visited by Spratt and other important members (Muzaffar Ahmad, Sohan Singh Josh, Abdul Majid and Sehgal) of the conspiracy. (3) It is a convenient central place for a trial. (4) Also conveniently situated for the government of India "who are really primarily responsible for the trial." (5) "It is probable that *objections will be raised on behalf of Spratt and Bradley that by having a trial at Meerut we are depriving them of the privilege of being tried by a jury which they, would enjoy at Calcutta and Bombay."*

The document further asserted that "If it is decided to institute the case, *government should remain quite firm about its being tried at Meerut and should not under any circumstances agree to its transfer to Bombay or Calcutta with a view to trial being held with a jury."*

Horton and Petrie raised the point of firmness with the government of India because they foresaw agitation being "got up in England on the ground that Englishmen are being deprived of the privilege of trial by jury."

"Viceroy directed that these proposals be circulated to all Hon'ble Members—20-2-29. All members agreed on 21-2-29."

The government of India even got it verified from the governor of UP whether cases under Chapter VI IPC were triable by jury or not in the province. The governor wrote to Haig "Not triable by jury—27-2-1929".

The government did not remain content with only this. Home political department wrote to the prosecuting counsel Langford James to know when the case would open and said.

"2 (a) *A judicial pronouncement is required as early as possible which will enable us to deal with further manifestation of communist and to prevent the communist movement recovering from the blow which the arrest of the leaders has dealt. We hope to be able on the result of the case to make further communist activities both difficult and dangerous for those who wish to indulge in them... wanted clear pronouncement from the court these activities are illegal"* (emphasis added).

"(b) From the political point of view, it would be in advantage to be able to convince the public in general as early as possible that *communism is not the kind of movement that should receive the sympathy of nationalists. The opposition to the Public Safety Bill has created an artificial and fake atmosphere and we want to set that right as soon as possible"* (emphasis added).

"Government will not agree to a transfer." (of the case to some other place). (29 April, 1929).

This document gives away the mind and strategy of the government of India on the inception of the Meerut Communist Conspiracy Case. It laid down how the 'conspirators' were to be tried and where. It did no mince matters. It said that the government was predetermined to convict the accused and the force of the trial was only to hoodwink the public. It also meant what sort of legal defence facilities the accused in the case were to be given.

This document is very important and it should be taken note of because the points it raised in it were going to be raised again by the defence in the course of the case and the courts were to decide on those points in favour of the government even if the law went against them. The truth was that under the British regime, the executive was all-powerful, the courts and the Central Legislative Assembly were subordinate to it.

People Arrested

On 20 March 1929 there were police raids in four provinces of India—Bombay, Bengal, UP and the Punjab to arrest the communists, prominent members of the workers' and peasants' parties and leftwing trade union and peasant leaders. The raiding parties, it seems, were instructed to thoroughly search all the places having any connection with them and take possession of all papers—printed or hand-written, correspondence files, newspapers, pamphlets and books which they could find in their offices or homes. Thus several cartloads of material was brought to Meerut district jail along with the arrested men for the prosecution to sort out, study and utilise it in the conspiracy case.

Thirtyone alleged 'conspirators' were arrested on 20 March. Lester Hutchinson was arrested later and brought to the jail, making a total of 32. But there were more who were wanted in the case who were not yet arrested; and there were others "not resident in India but amenable to Indian law". Most of the latter category belonged to the CPGB. They were—R. Page Arnot, R.P. Dutt, S. Saklatvala, Harry Pollitt, George Allison *alias* D. Campbell, N.J. Upadhyaya" Graham Pollard. "The above list is by no means final or exhaustive." R.A. Horton, (15 January 1929) M.N. Roy and others were added later.

The first category consisted of Amir Haider Khan, Abdul Halim, Hemanta Kumar Sarkar, Pendse and Kulkarni. Their activities are given in the government report. These comrades were later not proceeded against.

The men against whom the conspiracy case was launched were—

1. *West Bengal:* Philip Spratt, Muzaffar Ahmad, Dharani Goswami, Gopen Chakravarti, Gopal Basak, Radha Raman Mitra, Shibnath Banerji, Shamsul Huda, kishorilal Ghose.
2. *Maharashtra:* B. F. Broadley, S.V. Ghate, S.S. Mirajkar, K.N. Joglekar, R. S. Nimbkar, S.A. Dange, A.A. Alwe, G.R. Kasle, D. Thengdi, M.G. Desai, G. Adhikari and S.H. Jhabvala and later L. Hutchinson.
3. *UP:* P.C. Joshi, Ajodhya Prasad, Gauri Shanker, Bishwanath Mukherji, Dharambir Singh, L. Kadam and Shaukat Usmani.
4. *Punjab:* Abdul Majid, Sohan Singh Josh, Kedarnath Sehgal.

These people were prominent leaders of the workingless peasants and youth. S.A. Dange was the general secretary of the Girni Kamgar Union, the revolutionary union of Bombay's textile workers and was assistant secretary of the All India Trade Union Congress and a leading member of the Workers' and Peasants' Party of Bombay. S.S. Mirajkar was secretary of the Workers' and Peasants' Party of Bomaby and secretary of the British Steam Navigation Co. Union. Muzaffar Ahmad was secretary of the Workers' and Peasants' Party of Bengal and editor of *Ganavani* its organ and vice-president of the Calcutta Scavengers 'Union, etc. Dharani Goswami and Gopendra Chakravarti were both leaders of the Youth League in Bengal and active peasant organisers. Dr. G. Adhikari, after securing his doctorate in Germany had come to India and stayed only 100 days wrote articles for the *Spark* edited by M.G. Desai, a young journalist holding socialist views. Joglekar and Nimbkar were members of the All-India Congress Committee and also of the Workers' and Peasants' Party, etc.

Three Englishmen sent by the CPGB had played a

big part in building the trade union and workers' and peasants' movement in India and they occupied prominent positions in these organisations. Bradley was a member of the executive council of the GIP Railwaymen's Union and the Girni Kamgar Union. Philip Spratt likewise held prominent positions in the trade unions in Calcutta and he wrote a booklet *India and China* for which he and Mirajkar were arrested but the jury had released them. Hutchinson had taken up the work after the Meerut arrests and begun to edit the new *Spark* when he was arrested and brought to Meerut.

The arrest of these three Englishmen along with the Indians showed that all Englishmen were not enslavers of India, that there were others, specially communists among the Englishmen who were fighting their own colonialists for India's freedom.

Sohan Singh Josh from the Punjab was the president of the first All-India Workers' and Peasants' Party Conference, general secretary of the Workers' and Peasants' Party in Punjab and president of the Naujawan Bharat Sabha. Abdul Majid was organiser of the Press Workers' Union and other unions. He was Moscow-returned, had been tried in the Peshawar Conspiracy Case and sentenced. Shaukat Usmani of the Peshawar Conspiracy Case fame was also a Moscow-returned Hijrati who wrote the booklet *Moscow to Peshawar*.

P.C. Joshi, was a student of law at the Allahabad University, secretary of the UP Workers' and Peasants' Party, member of the executive of the All India Workers' and Peasants' Party, editor of the *Krantikari*. S.H. Jhabvala, 'father of fifty trade unions' in Bombay. D.R. Thengdi, an old man of 65 with a fighting spirit, a former president of the AITUC and secretary of the Workers' and Peasants' Party, Bomaby. Kishorilal Ghose, a lawyer and journalist from Calcutta. Kedarnath Sehgal, former president of the Naujawan Bharat Sabha. Shibnath

Banerji was a trade unionist. Others were working among the peasants and workers.

The immediate object in arresting these people was to "break up the existing organs and remove the more dangerous leaders." In the government's view this would strike a blow "against the indigenous communist movement from which it is likely to take some time to recover." "This combined with the exclusion of foreign communists would give us a valuable breathing peace." (H.G. Haig, 31 August 1928).

Here the admission of the British government is noteworthy. The government knew that it could not wipe out the communist movement which had come to stay. It could only weaken it for some time to time. These arrests plus the exclusion of the British or international communists' held from outside would give the government 'a valuable breathing space'.

It was truly an international gathering of Englishmen, hindus, muslims and a sprinkling of other communities, all well-known leaders in their own right.

But there was more to it than the political evaluation given above. The conspiracy case was firstly going to be a weapon to start a hair-raising smear campaign against the communists in order to frighten the people to beware of them and to mobilise the propertied classes behind the government. The government had decided to conduct horror-striking propaganda against the communists for isolating them. Secondly, the conspiracy case was a pawn in the political game of the conservative British leaders for the elections to the British parliament.

British Labour Imperialism

It was Baldwin's Conservative government which sanctioned the launching of the Meerut Conspiracy Case with a view to taking advantage of the impending parliamentary elections. Conservative colonially exploiting Britain was very allergic to communism. The forgery of so-called Zinoviev letter paid it earlier rich dividends in the elections. General elections to the parliament were held in May 1929. But the Baldwin government suffered a defeat in the elections and the British Labour Party came to power on 8 June 1929 and MacDonald became the Prime Minister. Public opinion was strongly in favour of withdrawing the Meerut Conspiracy Case but the MacDonald government refused to do that.

On 12 June 1929 the accused in the Meerut case asked the judge Milner White to permit them to send a telegram to prime minister MacDonald requesting him for restoration of the unlawfully abrogated rights of the defendants and for referring the trial to a jury court in Britain. The telegram was a follows:

"Now that British Labour has returned to power, will Indian labour be restored to its rights? Will the anti-labour legislation be repealed and will the Meerut case in view of its significance for the Indian and international movement be withdrawn from the backward part of the country and referred for trail by jury in the mother country?"

The telegram was neither acknowledged nor replied to. The British Labour Party government of MacDonald was following the same imperialist policy as the previous Conservative government. It was a labour government in name only and continued the imperialist practices. MacDonald, when he was prime minister of the first Labour government, had bluntly said in 1924, "No party in Great Britain will be cowed down by threats of force or by policies designed to bring government to a standstill, if any section in India are under delusion that that is not so, events will very sadly disappoint them...Come nearer to us rather than stand aside from us to get at our reason and goodwill."

And in a speech at a public meeting in 1929, MacDonald said: "Let us come to power. I will cut short the criminal work of this organisation (the Communist International) not only in India, but in the whole colonial East."

He pursued exactly the same line that the British bourgeoisie pursued unashamedly. There was no distinction between the two policies—conservative or labourite.

Petitions for referring the Meerut cases for trial by jury were filed again and again. Appeals to this effect were sent to the judicial council of the viceroy of India, to the India office as well as to the judicial authorities directly concerned with the trial. Objections were also raised to the effect that a case of a national communist conspiracy was not within the competence of the Meerut magistrate's court and later the sessions court. Even Sections 275 and 443 of the IPC referring the Meerut case for trial by jury did not come to their help. The fate of the Meerut prisoners was left entirely in the hands of the conservative Viceroy Lord Irwin who had already decided that neither transfer nor trial by jury could and would be allowed.

That was the policy of imperialism under MacDonald's Labour government. No release, no transfer of the case and no trial by jury. Lord Irwin was left to deal with the fate of the Meerut case prisoners who lodged in the Meerut jail were shut in separate cells and not allowed to see each other's face, let alone talking to each other. They were treated worse than criminals. Their turbans and towels were taken away from them forcibly and kept outside the cells so that the prisoners might not hang themselves! No books were allowed to them insider the cells. The warders were running about to see that nobody talked to the occupant of his next cell. An atmosphere of terror—which the jail was—was further intensified to terrorise the inmates. And they were kept in that miserable atmosphere and condition for weeks on and until agitation both inside and outside completed the jail-cum-government authorities to take them out the separate cells and put them in a big barrack.

Meanwhile Horton and his gang, Hairat Nabi, Tasadduk Hussain and their office paraphernalia and the prosecuting counsel Langford James, young Bengali barrister Mitter were busy neck deep going through several cartloads of material in order to decide what to put and what not to put before the trying magistrate, Mr. Milner White. The government wanted to open the case as early as possible. Lot of correspondence took place between the government and the prosecuting counsel on this point. The latter was asking for more time again and again. Ultimately the government threw up its hands and decided: He must be allowed to run the case in his own way. (Haig, 4 May, 1929).

Special Magistrate's Court

It was the same old story again. The charge that had been brought up in the Peshawar and Kanpur Bolshevik conspiracy cases against the communists accused was repeated this time on a bigger scale and with greater propaganda show in the Meerut Communist Conspiracy Case.

The case was actually opened after about three months on 12 June 1929 by Mr. Langford James before Mr. Milner White, special magistrate of Meerut. This prosecuting counsel was president of the European Association in Calcutta and was the bitterest enemy of Indian freedom and communism. In the beginning of December 1926, at a banquet in Calcutta in honour of Lord Irwin, the viceroy, he said that for reasons of "moral nature" the continuance of British rule in India was "necessary for the good of the Indian themselves".

This was the same notorious European Associates, which tried to make general Dwyer, the perpetrator of the Jallianwala Bagh massacers of the innocents, a hero and presented a big purse to him to known him. But their of the Indians made the government retreat and call him back in sock cloth and ashes.

He was the most highly paid counsel of his time. According to Muzaffar Ahmad, Langford James was getting "a fee of eighty guineas per day and his junior J.P. Mitter was paid a fee of five guineas a day for the entire period of the trial. In those days the guinea had the constant value of Rs. 17 and the government paid such big fees whether the court was in session or not and irrespective of holidays. It was estimated that the government used to pay a sum of Rs. 34,000 per month to Mr. James alone.

Some time after the Meerut case accused persons' arrest and their lodgement in the Meerut district jail several national leaders came to see them. Most important among them were Mahatma Gandhi, Pandit Motilal Nehru, Pandit Jawaharlal Nehru, Faridul Haq Ansari and Delhi's national leaders. B.T. Ranadive came to help them sometime later in defence matters but he was also arrested. The national leaders assured the accused that they would do something for their defence.

On the opening day of the trial, the trying magistrate, several national advocates, lawyers, barristers came to the court from different parts of the country besides the local ones. They had all come on their own.

So the defence arrangements of the Meerut prisoners were in doldrums. A defence committee had been set up in England on the initiative of the CPGB. Some help was coming from there now and then. Some collections were made by the Indian working people.

But the defence was always short of funds and was living from hand to mouth. There were many occasions when they did not have even a morsel in hand to be put in the mouth. If the trial had taken place in Calcutta or Bombay, the working class would have come to their aid and contributed every month to keep the defence pot boiling. But the almighty government ordained that the case would not be held there and further passed two more anti-labour laws for-bidding any money for defence or help from international sources.

Surprisingly, Congress leaders advised the Meerut prisoners to plead guilty to the charges. The accused rejected this advice out of hand. Their plea was that the case would soon came to an end and the defence ends would no longer be necessary. To plead guilty meant to abandon communism and blacken their face before the working class and the Indian people at large. The communists had their own plans of fight their case.

Lester Hutchinson's mother Mrs. Knight was doing lot of work in England for the release of the Meerut prisoners, and securing facilities for them. She was approaching members of parliament, supplying them with material for putting questions in the parliament about the Meerut undertrials. On 23 October 1930 she complained to British authorities that 'her son was not treated properly'. She was not getting any letter from him. Se sent to him two parcels, one containing a copy of Upton Sinclair's *Mountain City* and the other a novel by H.G. Wells, but they were not delivered to him, etc.

Miss Lee, MP put questions in this regard on 10 November and again questions were put in the House of Commons on December 1930. The British government had to provide answers supplied by Khairat Nabi of the Indian intelligence branch on the floor of the house. The answer said: "It is in the nature of the accused and their relations to take up one point or another...for their own propaganda purposes, in England... Sometimes slight delays in posting their letters.... not withheld, but certain portions of one scored out."

Mrs., Knight approached even a high official in the office of the secretary of state for India who threw up his hands saying he could not get her son's release. Besides the *Daily Worker*, organ of the CPGB, was carrying on propaganda, exposing the bad conditions in which the Meerut prisoners were kept inside the jail. At one time papers were thrown from the parliamentary gallery demanding release of the Meerut case prisoners.

Langford James' opening speech before the trying magistrate took ten days to finish. It was downright amusing and entertaining. It drew adverse comments from national leaders. Pandit Jawaharl Nehru wrote to Walter Citrine, general secretary for the prosecution self forth as if he was addressing a Hyde Park meeting and the government of India sent down their head publicity officer from Simla to Meerut simply to organise propaganda."

It is a fact that government files show that it did send its publicity officer to organise propaganda against communism, the Third International and the Red International Trade Unions (RILU), etc. And the prosecuting counsel was by conviction fully at one with the government to damn communism, the communist party, the international communist organisations and to show to the world that they were in fact fighting against communism in India to defend the world capitalist system. So James' vehemence is quite understandable.

Intelligence files show that the government was very keen that the communists should be isolated from the nationalists in India. It wanted to convince the public that "communism is not the kind of movement that should perceive sympathy of nationalists". The opposition to the Public Safety Bill by the nationalists in the Central Assembly had created the congress-communist get together atmosphere which the authorities wanted to disrupt. Horton and the government publicity agent were at great pains to show that this was a Moscow intrigue and had nothing to do with nationalism." That was why Langford James harangued in the magistrate's court: "communists are anti-national, anti-religion and anti-everything". He was carrying out the bidding of his masters. The policy of world capitalism-imperialism was to show up the communists as 'Moscow agents', as anti-religion, anti-marriage, anti-family and so on and create an atmosphere of contempt, ridicule and hatred against them and discredit them, isolate them from the nationalists and the general masses.

That explains as to why Jawaharlal Nehru was not implicated in this conspiracy case. He had written many letters to the secretariat of the League Against Imperialism at Brussels and received replies from them. He had himself taken part in the league conference and had been elected as one of the presidium members. He had persuaded the Indian National Congress to become its associate member and his sympathies were with the Third International rather than the Second International. He had visited the Soviet Union, which 'crime' had landed almost all men in jail in other cases. He was praising the progress made by Soviet Russia. Besides, he knew, according to him, more of communism than the Meerut accused. The only reason for not arresting him was the government's policy was directed towards isolating the communists from the mainstream of the national movement which has been described earlier.

From beginning to end, Langford James' address was nothing but propaganda for the government, against the communists, against the Soviet Union. According to the prosecution, the main criminals were the Russian government and the communist international. Langford James denounced Marx, Lenin and other Russian revolutionaries with equal zeal. He spared no pains to 'expose' the ugly 'murderous' nature of communists from whose hands blood was dripping.

But all of this mostly fell on deaf ears because all government propaganda was suspect in the eyes of the Indian people. It would however be wrong to deny that this poisonous propaganda against communism and communists did not cut some ice among nationalists and ignorant people. Prejudices sown against the communists and communism from the early days still persist and refuse to die even in some sections of the rural and urban poor even today.

Committed to Sessions

Mr. Milner White, the trying magistrate, was a very tactful person. He did not want to displease the accused as far as possible. The implication of three British communists in the case was a factor in determining his attitude towards the prisoners. Because of this tactful handling of the case, few and far between exchanges took place between the magistrate and the accused. He successfully piloted the case and committed the accused to the sessions court on 11 January 1930 after about seven months.

Milner White did one good thing. He sanctioned that all the prohibited or proscribed literature be provided to the accused inside jail to help them prepare their case. All the pamphlets, books etc. which were not available to them outside were now made available inside jail. They had been listed, put in an almirah and kept under lock and key and the key was given to one of the communists. This satisfied their hunger for communist literature. And they studied the literature voraciously to equip themselves politically and theoretically for future work. So the period of trial became one which benefitted the communist accused tremendously.

"The one bright feature of our imprisonment was", wrote Hutchinson, "that there was no restriction on our reading. We had been allowed to form a small library of proscribed literature to enable us to prepare our defence, but which also served the more useful purpose of enabling us to increase our political and general knowledge. The library was under close supervision in case any of the 'poison' should escape into the outside world and it was periodically inspected to see whether any books were missing. But it was of inestimable value not only to our defence but to our own educational development."

On 11 January 1930, Mr. Milner White, the magistrate framed the following charges against the 31 accused:

"That you in and between 1925-29 within and without British India agreed and conspired together with one another and with Amir Haider Khan, the absconding accused and persons and bodies mentioned in the list attached and other persons known and unknown and not before the court to deprive the king of the sovereignty of British India and thereby committed an offence punishable under Section 121-A, Indian Penal Code and within the cognisance of the court of sessions and I hereby direct that you should be tried by that court under the said charge."

The case was committed to the special sessions judge, R.L. Yorke on 14 January 1930. The magistrate let off only one accused named Dharambir Singh against whom we find very severe strictures made in the government reports. He wrote on 26 November 1929 a statement—rather an apology to the government—that he was not a communist. Then he wrote an amendment to that statement with regard to the Workers' and Peasants' Party. Langford James was not satisfied with his statement and dubbed him as 'extremely foolish'. He wanted from him "a statement disavowing any connection with communists and explaining his connection with the Workers' and Peasant's Party...he made a verbal statement (earlier of which approximately eighty per cent was not only untrue but a terrible petty-bourgeois vacillator. He cut a very sorry figure in the case. Apology and his reiteration that he was a Gandhian and that he believed in non-violence helped to be let off."

After the prosecution counsel concluded his arguments in the magistrate's court, the accused moved that they be allowed to go to the Allahabed High court to get the case transferred to some other province. The transfer application was moved on behalf of the accused by Pandit Motilal Nehru and Sir Tej Bahdur Sapru, two topmost lawyers of the time. The arguments were so reasonable and convincing that it was impossible to refute them. But what could reasonable and convincing arguments do when it had already been decided by the government beforehand, as we have shown earlier, that the venue of the case would remain at Meerut and no jury would be allowed even if the heavens fall. So the transfer application was rejected not because of Langford Jame's convincing refutation of the defence arguments but because the government had already decided so. Sir Edward Grimwood Mears discussed the application. It took three weeks' time to decide on the application.

Sessions judge R.L. Yorke was a sickly person. There was something wrong with his throat. He was coughing and spitting mucus in his handkerchief not a few times a day, dirtying half a dozen handkerchiefs. The strain was very much and it was the cause of irritation by our remarks, questions and interjections. The accused had made it not easy for him to carry on his work smoothly and peacefully. All happenings of a political nature in the country at that time were brought in the court and given expression to now by one prisoner, now another. His shouting notwith-standing, the prisoners put their points undaunted. His threats to charge them of contempt of court and punishment did not weight much with the accused. The hungerstrike of the Lahore Conspiracy Case prisoners. Jatindara Nath's death, Bhagat Singh, Raj Guru and Sukhdeve's hanging—all these political issues were raised in the court and the British government was condemned for these heinous crimes despite threats from the sessions judge R.L. Yorke and his shouts of 'order, order' and 'sit down'.

About this Hutchinson wrote,

"For three years he had toiled, tappng down the evidence on his little typewriter and his task had not been always easy. Hardly a day had passed throughout the three years without a 'breeze' with one or the other of the accused. His powers for contempt of court were too inadequate to be impressive...yet, although he must have realised that his powers were so limited, he often seemed to go out of his way to provoke trouble unnecessarily by seeking to impose petty restrictions and by occasional outbursts of rudeness."

After the committal order it had become clear which of the accused stood where. Those who denied being communists formed a separate group. The communists consolidated themselves separately and began to function in a communist way, holding their meetings and deciding democratically on each problem as it arose on what attitude to take in regard to it in the court or inside the jail. There were some others who agreed with the communists but were not in the communist group. Dange was not in the communist group.

It was at this time that the communist group took a very important decision. It decided that the sessions court be utilised as a platform for communist propaganda. The government wanted to discredit and crush communism, the communist group would face this challenge boldly, stand by communism and propagate it without fear of the consequences. The group, it was decided, should not put up defence to find legal loopholes in the case, to save its skin but to challenge the very nature of the charge of communist conspiracy and the intention and purpose of the British rulers working behind it.

With this political objective in view, the communist group decided to conduct its own defence. Generally the lawyers derailed the clients by saying that a certain point would go against you, another point would strengthen the hands of the prosecution, concentrating only on legal quibbling. The group decided not to accept the advice of the lawyers in this matter. This line was accepted by the group as a whole enthusiastically and unreservedly.

Two tasks emerged from this line. *One*, any comrade who spoke in the court should always have in mind that resolution and should in no case deviate from it. *Two*, comrades should begin seriously studying the case and preparing statements to defend boldly their political revolutionary activities, refuting wrong and distorted facts and upholding the democratic right of freedom of speech, assembly and organisation, etc. They should fearlessly defend the Russian revolution, Marxism- Leninism and the right to have international connections. All the above if it was legal in Britain; why was it illegal in India? They should stand four square for complete freedom for India and should denounce the Nehru Report and the draft constitution framed by it.

To sit in a case, week in and week out, month after month for three years and a half was not a joke. One loses all interests if the same thing is repeated nauseum hundred and one times. As long as Langford James was alive (he died on 28 March 1930) and conducting the case, some entertainment was there. He was a crusader against communism, clever, quick-witted, possessed and sardonic humour and an inexhaustible fund of invectives. He fitted political oratory into legal verbosity very shrewdly. He was also keeping the court in good humour.

While he was alive, the accused used to pour fun on his gesticulation, flourishes and humour. They wrote skits on him in English, Bengali, Marathi, Hindi and Punjabi. Hutchinson wrote the following skit on him:

Hail Langford James,
Saviour of Britain's grace
Whose fees are more handsome
Than his face!

Then came K.Mc J. Kemp to replace him as the chief government counsel. He was humourless dry as dust man, not vociferous like his predecessor. Mitter, the junior counsel, was in reality conducting the case after Langford James' death. Sometimes he fumbled for want of good arguments.

Most of the time in the court was spent by the prisoners in cutting jokes at each other, doing some cartoons and doodling facial expressions of somebody or the other which made one laugh. Dr Adhikari was adept in this art. Then sometimes a serious, another time a ludicrous caricature of somebody would be drawn and circulated among the accused and would be enjoyed by them. Some court titbits were written almost daily and circulated. These things were of transitory nature and torn off after reading. Had they been kept they would have amused even today. That was how the accused used to keep away monotony and boredom and maintained them fit and in fighting spirit.

The case was looked after by Nimbkar, Joglekar and Muzaffar Ahmad on the communists' behalf. The communists engaged Mr Sheoprasad, a junior lawyer of Meerut, to represent them only in case any of them fell ill and was unable to attend the court so that the proceedings were not held up. Communists used to pay him a very small sum as fee for his services yet he remained with them till the end of the trial at the sessions court. Sheoprasad had developed an attachment to his clients because of his long association with them.

Shibnath Banerji and D.R. Thengdi, both non-communists, engaged at government cost Mr Deokiprasanna Sinha at a fee of Rs. 1500 per mensem. He was looking after the cases of other non-communists as well. The communists were approached by Mr Langford James on behalf of the government to have free legal aid, but they refused to avail themselves of it.

While going to the court, the accused used to sing many a revolutionary song and shout slogans. The slogans were "Inquilab Zindabad!" "Communist Party Zindabad!", "Soviet Russia Zindabad!", "Workers of the World unite!" "Imperialism and Colonialism Murdabad!" "Freedom of India Zindabad!" Sohan Singh Josh had composed a few songs in Urdu in consonance with the English tunes of the red flag and other songs. They used to sing them daily. They also sang Bismil's *Sarfaroshi-ki tamanna ab hamare dil men hai, Dekhna hai zor kitna bazue-Qatil men hai.*

The case was the longest one in judicail history of India. It took three years and a half till the final appeal in the Allahabad High Court which reduced imprisonment terms of the accused. Many skirmishes, bickerings, hot exchanges took place during this period making it lively. But most of the time it was boring and repetitive, sickening.

In order to understand the magnitude of the case, a few facts would suffice:

(1) The total number of prosecution exhibits came to 4859 pages. In the sessions court the prosecution evidence took over 13 months.

(2) Total number of defence exhibits—1406 pages. The defence evidence lasted for about two months.

(3) Speeches of the accused used by the prosecution came to 582 pages.

(4) Statements made by 281 prosecution witnesses before the sessions court—came to 900 pages.

(5) Statements made by the accused in the sessions court covered 3092 pages—printed in four volumes and occupied over ten months.

(6) Judgement delivered by the sessions judge was 676 pages in two volumes. He took over five months to write it.

(7) Committal orders passed by the additional district magistrate Meerut came to 287 pages.

(8) The arguments continued for over four months and a half... and so on. We have given only important items.

That was the gigantic scale on which the case was conducted.

The judgement of the sessions judge was not a balanced one. Our sharp and condemnatory criticism of British imperialism, its leaders in Britain and India, the imperialist law courts and their justice and last but not the least, our defiance of sessions judge Yorke's authority, had bitterly upset him. Some personal element therefore seems to have played its part in writing the judgement against the communist accused. In such conspiracy cases, judges always stood on the right side of the British government and acted on the hints or advice of the executive. For this they were rewarded with long holiday for rest and then given promotion.

Sessions judge Yorke took five months to write the judgement. He acquitted only three of the accused—Kishorilal Ghose and Shibnath Benerjee, both of Calcutta and Biswanath Mukherjee, of Gorakhpur, U.P. All the rest were given very heavy sentences:

1. Muzaffar Ahmad	transportion for life
2. S.A. Dange	
3. Philip Spratt	
4. S.V. Ghate	each to transportation for a
5. K.N. Joglekar	period of 12 years
6. R.S. Nimbkar	
7. B.F. Bradley	each to transportation for a
8. S.S. Mirajkar	period of 10 years
9. Shaukat Usmani	
10. Mir Abdul Majid	
11. Sohan Singh Josh	each to transportation for a
12. Dharani Goswani	period of 7 years
13. Ajodhya Prasad	
14. G. Adhikari	each to transportation for a
15. P.C. Joshi	period of 5 years
16. M.G. Desai	
17. Gopendra Chakravarti	
18. H.L. Hutchinson	
19. Radha Raman Mitra	each to 4 years rigorous
20. Gopal Basak	imprisonment
21. S.H. Jhabvala	
22. Kedarnath Sehgal	
23. Shamsul Huda	
24. A.A. Alwe	each to three years rigorous
25. G.R. Kalse	imprisonment

26. Gauri Shanker
27. L.R. Kadam

The sentences were not unexpected. The Meerut case prisoners were prepared for anything. This minion of law and order could not give more than transportation. There was howl raised against this judgement everywhere in the world. And the worst of it was that the judge put every one of the accused in C-class.

The appeal against the judgement was filed in the Allahabad High court and heard by Chief Justice Dr Suleiman and justice Douglas Young. They took only eight working days to deliver the judgement in a case which had taken four years and about six months in the magistrate's court and the sessions court. It is humanly impossible to wade through thousands of pages of prosecution exhibits, defence exhibits, speeches of the accused, statements made by 281 prosecution witnesses in the sessions court, 320 witnesses in the magistrate's court and three dozen defence witnesses in the sessions court, etc., etc.

That is not all. The statement of the accused alone consisted of 3092 pages and the session judge's judgement of 676 pages, let alone the harangue of Mr Langford James before the magistrate's court and the committal order delivered by the magistrate running into 287 pages. It seems to the High Court judges heard the arguments of the prosecution as well as defence side, went through Mr Yorke's judgement and then delivered their judgement in just eight days. The shortest period taken for such a long case!

The High Court judges released some of the accused and reduced the sentences in the rest of the cases as follows:

Those released were—(1) M.G. Desai, (2) H.L. Hutchinson, (3) H.S. Jhabvala, (4) Radha Raman Mitra,

(5) K. Sehgal, (6) Gouri Shanker, (7) L.R. Kadam, (8) A.A. Alwe, and (9) Kasle. They were acquitted of all charges.

Those sentenced to period already undergone: The sentences of (1) Ajodhya Prasad, (2) P.C. Joshi, (3) Gopal Basak, (4) Dr G. Adhikari and (5) Shamsul Huda under Section 121-A, IPC were upheld but considering the sentences already undergone by each of them as sufficient punishment, the court ordered their release. The sentence passed against Gopendra Chakravarti was reduced to seven months, but he had to stay inside jail for a few days more due to the delay in reaching the court's order.

Three-year-term: (1) Muzaffar Ahmad, (2) S.A. Dange and (3) Shaukat Usmani had their sentences reduced to three years rigorous imprisonment each.

Two-year-term: Philip Spratt's sentence was reduced to rigorous imprisonment for two years.

One-year-term: Sentences passed against (1) S.V. Ghate, (2) K.N. Joglekar, (3) R.S. Nimbkar, (4) Ben F. Bradley, (5) S.S. Mirajkar, (6) Sohan Singh Josh, (7) Dharani Goswami and (8) Mir Abdul Majid were reduced in each case to rigorous imprisonment for one year.

Thus the Meerut Conspiracy Case trial came to an end on 3 August 1933 with the delivery of the High Court judgement. It was the longest drawn out conspiracy case trial in judicial history. The inordinate duration of the trial which lasted four years and a half from the date of arrests to the delivery of the final judgment and appeal and confinement of most of the prisoners in jail for the whole of that period, as well as the denial of trial by jury, drew protests from nearly every quarter, including indignant statements from such international celebrities as the archbishop of York, Mr. H.G. Wells, Professor Albert Einstein, Romain Rolland, Professor Harold Laski and A.H. Tawney. President Roosevelt himself is reported to have interested himself in the case.

The heavy sentences of the accused were greatly reduced because of the pressure of the international working class movement and protests of intellectuals. This fact was noted by Professor Brecher of Canada in his book *Nehru—A Political Biography*.

Hutchinson made an effective point in his book *Conspiracy at Meerut* when he wrote—"The arrest of Englishmen with Indians on the same charge not only attracted the critical attention of the world, but was also object of lesson in international working class solidarity. What had been intended as propaganda against communism had turned into propaganda for communism."

The Statements

The statements of the communist accused in the Meerut Communist Conspiracy Case are a proof positive of the revolutionary spirit with which they were imbued. They bearded the so-called 'British lion' in his own den. They hurled defiance at the prosecutors in the Meerut trial. They ignored the threats of the sessions judges from time to time to punish them for contempt of court and carried on communist propaganda utilizing the sessions court as a platform. The ideal of building a new society based on the working class revolution and toppling the old one had made them death-defying.

I will just quote a few paragraphs from the statements of some of the communists to show the dare-devil way in which they faced their prosecutors. They acted fearlessly according to the resolution they had passed earlier. In fact, they set an example before the revolutionary fighters against British imperialism on how to conduct oneself in a bourgeois court. The youth of today should get hold of and read the full statements which will enrich their political and economic knowledge. They contain a mine of information.

S.V. Ghate as the general secretary of the Communist Party of India till his arrest, considered it his duty to place certain facts before the court. He said:

"What is there in communism that frightens them so much? To me it seems that it is because we believe in the irreconciliability of the antagonisms between the classes that comprise the Indian society because we believe in class-war; because we believe that the interests of the toiling masses are fundamentally opposed to the interests of those that represent the ruling class; because we believe that their class has long outlived its usefulness and as such has no right to be in the position in which it is today; because we believe that the vast majority of the workers and peasants have a right to all the things they produce—because of all these facts this class a mighty opponent, its future hangman is the class that we represent—and hence this movement of frenzied falsehood and insensate hurry to crush its opponents before it gains that might."

Muzaffar Ahmad in the very beginning of his statement said, "I am a revolutionary communist... had been a member till the day of my arrest... the Communist Party of India on the day of my arrest was not officially a section of the Communist International. We did not duly affiliate our party with the Communist International for the reason that we had been weak numerically. Otherwise our party fully believed in the policy, principles and the programme of the CI and propagated them as best as it could under the circumstances."

Ben Bradley discussed all the national and international issues brought against the accused in the course of the trial in a bold statement and exposed the hypocrisy and double-dealing with regard to their defence. He said:

"Thus the position was that while the prosecution

with their unlimited resources could bring eight witnesses from England, several from French possessions in India and one from and Indian state, the defence could not even get summonses issued for their witnesses.

"... This trial is an attack upon the working class movement and specially the militant trade-union movement. The trial as such is a political trial and a political trial of this character only masks the state of panic that the bourgeoisie have got into and it has also registered the fact that they are going along the path to their own destruction...

"I believe that the proletarian revolution will come and that communist will triumph...

"I am confident that this trial will have the very opposite effect to that which the prosecution desire, it will awaken the consciousness of the masses of India and at the same time will focus the attention of the workers of Great Britain on the struggle of the colonial masses, and will undoubtedly be responsible for rousing the workers of Great Britain to take a more active part in the fight against imperialism and for the freedom of the colonial slaves.

"The British Labour Party is acting as the lackey of imperialism and outdoing even the diehard Tory Party in carrying on a reign of terror in India and throughout the empire."

Joglekar's 350 page statement condemned British imperialism and its policies and explained the part the Communist Party of India had played in strengthening and broadening the national freedom movement and popularising the slogans of the revolution and complete national independence. The following passage from his statement gives an evaluation of the case. On 5 November 1931 he said:

"I must congratulate the Indian government and

their foolish counsellors, the Bombay and Bengal bourgeoisie, for their stupidity in cooking up this case and raising a mountain out of a molehill. They have done unconsciously the greatest service to Indian revolution by glorifying and raising our ordinary innocent elementary trade union and national emancipatory work to the heights of scientific revolutionary deeds. By prosecuting us they have given tremendous prestige to the cause of communism and have directly accentuated the growth and spread of communist philosophy by kindling a keen desire in the minds of the intelligentsia to dive into the depths of communist principles and philosophy. What we could not have achieved, left to ourselves, in ten years of free activity, we have achieved in three years of prison life... The masses during these (1929, 1930, 1931) years have gone through the experience of a terrible economic crisis and they have seen the inability of capitalism as well as of Indian nationalism to meet with their requirements... They have realised the revolutionary need of a revolutionary organisation and have begun to find hope in communism and our trial during all these eventful years has helped the process of attraction of their attention towards the study and application of communist principles in the present Indian situation."

Philip Spratt in a 100-page statement, replying all the charges levelled against him, straighforwardly said.

"We work under the initial—one may say fundamental disadvantage of being tried by our enemy's court and under our enemy's law. An almost equally formidable obstacle in the disparity between our opponent's financial resources and ours... on general grounds such as these we maintain the impossibility of impartiality or a fair trial in a case between the ruling class and the representatives of its political opponents...In the first place, the case was launched at

Meerut... Then we have been refused a jury... We have been refused bail... We have found that while the prosecution could bring witnesses from abroad we cannot... While they have a more or less unlimited staff of CID men and other officials and technical experts and so on to assist them, the people who come to assist us turn out to be suspicious characters who have been put away under Regulation III... But nevertheless, the pretence of fair trial and even-handed justice is kept up... Our case which is already on the way to becoming a public scandal is helping appreciably to expose the gigantic fraud of the civilising mission and the impartial justice of British imperialism in India."

Mirajkar in a very challenging statement running over one hundred pages before the sessions court refuted the charge of adopting dilatory tactics to prolong the case. He said: "I definitely charge the prosecution that it has deliberately and consciously prolonged this prosecution in order to harass us by producing all sorts of unnecessary and irrelevant evidences, books, pamphlets and papers. Let Mr Wedgewood Benn, the late labour state secretary and Sir Samuel Hoare, the present national government state secretary understood these facts. Let them not like parrots repeat what their underlings in India ask them to do from the platform of the House of Commons.

"The junior public prosecutor... said that if there were any genuine trade unionists and congressmen among the accused, well, they should not be committed to the sessions. Well, Sir,... several of them promptly told you as well as the magistrate, that they were not communists, that they were (N.M.) Joshi brand trade unionists... Has the magistrate let them off in spite of their explanation?... I wish to recommend to your honour for immediate release of all those who are not communists..."

"In conclusion therefore I once again reiterate that I do not expect any justice from this court... The purpose of my defence statement is to tear the mask of the so-called 'impartial justice' and show it in naked and brutal form of 'class justice'."

P.C. Joshi, after explaining the communist programme of revolution, the rules of the Workers' and Peasants' Party and the Youth Leagues in it ended his statement thus: "...We take the trial itself very seriously. In this case we are not on trial but British imperialism is on trial before our final judges, the Indian masses. We are not the accused but prosecutions. We have no doubt that the final judgement of our real judges will be 'forward to revolution!"

Sohan Singh Josh, defending his revolutionary activities vehemently in the court in a long statement concluded by saying: "I shall rather choose a heavy sentence than forego my opinions that are not to the taste of British imperialism... The case is so serious, so very serious that any man washing his hands of his radical opinions and giving an undertaking like Dharambir that he will not be a communist will never ally with them... can easily get off scotfree. I abhore to buy my release like this... I, therefore, challenge the British imperialism to do its worst, for I believe that no power on earth can crush our movement, because even if crushed for a while, it will rise phoenix-like from its ashes and will crush British imperialism our enemy."

Dange, concluding his 500-page statement said: "A question has been sometimes put whether what we say is defence or defiance... We are putting up a defence, if such a thing is allowed under bourgeois law. But if defence means desertion of principles we cannot put up with it. It is not defiance because thereby I do not gain my objective. It is defence and not defiance in deadly earnest... defence of the right to propagate the principles for which the individual stood and stands.

"I do not defy, but defend and urge that this court do recognise the right of every Indian to hold communist principles, to belong to a communist party, to be one with the international of the world proletariat to carry on trade union and literary activity, while subscribing to Leninism—a right which exists in all the advanced bourgeois democracies and in England itself, on the basic principles of whose judical system and political liberties this country is said to be governed."

The Government Reports

Viceroy lord Lrwin had started the case with a fanfare, but as the case preceded and got prolonged, he began to repent for having launched the conspiracy case trial. In December 1930 he remarked that he 'wished to heaven', he 'had never embarked on the Meerut trial'. But at the same time, he expressed his satisfaction at "having these communist patriots (sic.) out of the way at a difficult time."

We find the highups in Britain and Indian rulers expressing their dissatisfaction over the outcome of the Meerut case. The general admission on their part was that the government had failed to achieve the objective for which the case had been launched.

In the beginning the government expressed 'pleasure' over the trial. But soon after their 'pleasure' turned to concern as the expected propaganda dividends failed to appear. Governor Hailey of UP at that time, earlier in July had expressed his unease at the likely failure of a prosecution which was 'concentrating on propaganda rather than conviction'. (Hailey to de Montmorency, 12 July 1929). He was for confining the case strictly to the evident necessity to secure conviction. The under secretary of state Hertzel 'shared Hailey's horror at the protraction of the Meerut proceedings'.

Mr Wedgewood Benn was the secretary of state for India under the 1929 Labour government. Public protest was making him the target for continuing the case. His correspondence with India government at that time reveals the impact the campaign conducted in Britain by the Meerut prisoners' defence committee was having. He openly backed the prosecution. He complained to the Viceroy Lord Irwin that 'good many' Labour Party members were going to see him about the trial and added: "This is the echo of the considerable campaign which the Meerut prisoners' defence committee is making in this country." On this occasion (and others) he wrote to the viceroy, "I shall be devoutly thankful when the whole thing is over and done with."

The new Viceroy Lord Willingdon talked to the secretary of state for India, Hoare, in February 1933 about 'these terrible conspiracy cases' and said that he would 'pretty well assure' Hoare that he was 'going to have no more conspiracy cases' while he was viceroy.

There was widespread sense of outrage in England at the savagery of the sentences passed on the Meerut accused. The resentment, sweep and vigour of the agitation against these sentences was so much that the worried secretary of state. Hoare, in April 1933 sent Willingdon a cutting from the *Daily Express* on the subject with the comment:

"You will see from the cutting that the agitation is by no means confined to the *Daily Herald* and the Labour press, but their is a general feeling, even amongst conservatives that sentences are too heavy and there might fairly be some remission." (28 April 1933)

Even that cunning bureaucrat Hailey told the governor of Punjab in January: "I do not suppose that they can let the sentences stand; they are rather out of scale for this kind of offence and are much more appropriate to Bengali terrorists." (29 January 1933)

Calculating the profit and loss of the Meerut Conspiracy Case trial, the British imperialists decided not to start such a conspiracy case again. Even when the British rulers banned the Communist Party of India and other political organisations under the influence of the communists and progressives in 1934, they did not arrest anybody. The overall estimate of imperialism of the outcome of the trial was one of failure.

The British Communists deserve our heartfelt comradely thanks for the role they played under the leadership of the CPGB in launching a big campaign in England for the Meerut prisoners' release, for collecting funds for their defence and for mobilising the Labour press against the heavy sentences passed on the prisoners. Rajni Palme Dutt and other communist leaders did yeomen's service in keeping the crying injustice of the Meerut case trial before the public eye.

A great lesson of Meerut trial was that the combined forces of the Indian working class movement and all anti-imperialist sections in India, backed by the international progressive opinion, were capable of frustrating the objectives of imperialist repression. The Meerut Conspiracy Case trial even today underlines the necessity for united action of all anti-imperialist democratic and left forces against the dark forces of reaction, obscurantism and overt or covert fascism.

The End

The British government started the case to do virulent propaganda against communism, against Soviet revolution, the Third International, against the communist movement and the communist party. It wanted to damn the whole movement by stigmatising the accused as anti-national, anti-religion, anti-family, anti-everything that was decent and so on in order to isolate the communist accused from the Indian people and tried to rouse religious prejudices and national hatred against them. Its second aim was to pass very heavy sentences against the accused to terrorise and terrify the communists and would be communists.

The communist accused therefore as we have seen decided to meet the government propaganda with a vengeance. They not only turned the table on the government but also paid the latter back in the same coin in a manner which made it to charge the accused of not asking the case seriously. This meant that the government realised at long last that the communists could play the game of propaganda better than it did.

The communist accused defended the communist movement steadfastly and took the offensive on the black deeds of British imperialism, colonialism, its blood-sucking exploitation of India and other colonies under it; they showed that British imperialism's main aim was (and is) to squeeze profits, more profits and still more profits at the cost of the sweat, blood, toil, tear and death of the enslaved peoples. The government found and realised that their game had been lost badly. The communist accused's statements brought not only glory to them but they also strengthened the communist movement outside in the country.

You have a proof of this from the horse's mouth. The Bombay government on 21 June 1933 wrote to the government of India: "The problem of dealing with communists and their activities had again been forced on the government of Bombay by the efforts which have been made for some months in Bombay city, Sholapur and Ahmedabad to bring about a general strike in textile factories. The position which at present exists...affords a close parallel to that which existed at the beginning of 1928..."

The communists taught the government a lesson to think a hundred times before starting such a conspiracy case against them in future. The Meerut courtroom was successfully utilised by them to make known the true stand of the Communist Party of India. British Intelligence in 1935 admitted that the "Meerut prisoners... extracted... more of advertisement and political capital from their trial them did their predecessors at Cawnpore." Then the main purpose for which the case had been started was miserably defeated and the results achieved were quite the contrary to what they wanted.

This was the victory the communist prisoners won in the Meerut Conspiracy Case!

In conclusion I may add that certain favourable factors in the situation that existed at that time helped the growth of the communist ideas, the communist movement and the influence of the Communist Party of India. Important among these factors were—(1) On the internationall plane, Saklatvala's (British MP) visit at the time of the Meerut Conspiracy Case trial helped in negating to no small extent the British anti-communist propaganda in the Meerut case and outside in the country as a whole. He advocated communism boldly during his stay in India and enthused the youth and progressive people by his uninhibited propaganda of communist views, spotlighting the achievements of the Russian revolution, the achievements of the Russian working class, peasantry and people at large. He underlined the effect of the Russian revolution on the working people all over the globe and on the national-liberation movements in the colonial world.

The Communist Party of Great Britain took keen interest in the Meerut case trial. It sent some financial aid and continuously exposed the rotten conditions in which the Meerut prisoners were kept. The British progressive press, the pamphlets and poster propaganda carried on by the CPGB contributed in a big way to highlight the case of the communists in the Meerut trial. Internationally, it helped in forging a united front against British rulers in India. Some members of parliament in Britain played a good role in the campaign against the British government for launching and handling the Meerut case.

The protest of the industrial workers of the Soviet Union and in the Soviet press against the launching of the conspiracy case and their financial contribution to help the defence of the accused in the case emphasised the internationalism of the working class. The campaign started by the League Against Imperialism against the Meerut trial was of great help in positively strengthening proletarian internationalism.

On the national plan, the appointment of the Simon Commission by the British government with anti-self determination mandate and the support extended to it by the British Labour Party and its government not only shattered illusions about the latter in the Indian people, but it also helped in uniting all the nationalist forces against the Simon Commission. Besides, the British government in India introduced at this time two anti-working class and anti-communist bills—the Trade Disputes Bill and the Public Safety Bill which mobilised the working class in a big way in opposition to them. The appointment of the Whitley Commission to bind still further the working class hand and foot added further fuel to fire. In this way all the political forces in India which mattered were drawn closer to fight the machinations of the British rulers in India.

The cumulative effect of the repressive policies of the British imperialist rulers was that they united the Indian people in a big struggle against the British imperialists to secure the freedom of the country. In this struggle, the working class and all patriotic classes in the national movement unitedly played their glorious part.

This was what the British rulers did not want to happen. But it came about because of the blind repressive policies of the British rulers. The country's freedom movement advanced by leaps and bounds.

Today to solve the post independence problems faced by the country, the need of the hour is to forge a left and democratic front to wrest power from the hands of the bourgeois parties which have over the last thirty-two years failed to solve the fundamental problems of the country. Socialism is the only way out of the ills afflicing India today. Let all the left and democratic forces in the country unite and oust the bourgeois parties from power and take the country along the road to socialism.

(Curtesy—People Publishing House—New Delhi and Sohan Singh Josh—The Great Attack—Meerut Conspiracy Case PPH—N.Del,1979).

Meerut Conspiracy Case and Arrests of the Accused Persons

On 14th March the Viceroy's Council sanctioned the arrest of thirty-one leftist leaders with the charge of having "entered into a conspiracy to deprive the King of the sovereignty of British India, and having thereby committed an offence punishable under Section 121-A of I.P.C." The Council, under the provisions of Section 196 of Criminal Penal Code, 1898, ordered Mr. M.A. Horton, Officer on Special Duty, under the Director, Intelligence Bureau, Home Department, to file a complaint against those thirty-one persons in the Court of the District Magistrate at Meerut.

The thirty-one persons accused of conspiracy represented the leadership of the working class movement of India. They were:

1. *Phillip Spratt:* former Executive member of the Trade Union Congress, prominent member of the

CPI, the WPP and the GKU.

2. *Benjamin Francis Bradley:* former member of the London District Committee of the Amalgamated Engineering Union in Britain; Executive member of the G.I.P. Railwaymen's Union and of the GKU; Vice President of the All-India Railwaymen's Federation; Treasurer of the Joint Strike Committee in the Bombay textile strike; prominent member of the CPI and the WPP.
3. *Ajodhya Prasad:* active member of the Bengal WPP.
4. *Shaukat Usmani:* sentenced in the Kanpur trial; Editor of a Urdu working-class paper in Bombay and a newly elected member of the Comintern Presidium.
5. *Puran Chand Joshi:* Secretary of the U.P. and Delhi WPP.
6. *Gauri Shankar:* Executive Committee member of the U.P. WPP.
7. *Lakshman Rao Kadam:* organiser of the Municipal Workers' Union at Jhansi.
8. *Dr. Viswanath Mukharji:* President of the U.P. WPP.
9. *Chowdhury Dharamvir Singh,* M.L.C.: Vice-President, WPP, Meerut.
10. *Dharani K. Goswami:* Assistant Secretary of the Bengal WPP and a prominent trade unionist.
11. *Shib Nath Bannerjee:* President of the Bengal Jute Workers' Union, previously sentenced to one year in connection with the Kharagpur Railway strike.
12. *Gopal Basak:* President of the Socialist Youth Conference in 1928.
13. *Muzaffar Ahmad:* Vice-President of the AITUC; Secretary of the Bengal WPP; sentenced in the Kanpur trial.

14. *Samsul Huda:* Secretary of the Bengal Transport Workers' Union.
15. *Kishorilal Ghosh:* Secretary of the Bengal Provincial Federation of Trade Unions.
16. *Gopendra Chakravarty:* official of the Eastern Railway Union; previously sentenced to one and a half Years in connection with the Kharagpur Railway strike.
17. *Radha Raman Mitra:* Secretary of the Bengal Jute Workers' Union.
18. *Sripad Amrit Dange:* Assistant Secretary of the AITUC; formerly sentenced in the Kanpur trial; General Secretary of the GKU; prominent member of the CPI and the WPP.
19. *Sachidanand Vishnu Ghate:* Assistant Secretary of the AITUC (1927) and Vice-President of the Bombay Municipal Workers' Union; prominent member of the CPI and the WPP.
20. *S.H. Jhabwalla:* Organising Secretary of the All-India Railwaymen's Federation; former Vice-President of the GKU.
21. *Dhondi Raj Thengdi:* Ex-President and Executive member of the AITUC; member of the AICC.
22. *Keshab Nilkant Joglekar:* Organising Secretary of the G.I.P. Railwaymen's Union; member of the AICC.
23. *Shantaram Savlaram Mirajkar:* Assistant Secretary of the GKU.
24. *Raghunath Shivram Nimbkar:* Secretary of the Bombay Trades Council and of the Bombay Provincial Congress Committee; General Secretary of the All-India WPP; member of the AICC.
25. *Gangadhar Moreswar Adhikari,* Ph.D.: joined both the Bombay WPP and the CPI after returning to India from Germany in December,

1928; contributor to the Bombay socialist paper *The Spark.*

26. *Motiram Gajanan Desai:* Editor of the Bombay socialist journal *The Spark.*
27. *Arjun Atmaram Alve:* President of the GKU; a prominent member of the CPI and the WPP.
28. *Govind Ramchandra Kasle:* important official of the GKU.
29. *Sohan Singh Josh:* President of the All-India Workers' and Peasants' Conference and an important member of the Punjab Kirti Kisan Party.
30. *M.A. Majid:* left India in 1920 with the Khilafat movement; visited Russia and was imprisoned on return. Secretary of the Kirti Kisan (Peasants) Party, Punjab; important member of the All-India Youth League.
31. *Kedar Nath Sehgal:* President of the Punjab Congress Committee and Financial Secretary of the Punjab Provincial Congress Committee; member of the All-India Youth League.

On March 20, 1929, large scale arrests were carried out simultaneously in half dozen different towns. In some cases prolonged house searches were made. All the prisoners were taken to the inland town of Meerut. Of the thirty-one accused, thirteen came from Bombay, ten from Bengal, five from the United provinces and three from the Punjab.

In June the number of defendents was increased to thirty two with the arrest of Lester Hutchinson, an English journalist who arrived in India in September, 1928. He was the editor of a Bombay labour journal *The New Spark* and also the Vice President of the GKU. The Home Department investigated him closely and decided, they had enough evidence to prosecute him with the other accused in the Meerut Conspiracy Case.

The Viceroy informed the Secretary of State on June 8, 1929:

As a result of the examination of the evidence against Hutchinson it is found that there is a very strong case against him, and that if he is included as an accused in the Meerut Case it will be of material benefit to the prosecution of the other accused. To proceed against him under the Public Safety ordinance may it is thought be reasonably criticized as prejudging the Meerut trial. Governor-General-in-Council has therefore sanctioned prosecution of Hutchinson as an accused in the Meerut Conspiracy Case.

A warrant was also issued for the arrest of Amir Haidar Khan who was described as a "secret agent of communications between India and Moscow," and an active member of the CPI, but he absconded before he could be brought to trial.

(Courtesy—Meerut Conspiracy Case and left-wing in India-Pramita Ghosh).

The Meerut Arrests and the Government Actions

The Government of India's growing concern with the development of left-wing activities in the country during 1928-29 was responsible for a series of measures undertaken to curb and crush the Communist movement in India, leading up to the arrest of thirty-one principal active leaders of the movement on March 20, 1929, in connection with the Meerut Conspiracy Case. However, the launching of the Meerut Communist Conspiracy Case did not end the efforts of the officials to proceed with other measures which they had already envisaged with a view to arresting the growth of Communism in India. Some of the notable Government measures undertaken during March, 1929 to December, 1929, in this connection, will be discussed in the following pages.

Fawcett Committee Report

The large number of mill strikes in Bombay in 1928, a Riot Enquiry Committee under the chairmanship of Charles Fawcett was appointed in October, 1928, to consider the introduction of the Standardisation Scheme. Three days after the arrest of the thirty-one labour leaders on March 20, 1929, the Fawcett Committee published its official report on March 23, 1929. In this report the Committee recommended:

...We regard the proposals of the Millowners' Association (a) for Standardisation of wages, duties and numbers of operatives in a mill...and (b) for Standing Orders for the operatives about the conditions of their employment, as being in the main fair and reasonable. On the other hand we consider that, while there is justification for the Associations' proposal to make a cut of 7-½ per cent in weavers' wages,...there are reasonable objections to be urged against its adoption in the present circumstances, and we recommend that it should be dropped by the Association, provided the Labour leaders undertake to co-operate in working the Standardisation Scheme.

The Committee in its report further recommended that "the Government should take drastic action against the activities of the Communists in Bombay", and also raised the question whether the Trade Union Act should not be so amended as "to exclude communists from management in registered trade unions."

On the whole, the findings of the Fawcett Committee were definitely unfavourable to the interests of the trade unionist movement of the period.

Some of the leading moderate nationalist papers termed the Fawcett Committee Report as "fair" and "justifiable". The *Indian National Herald* (Bombay) considered that the Committee "have done their work in a spirit of justice and with a clear desire within the lights to hold the scales even between owners and the workers." The *Bombay Chronicle* of March 25 remarked that

The report of the Fawcett Strike Enquiry Committee makes, on the whole, a fair recognition of the claims of industrial workers engaged in the city's principal industry. Though the Seventeen Demands of the workers are not conceded equally, the balance of the Committee's findings is distinctly on the side of the workers.

However, the more radical section of the nationalist press was bitterly critical of the report. Thus the *Indian States Journal* (Bombay) of April 6 wrote:

We can hardly congratulate the Fawcett Committee on their report. Their recommendations have erred sadly by being one-sided almost from start to finish...If the Committee have been acting as counsel for the Mill representatives they could not have done better...The whole thing seems to be a farrago of nonsense and we are constrained to think that the Committee could not have made a worse exhibition of its ignorance of human psychology or strong class prejudice.

The *Kranti* (Bombay) of March 31, commenting on the report noted:

On Saturday the 23rd of March 1929 ended the period of truce as the Report of the Fawcett Committee was out on that day...The reasons set forth by the Committee in justification of the cut in the wages in the weaving departments are quite unconvincing to labour. The system of calculation given in the new project is very intricate. In this calculation the owners will surely try to deceive the labourers. The demand that no labourer should receive anything less than thirty rupees has been brushed aside by the Committee with the remark that they were not bound to consider such new proposals...On the whole we are forced to say that the

Report has been written with an eye to the capitalist interests and whatever few suggestions beneficial to labour it contains are made through sheer necessity and taking into consideration the increasing strength of the labour movements.

Public Safety Ordinance

The Government effort to secure the passage of the Public Safety Bill in the Legislative Assembly having failed in September, 1928, the bill was referred to a Select Committee during the winter session of the Assembly. As reported by the Select Committee, the Public Safety Bill was scheduled for discussion once again in the Assembly on March 21, 1929. However, the President of the Assembly, Mr. Vithalbhai Patel, ruled on that date that the consideration of the bill be postponed till April 2. When the issue was taken up on April 2, Mr. Patel suggested that the fundamental basis for the bill was virtually identical with that of the conspiracy case launched by the Government and consequently that it would not be possible to argue the case for the bill without arguing the case for the prosecution and making statements which were likely to prejudice the trial. The President accordingly advised the Government either to "postpone the bill pending the Meerut trial or, if they attach greater importance to passing this bill at this juncture, to withdraw the Meerut case and then proceed further with the bill."

On April 4, Mr. Crerar delivered the Government's response to the President's earlier ruling by declaring that the Government refused to accept either of the alternative suggestions put before them by the President, and concluded:

The submission of government, therefore is that in accordance with the rules of the House you [President] should direct the House to proceed, as soon as may be, with the consideration of the Public Safety Bill.

After duly considering the government's reply, the President of the Assembly re-affirmed his view on April 11, 1929, saying that he was convinced that no debate was possible on the bill during the tendency of the trial and any debate on it under the circumstances would be a fraud and a farce. So he ruled that the further consideration of the bill under the circumstances was out of order.

On April 12, the Viceroy Lord Irwin addressed a joint session of both Houses of the Indian Legislature. Referring to the President's ruling he announced his decision to issue an ordinance embodying the Public Safety Bill and to secure the amendment of the rules to prevent the President of either House from interrupting normal legislative procedure.

On April 13, 1929, the Viceroy acting under the authority of Section 72 of the Government of India Act which enabled him in case of emergency to promulgate ordinances for the peace and good government of British India, issued the "Public Safety Ordinance, 1929" which granted the Government the same powers it had sought to secure through the legislation.

The invoking of the Public Safety ordinance was criticized severely by prominent Indians as well as by the nationalist press. Mahatma Gandhi commenting on the ordinance wrote in his Gujarati weekly *Navajivan* (Ahmedabad) of April 21:

> By issuing the Ordinance His Excellency the Viceroy has showed the futility of the Councils. The institutions like Councils, etc., are toys in the hands of the Executive officers with which they play till like and destroy them when they do not give them satisfaction. Hence Swaraj cannot be secured by such toys.

The *Basumati* (Calcutta) of April 13 noted:

The country will hold that the passing of the Bill by Ordinance is quite uncalled for, it as much as the situation is not such or so very grave as to necessitate a drastic step like the one the Viceroy has chosen to take. We should have been glad if in overruling the President's ruling, his Government preferred to bring forward a vote of censure on the President, or better still dissolve the Assembly and made the question an electoral issue. That would have been a constitutional procedure. Ordinance has the practical effect of supplanting the constitution.

The *Amrita Bazar Patrika* (Calcutta) of April 14 wrote:

As for the new weapon in the armoury of the government, it is better that it has had to be obtained by them through the agency of the Governor-General independent of the Legislature. Constituted as the latter body is, it is almost sure that had the Public Safety bill been proceeded with, it would have been passed with the help of the officials and their *jo-hukum* [as the master commands] henchmen. That would have had the effect of misleading the uninformed world opinion and giving an opportunity to the Government to parade the vote of the Assembly as the voice of the country.

The *Tribune* (Lahore) commented on April 17:

We have no hesitation in saying that the decision arrived at by Lord Irwin's Government with respect to the situation created by President Patel's ruling on the Public Safety Bill is entirely and fundamentally wrong. The promulgation of the Public Safety Ordinance involves a two-fold invasion upon the rights of the public. The substance of the Ordinance is open to all the grave objections to which the Public Safety Bill was open. Not only is it unnecessary and uncalled for, but it amounts to the taking away in an important class of cases of one of the elementary rights of accused persons, the right of open and fair trial by an independent and properly constituted tribunal according to the ordinary forms of law. The manner in which the Ordinance has been passed is just as objectionable as its substance. An Executive-made law is in its very nature a lawless law because the assumption by the Executive of the power of making laws deprives laws of their essential character of being the expression of what Rousseau called "the general will."

The *Mahratta* (Poona) of April 21 remarked:

We would not have demurred to the assumption of extra-ordinary powers by Government, had there been the slightest necessity for it. As things stand, there is none. The power are required to deport British subjects carrying on subversive propaganda in India. At the most liberal computation there are hardly three of such undesirables whom government can publicly name. The Viceroy spoke of "the full knowledge of much that can necessarily not be publicly disclosed" but obviously it was unfair to ask for special powers from the Assembly without taking that body into confidence. Just as foreigners of the description can be dealt with under the present powers, just as, again Indians of the same type can be disposed of under the present law, so it was not impossible for Government to have done with British subjects by methods now within the control of Government, say by severe application of the passport regulations. Foreign money too could be intercepted by government in more than one way, if they meant to do so. There was, thus, no reason at all for the special measures at the cost of the popular furore and even the constitutional forms of the ordinary administrative and legislative work.

Trades Disputes Act

As noted earlier the Trades Disputes Bill was

referred to a Select Committee in the Assembly on February 11, 1929. The bill slightly modified by the Committee, was taken up for consideration in the Legislative Assembly on April 2, 1929. Once again a debate raged over the bill and finally after four days of deliberation and speeches by both the Government representatives and the members of the Opposition, on April 8, the whole bill, as modified by the Select Committee, was passed by fifty-six votes to thirty-eight.

Coming so soon after the Meerut arrests, the enactment of the Trades Disputes Act was considered as yet another government attack upon the working class and the labour organizations of India. The *Railwayman* (Bombay) of April 13 commenting on the passage of the Act noted:

The Government is trying to put down the labour movement by passing laws like the Trades Dispute Bill in order to protect itself and the capitalists. In passing this Bill the Government and the Capitalists seem to have the idea that the Bill will suppress the present labour movement which is in full swing and then being able to crush the labourers they will be quite at ease. But we emphatically declare it to-day that this idea of the Capitalists is quite false and erroneous. For the labour movement in this country is based on legal and constitutional grounds and the present Bill will have no effect whatsoever on it. The Bill containing as it does some sections unfavourable to the labour movement, met with the disapproval not only of the various labour unions but of several owners also. Not only this, but many of the members of the Assembly also vehemently opposed it. Even thought the Government decide to pass the Bill into law and thus try to deprive the labourers of their rightful privileges nothing good will come out of it. But on the contrary the unrest among the labourers in the country will increase and there is a probability of a recurrence of the atmosphere which was created at the time of the Rowlatt Act.

The *Kamkari* (Bombay), a Marathi weekly, wrote on April 14, 1929:

The Trades Disputes Bill has totally deprived the workers of their independence. A Bill has been passed which turns the labourers into slaves from Africa or cattle in the stable. Henceforward the labourers must not try to redress the grievances nor must they show by their conduct that the oppression has become intolerable. And if anyone tries to give vent to his feelings, if anyone leaves the hell in the form of the workshop, he will be sent to prison...The members of the Assembly are interested in the mills; the capital belonging to their relatives is locked up in the industry. And these people will suffer loss if the labourers go on strike as a protest against oppression. The Public Safety Bill is being opposed because it is likely to deprive a few persons of their vocation. But the Trades Disputes Bill will make the labourers suffer the tortures of hell while yet living.

Some of the noted left-wing papers in condemning the Trade Disputes Act blamed the nationalist leaders as well as the Government for the passage of the Bill. Thus *Kranti* (Bombay) commented on April 10, 1929:

The storm raised by the President of the Legislative Assembly over the Public Safety Bill proved of use to Government and the capitalists in getting the Trade Disputes Bill safely passed through the Legislative Assembly. It does not seem possible that the members of the Legislative Assembly did not know that the provisions of the Trade Disputes Bill were more dangerous than those of the Public Safety Bill. But the friends of the capitalists in the Legislative Assembly hatched a plot to raise a storm over the Public Safety Bill which has become useless owing to the arrest of

Messrs Spratt and Bradley and to pass a Bill which strengthens the position of the capitalist and strikes at the very root of the labour movement.

Whitley Commission

As announced by the Viceroy on January 28, 1929 an Enquiry Commission was proposed to be set up under the Chairmanship of Mr. Whitley to examine the conditions of labour in India. The Commission was duly selected on July 4, 1929; its duties were to inquire into and report on "the existing conditions of labour in industrial undertakings and plantations in British India, on the health, efficiency and standard of living of the workers, and on the relations between employers and employed, and to make recommendations."

The Commission started its work at Karachi on October 15, 1929, and visited all the major Provinces and administrative areas except Burma, before it sailed for England towards the end of March, 1930. At almost every important centre visited by it, the Commission received a great amount of co-operation from employers and employed alike, and collected valuable evidence, both written and oral. The only notable difficulty experienced during the tour was the boycott declared against the Commission by the All-India Trade Union Congress during its session held at Nagpur at the end of November, 1929. The subject of boycotting the Commission became a major issue in the Nagpur session of the AITUC and representatives of thirty unions, including some *ex-official* members of the Executive Council of the AITUC resigned as a protest against the decision in favour of boycott and formed an independent organization known as the All-India Trade Union Federation. The Commission resumed its work in the later part of 1930 and submitted the complete report in June, 1931. The report is a precise and insightful study of labour conditions and industrial problems in India in the pre-1930 period. After an exhaustive enquiry, the Commission recommended in 1931 that employers should adopt a more liberal policy towards "recognition" of unions, and that Government should take the lead in the case of their own industrial employees. It favoured a liberalization of the provision in the Trade Union Act, 1926, relating to the inclusion of "outsiders" in trade union excutives. Further, the Commission was particularly critical of the Trades Disputes Act and the prevailing Government approach to the settlement of industrial disputes, as being influenced unduly by considerations of public order.

Thus while a conspiracy case was launched to make the notable left-wing leaders inactive in the Indian political scene, the Government continued its operation against Communism in India in other fields as well. Aside from the significant role that the foreign Communist agents had played in India, the other factor which has posed an immediate problem for the Government of India was the situation on the labour front. The Communist accomplishments in the labour movement in general and the trade union movement in particular during 1927-28 were perilous in the official point of view. Several measures were contemplated to meet the situation, the most important of which were the proposed Trades Disputes Bill, the appointment of the Fawcett Committee and that of the Royal Commission on Labour. Of these, the Trades Disputes Bill was designed in a fashion to restrict the outbreak of industrial strikes which were causing a great deal of hardship for the government as well as for the private businessmen of the country. The Fawcett Committee was an answer to the pressing crisis in the textile mills of Bombay Province. It was an attempt on the part of the government to mediate between the mill owners and the mill workers of Bombay. The Royal Commission (or the Whitley Commission) was appointed by the Parliament in response to the presistent demands both in England and in India for a thorough enquiry into the actual conditions of labour in India. Lastly, the Public Safety Bill was legalized as an ordinance more as a preventive measure against the danger of future foreign Communist agents working in India, than as a punitive measure.

Meerut Conspiracy Case: Significant Features

Some of the important events that occurred over the period following the Meerut arrests, from March to December, 1929. A relevant event of that period which was not discussed therein was the beginning of the actual Meerut trial. The trial was formally inaugurated in June, 1929, and the first phase of its enquiry was completed by December, 1929. This initial portion of the trial proceedings which took place during the time span of our inquiry (upto the end of 1929) will be discussed in the following pages. A detailed examination of the entire legal proceedings in the case, which lasted for almost four years, however, is outside the scope of this study. But in order to appreciate the full significance of the Meerut Conspiracy Case as a British reaction to left-wing politics in India during 1928-29, and to get a historical perspective of the case in the context of events of that period, some of the notable features of the case, as a whole, will be mentioned briefly.

Beginning of the Trial

The thirty-one persons arrested on March 20, 1929, at various parts of the country were all gathered together at Meerut and were held in jail by the local police, who took a fresh remand at the expiry of every two weeks. As a result of the numerous searches carried out by the police following the arrests, a large number of papers, letters, documents and books were seized and the prosecutors had a difficult time sorting out the incriminating documents they needed to use against the accused in the trial. A conspiracy trial under British Indian Legal Code had to be proceeded by a preliminary enquiry by a Special Magistrate. This enquiry for the Meerut prisoners had a very delayed start due to the massive documents collected as a result of the searches. The Indian Government as well as the Home Office in London were keen on starting the enquiry without delay. The Home Department of the Government of India sent a series of letters to the chief prosecutor Mr. Langford James urging him to begin the trial as early as possible. Mr. H.G. Haig, the Home Department Secretary, Government of India, in a letter dated April 29, 1929, to Mr. Langford James made the Government's anxiety very clear:

> We are rather uneasy at the suggestion made in two recent letters from [Special Investigator] Horton that so much material has been recovered in the searches that it may be at least another two months before you are ready to open the case...We are definitely of opinion that earlier the case can be started without prejudice to the result the better it is from our point of view, and while it might no doubt be possible to elaborate considerably by taking another two or three months so as to fit every bit of evidence discovered at the searches into its appropriate place. From the practical point of view are disposed to think that this elaboration might be purchased too dearly.

The Secretary of State for India was also putting pressure on the Indian Government to begin the enquiry at an early date. In reply to the Secretary of State's telegram in this connection, the Viceroy informed him on May 7, 1929:

Material recovered in searches was very voluminous, and work of examination, which must be confined to a limited number of people who appreciate what it means, take considerable time. Langford James is clear that start cannot be made until this material has been fully examined, and he knows precisely what it contains... Already fresh evidence discovered will enable him to dispose with a good deal of evidence originally relied upon...We feel there is considerable force in views of Langord James and that we cannot interfere with what he regards as essential preliminary work.

However, the Secretary of State was evidently getting uneasy with the growing criticism in England and informed the Viceroy on May 28:

Sincerely trust that Langford James is now in a position to start conspiracy case according to programme on 1st proximo or very soon after. Further delay is likely to provide severe criticism in Assembly (or) Parliament.

In spite of this desire on the part of the Government to start the case early, the preliminary enquiry did not begin till June 12—almost eleven weeks after the arrests. Meanwhile numerous applications for bail made on behalf of the accused, individually and collectively, were refused. One of the principal grounds advanced by the prosecution for rejecting bail applications and accepted by the Magistrate was that the case had been started by the Government of India after due care and therefore it was very likely that the accused were guilty.

The preliminary enquiry in the case commenced on June 12, 1929, before Mr. Milner White. Special Magistrate, at the District Court of Meerut. After the hearing on June 13, however, and adjournment of ten days was granted and the hearing was resumed on June 24 and continued till June 25. Meanwhile on June 19, 1929, the number of accused increased to thirty-two with the addition of Lester Hutchinson. The first four days of the trial (seventeen and one half hours) were totally occupied by the opening address of the chief counsel for the prosecution, Mr. Langford James. This opening address was remarkable as the like of it is rarely heard in any court of justice. It was an attack on the theory of Marxism and Leninism, the policy and the Government of Soviet Russia, the Communist International and an attempt to show the anti-national character of the accused. Very little was said about how a "conspiracy" was afoot to "deprive the King of his sovereignty over British India."

Mr. Langford James emphasized the role of Moscow and the Third International in carrying on Communist propaganda in India. Giving a detailed description of the origin, objectives, organization, methods, and tactics of the Third International, he said that a large number of people connected with the Bolshevik movement had "indulged in ruthless bloodshed and a reign of terror" at the direction of the Third International. And according to the "programme of this body in Moscow violence, bloodshed and civil war and a reign of terror were unavoidable."

He also described at length the creed of the Communist Party as propounded by Marx and Engles—the theory of class war and the dictatorship of the proletariat. "These men advocated war between capitalists, or those who had a stake in the country," he said, "and the proletariat, or those who had not stake in the country. This was clear from the origin of the word proletariat."

Lenin had prescribed blood red revolution for overthrowing capitalism. He had declared it as the duty of all Communists everywhere to bring about an armed uprising, with the aid of peasants and workers. Lenin had preached this doctrine both before and after the

Russian revolution.

Referring to the state of affairs in Russia under Bolshevism, he said:

A large number of people, when you mention Russia, connect it with bloodshed, a ruthless reign of terror. This contains the germs of truth. Bloshevism...I believe to be a festering sore on the face of Europe, a cruel and tyrannous autocracy masquerading under the mask of popular government.

In addition, the prosecution pointed out the relationship of various Moscow-controlled and directed front agencies such as the Red International of Labour Unions, the National Minorities Movement and the League Against Imperialism to the futherance of Communism in India.

Besides stressing the subversive character of the Comintern to the entire non-Communist world, Chief Crown Counsel Mr. James also emphasized the view that the Communists in Russia harshly oppressed their own people, and were bent on annihilating the social structure of India, notably the so-called national bourgeoisie.

Anticipating a defence argument to the effect that since there was technically no Indian Communist Party which was formally a branch of the Communist International and that therefore Indian Communists were not officially members of the Comintern, the Chief Prosecutor held that it was sufficient to show the Indian Communist were acting "at the behest of the Third International" to warrant the conviction of the Indian conspirators.

As to the charges against the accused themselves, Mr. James said:

The activities of the accused India consisted in faithfully carrying out the Communist programme contained in Communist literature and books. Spratt had assisted the formation of the Workers' and Peasants' party in Bombay and thereafter the activities extended to other provinces...The strikes in Bombay and Calcutta were instigated and carried on and prolonged by the accused and they were proud of it. They made vigorous efforts to capture the Trade Union Congress in 1927 and last year. They persistently adhered to the Moscow clique. They had newspapers everlastingly preaching the gospel of Communism and their activities consisted in poisoning the minds of the youths in the country by the formation of Youth Leagues...The accused had engineered, taken part in and spoken at various kinds of demonstrations which were intended by the accused to educate the proletariat in order to initiate them into the mysteries of class war and dictatorship of the proletariat.

A conscious effort was made on the part of the prosecutor to bring out the anti-national character of the Communists. Realizaing that the seizure of the Indian radicals was unpopular, to say the least, among influential Indians, notably in Congress circles, Mr. James stressed those features of Communism which he felt were utterly distasteful to the Indian nationalists. He said:

> The Indian National Congress was stigmatised as a misguided bourgeois body, which was to be captured or converted to the peculiar principles of the accused. Their [Communists'] opinions of some of the Nationalise leaders were:—
>
> Pandit Motilal Nehru—A dangerous patriot.
>
> Pandit Jawaharlal Nehru—A tepid reformist.
>
> Mr. Subhas Chandra Bose—Bourgeosie and ludicrous careerist.
>
> Mr. Gandhi—A grotesque reactionary.
>
> Lala Lajpatrai—A scoundrel, and politically dangerous.

> Mr. C.R. Das—A poltroon.
>
> The quarrel which the accused had with men of Nationalist thought in India was that the latter's ideology was all hopelessly wrong.
>
> Mr. Gandhi was charged with another crime by these people. He was religiously minded and there was no place for God in Communist ideals...
>
> Each of these accused is, I repeat, anti-nationalist.

He charged that the objective of the accused was "to remove the Government of His Majesty King George in India and in its place put the Government of the Third Communist International." Explaining further he said that the accused wanted to "substitute the Governement of His Majesty by the Government of M. Stalin as he is now known."

Mr. James described the accused as Bolsheviks and according to him, a Bolshevik had certain characteristics:

> To be a Bloshevik of an unimpeachable character you require certain definite qualifications to which an ordinary man does not aspire. You don't love your country, you are anti-country, you are anti-God, you are antifamily; in fact you are anti-everything which a normal man considers decent.

The defence was represented by a number of prominent Indian lawyers like K.F. Nariman, D.P. Sinha, M.C. Chagla, C.B. Gupta, K.C. Chakravarty and others. The senior Defence Counsel, Mr. D.P. Sinha maintained that this was the first systmatic prosecution by the Government of a group of men for holding certain ideals and cherishing certain beliefs even though their actions were not contrary to law. All trade unionists, he explained, believed that it was their elementary duty to make labour "class conscious" and to organize for collective bargaining. As for the allegation that the accused had attempted to deprive the King of his sovereignty, the Chief Counsel contended, that was no offence so long as the means employed were not illegal, and even if they were illegal the accused could only be tried for sedition and not for treasonable conspiracy.

Another defence attorney, Mr. K.C. Chakravarty argued that from the charges enumerated by the Prosecuting Counsel it seemed the Government was launching this case against the Soviet Government as much as against the thirty-two accused. Hence, he said, "the only law which applied to such a conspiracy case was the law of Nations" and "municipal tribunal" such as the District Court of Meerut had no true jurisdiction over the case.

All of the accused pleaded "not guilty" after the prosecution completed its presentation of the case, in the course of which they examined 320 witnesses and filed 12,500 exhibits (covering 7,000 printed pages). Most of the defendants did not exercise their rights to cross-examine the witnesses for the prosecution, or make statements, or gives evidence on their own behalf in court. Only three of the accused made specific statements in their own defence. Dr. Dharamvir Singh, a Member of the U.P. Legislative Council and the Vice-president of the U.P. Workers' and Peasants' party, pleaded "not guilty" on the plea that he had never been a Communist and as a follower of Gandhi was opposed to Communist objectives and methods. A.A. Alve and S.H. Jhabwalla, explaining they had joined the WPP because they shared its objective of working for the amelioration of working conditions, denied that they were Communists. While Jhabwalla argued he was a "Parsee humanitarian," Alve claimed himself to be an "agriculturist and a labourer."

The first phase of the Meerut Conspiracy Case, the Magisterial Enquiry, ended on December 15, 1929, after lasting for about seven months. On January 13, 1930, thirty-one of the thirty-two accused were committed to trial by Mr. Milner White. All the prisoners except Mr. Dharamvir Singh were committed to be tried by the Court of Special Session, Meerut.

The only one of the accused who was pronounced "not guilty" in the preliminary examination, was Dharamvir Singh, who was released after he submitted a written statement to the Court on November 26, 1929, saying:

> I am not a Communist and never have been one I have heard the description of communism put forward in this case and I have now looked at some of the books and I can say quite frankly that I do not agree with the object or the methods of the Communists. I am an ardent follower of Mahatma Gandhi and believe firmly in non-violence; and in practice I am a nationalist and propose to remain such. If I had the slightest idea that by attending the conference and writing to Dr. Mukerji I am helping the Workers' and Peasants' Party which is alleged to be a communist organisation, I would never have anything to do with those two things. As a matter of fact I had no idea of Workers' and Peasants' Party at all. I have always tried to do work among the farmers and labourers, but certainly not on communist lines, as I now understand them; nor have I the slightest idea to do such work in the future on those lines.

The efforts of the accused to get the trail transferred to a presidency town where they could be tried by a jury was rejected. The first application in this respect was made to the Chief Justice in Allahabad on July 16, 1929. He rejected it saying that the trial was being conducted under conditions "most normal in this country", that he did not believe there was any inconvenience and that "everybody will settle down comfortably at Meerut."

4. Political workers belonging to either the Peasants' and Workers' Association or Trade Unions or the Congress, who deny that they have ever belonged to any Communist organisation or joined in any conspiracy.

The High Court ordered the sentences to be reduced as follows:

Name	*Goupe placed in*	*Original Sentences*	*High Court Decision*
Muzaffar Ahmad	1	Life transporation	3 years r.i.
S.A. Dange	1	12 years "	3 " "
Shaukat Usmani	1	10 " "	3 " "
Philip Spratt	2	12 " "	2 " "
S.V. Ghate	1	12 " "	1 " "
K.N. Joglekar	1	12 " "	1 " "
R.S. Nimbkar	1	12 " "	1 " "
B.F. Bradley	2	10 " "	1 " "
S.S. Mirajkar	1	10 " "	1 " "
S.S. Josh	1	7 " "	1 " "
Abdul Majid	1	7 " "	1 " "
Dharani Goswami	3	7 " "	1 " "
Gopen Chakravarty	3	4 " r.i.	7 months "
Ajodhya Prasad	1	5 " transp.	Conviction uphled but released
P.C. Joshi	3	5 " "	"
Gopal Basak	3	4 " r.i.	"
G.M. Adhikari	1	5 " transp.	"
Samsul Huda	1	3 " r.i.	"
M.G. Desai	4	5 " transp.	Acquitted of all charges
S.H. Jhabwalla	4	4 " r.i.	"
H.L. Hutchinson	3	4 " "	"
R.R. Mitra	3	4 " "	"
K.N. Sehgal	4	4 " "	"
G.R. Kasle	4	3 "	"
Gauri Shankar	4	3 " "	"
L.R. Kadam	4	3 " "	"
A.A. Alve	4	3 " "	"

Thus the sentences were reduced considerably. Hutchinson and eight others were completley acquitted. The High Court, taking into consideration that the defendants had already been confined for more than four years, decided to be lenient. The sentences of Joshi, Basak, A, Prasad, Adhikari and Huda were reduced to the time they had already served and they were released immediately. The sentences passed against Bradely and nine others were reduced to one year and that of Chakravarty to seven months. The period of remission already earned by them was taken into consideration and all of them were released sometime in November, 1933. By the end of the year 1933, all the accused except Muzaffar Ahmad, Dange, Spratt, and Usmani had been released.

Special Features of the Case

In many respects the Meerut Conspiracy Case stands out as unique even in the history of British India. It was the longest state trail in that history, planned, carried out, and concluded under three different British Governments—Conservative, Labour, and National. The trial was conducted at an enormous financial cost at a time when the economy of the country could ill afford it. From a strict legal point of view also the case was unusual for its overt political tone. As the trial proceeded it was apparent that both the prosecutors and the defendants were using it for their respective political purposes. Moreover, the case attracted wide scale international attention mainly in the shape of criticism. Some of these notable features of the case will be discussed briefly in the following pages.

(a) The most significant feature of the case was its unusually long duration and cost. Formally the case was launched on March 20, 1929, with arrests of the thirty-one accused and was finally concluded with the

Appelate Court Judgement delivered on August 3, 1933. So the case lasted for almost four and a half years. A massive amount of documents were produced in evidence and numerous witnesses were examined in the course of the trial. Some idea of the huge scale on which the case was conducted can be had from the following extract from the Judgement of the Allahabad High Court:

The trial has become somewhat notorious on account of its unprecedented duration. All the accused persons, except Hutchinson, were arrested in March, 1929 (Hutchnison was arrested in June of the same year) and have all this time, except for the period during which some of them were released on bail, been detained in jail. The trial commenced in the Court of the Committing Magistrate on a complaint filed on March 15, 1929, and a supplementary complaint filed against Hutchinson on June 11, 1929. The entire proceedings have now lasted for nearly four years and a half. This is accounted as follows:—

(1) The preliminary proceedings before the Magistrate took over seven months, resulting in the commitment of the accused to the Court of Session on January 14, 1930;
(2) In the Sessions Court the prosecution evidence took over 13 months;
(3) The recording of the statements of the accused occupied over ten months;
(4) The defence evidence lasted for about two months;
(5) The arguments continued for over 4 - ½ months;
(6) The learned Sessions Judge took over five months thereafter to pronounce his judgement;
(7) The last of the appeals was filed in the High Court on March 17, 1933,...July 24, 1933 was fixed for the appeals, on which date the arguments

commenced, and having lasted for 8 working days were concluded yesterday (August 2, '33).

The case was conducted on a gigantic scale. The evidence consists of 25 printed volumes of folio size. There are altogether 3,500 prosecution exhibits, over 1500 defence exhibits, and no less than 320 witnesses were examined. The judgement itself is in two printed volumes covering 676 pages of folio size.

The trial was conducted at an enormous expense. Exactly what amount of money was spent on the case has never been declared anywhere. However, when the Sessions Court Judgement was delivered on January 16, 1933, it was officially estimated that the case had cost £126,000 or Rs. 16 lakhs up to that period. By the end of the appeal the figure must have had increased and one estimate is that the total cost to the persecution was in the neigbourhood of £200,000.

(b) Another important feature of the case was that, being a conspiracy trial, it was conducted without a jury and for most part it was a trial where bail was refused to the majority of the prisoners for the full four and a half years that the case lasted.

The Government of India was determined to have the case tried without a jury although only two of the thirty-two accused came from Meerut while fourteen of them came from Bombay and ten from Calcutta. Moreover, twenty-four of the prisoners had never even been to Meerut before the trial. The accused had appealed four times to get the case transferred to Allahabad High Court where it could be tried by a jury, and each appeal was refused. All this together with the fact that three British citizens among the thirty-two accused were also denied of a cherished British privilege to be tried by a jury, came under heavy criticism both in India and in England.

From the time of the arrests in March, 1929, up

until April, 1931, all the prisoners were kept in close confinement in prison. In spite of the effect of this confinement upon the health of men who were still at that time entitled to be treated as innocent men, the Sessions Judge consistently refused to permit their release on bail. Eventually ten out of the thirty-one were allowed bail after April, 1931, by the Allahabad High Court, who declared, that in their opinion they should have been released long before. The rest of the twenty-one accused were refused bail in spite of several appeals and were kept in prison for the entire period of the trial. It might be of interest to note that the ten who were granted bail were all non-Communists. Referring to this fact a number of defendants in their Joint Statement to the Court stated:

A test application was made by two of us in April 1931, after the Delhi Pact had been signed and the political tension of the previous years had partially relaxed. Owing to this fact coupled with the carelessness of the Crown Counsel, and the circumstance that they were fortunate enough to argue before a relatively independent and liberal-minded bench, they were granted a conditional bail. This established a precedent and almost all the remaining accused applied also. Only four non-communist accused succeeded in this Court. When we appealed to the High Court, a full bench was carefully arranged to decide this important question. Their decision was prepared before they heard argument, as is shown by the fact that their judgement of several typed pages was ready a few minutes after they had retired for decision. The decision itself was extraordinary. All the non-communists accused except one...and including three who had not applied, were granted bail while all those of the accused who had declared themselves communists by conviction, whether the evidence proved their connection with the

C.P.I., or not—were refused.

The fact that bail was refused to a majority of the prisoners for the trial's entire period of four and a half years indeed makes it an unusual instance of British justice in India.

(c) The Merrut trial was from the very beginning a political case. As the trial proceeded it assumed a propagandist character on both sides. This trend was set in motion by the Chief Prosecution Counsel, Mr. Langford James who vehemently attacked Communism, National and International, in the choicest phraseology, characterizing the Communists as enemies of civilized life. Throughout the trial the prosecutions's attack was aimed chiefly at Moscow, the Communist International and the theory of Marxism and Leninism. In fact none of the accused was ever charged with committing any "overt act" of illegality or having committed any act of violence in pursuance of the alleged conspiracy. This was expressed clearly in the Allahabad High Court Judgement in the following words:

It is conceded that the accused persons have not been charged with having done any overt illegal act in pursuance of the alleged conspiracy...It is clear that if there was any office committed it the nature of a conspiracy of a serious character, it was almost nipped in the bud...All that they have done is to hold meetings, study the principles of Communism and probably also to make an attempt to disseminate the teachings which are said to be dangerous to society...The defendants in their turn seized the opportunity of the trial to make political speeches and propaganda statements from the court. Most of the accused, particularly the Communists among them, had decided to make such statements as would help to publicize the ideology and programme of the Communist Party. To this end each of the accused delivered an individual statement of defence and a joint statement was issued by the Communists. As Muzaffar Ahmad recounted it later on:

> As soon as we came together, we, the Communist accused, came to the decision that by making statements day after day we would transform the courtroom into a political forum for the dissemination of our ideology and [agreed] to equip ourselves for this mission by study beforehand. It was decided further that besides statements to be given individually by every accused, the Communist accused would make a General Statement.

This General Statement is of particular interest because it embodied the Indian Communists' views on Marxism-Leninism and its applicability to the Indian scene, the nature of the Indian revolution and the role of the CPI in it, etc. In general, the Communists among the accused defended Marxism, proletarian internationalism, and admitted that they were Communists and had been members of the CPI.

Extracts from a few of the defendants' speeches are given below to show the propaganda character of their defence. S.A. Dange in his statement said:

> The aim of the communists is the overthrow of imperialism and capitalism and the immediate aim of the communists in India is the overthrow of British imperialism....The World Communist Party, that is the Communist International, is perhaps the most organised force of the working class of the oppressed peoples. An establishment of a new state suited to and for the quiet masses of workers and peasants will essentially mean the smashing up of the present state and the party of the working class can accomplish this.

Muzaffar Ahmad in his statement before the Sessions Judge, said:

> I am a revolutionary communist—our Party fully

believe in the policy, principle and programme of the Communist International and propagated them as best it could under the circumstances...At present the British Imperialism is in control of state power in India. As the workers and peasants will overthrow imperialism they will naturally capture the state power, but they will not capture the power in order to maintain the state form as it is now. They will smash the present state form into pieces and establish in its place, the Workers' and Peasants' Republic based on the organ of the real mass power, the Soviet.

G.M. Adhikari in conclusion to his speech before the court declared:

> The nature of the present case is such that the question of defending the individual does not arise. The question is to defend the Party, its ideology, its right to exist, its right to affiliate to and be assisted by the Communist International. If I have to deal with the Communist International at length...it is because the prosecution has made it the central figure in this case... We as Communists feel it our duty to defend it before the Court and the public and place imperialism and capitalism on trial. The prosecution have hurled the vilest abuse on Communism, Communists and the Communist International. They have said that our crime is not merely against the State, but against society as a whole. I shall treat their abuse with the contempt it deserves, but hurl back the charge of being criminals against human society as a whole, in the teeth of the Imperialists and their highly-paid agents themselves. Who are the social criminals? I ask the blood thirsty imperialists who carried fire and sword through entire continents, who have instituted a colonial regime of blood and terror, who have reduced the toiling millions of these

> continents to abject poverty, intolerable slavery and are threatening them with mass extinction as a people; or the Communists, who are out to mobilise the revolutionary energies of the toiling masses of the whole world and hurl it against this wretched system based on ruthless oppression and brutal exploitation, smash it and create in its place a new one and thus save human society and its civilization from the catastrophe towards which it is undoubtedly heading? The official representatives of social criminals in this case are sitting on the prosecution benches.

Similar statements were made by other accused as well. It is quite apparent from the above that the Meerut Conspiracy Case became the platform for political propaganda and speech-making for both the British Government as well as the Communist defendants.

(d) Finally, the publicity given to and the wide ranging interantional attention received by the Meerut Conspiracy Case helped it to become an unparalleled even in Indian history. The major bulk of the comments on the case was sharply critical of the Government's action. Following the arrests of the thirty one original accused in March, 1929, unrelenting criticism was expressed not only by the leftists and the Communists of England and Russia but even international celebrities like Professor Harold Laski, Albert Einstein, Romain Rolland and others publicized their unambiguous disapproval of the official measure. The extraordinary length of the trial and the refusal on the part of the Judges to grant bail to the accused were also critically commented upon while the case was dragging on in Meerut.

The strongest reactions to the case, however, came after the Judgement of the Sessions Court was delivered on January 16, 1933. The severity of the sentences produced immediately a storm of protest in the Communist circles throughout the world. A writer in an official Comintern publication declared that "the sentences are savage." The response was by no means confined to India or the Communists alone, as it was perceived in England and elsewhere as well. The British left-wing exerted great pressure upon the Government to reduce the sentences. The National Joint Council of the British Trade Union Congress and the Labour Party issued a pamphlet stating that "the whole of the proceedings from beginning to end are utterly indefensible and constitute something in the nature of a judicial scandal." The India Office in London was flooded with protest resolutions from various labour organizations in England and the Secretary of State had to face "uneasy moments" with critical questions from the Opposition in the House of Commons. Speaking at a Parliamentary debate on the Meerut Case, Mr. Lansbury (Labour) called the sentences "savagely severe" and commented:

> These men [the twenty-seven convicted] were tried at Meerut so that the possible inconveniences of trial by jury might be avoided, and they had been in prison or on bail for four years. No act of conspiracy had been proved against them, and it was as though Englishmen were to be sent to gaol for being or being presumed to be members of the Communist Party. Sentences of three, four, and five years' rigorous imprisonment were passed for organizing strikes, and all around me are honourable members who had organized strikes and who ought to be in prison...

The British press was also very critical as the *Daily Herald* (London) commenting on the "irregularity" of the trial described it as "one of the greatest judicial scandals in the history of the Empire." The *Manchester*

Government. This is evidenced from the Secretary of State's telegram of February 18, 1933, in which he informed the Viceroy:

> I am somewhat exercised in my mind over severity of some of sentences passed in Meerut Case and I think it is right to let you know that there is a general feeling of uneasiness on the subject in various quarters here. I realise that it is difficult of Government to take any action in the matter at present stage when an appeal is pending but my difficulties here will not be made easier if there is delay in hearing appeal and possibly another six months elapse before matter is settled in court. You are no doubt alive to difficulty of position and I should be glad to learn your view on it.

An American weekly the *Christian Century* (Chicago) commenting on the Meerut trial, wrote:

> It is the longest and costliest state trial in India in recent years, the country having become poorer by Rs. 1,700,000 on this account... A feature of the trial which has evoked much criticism is the judicial system in India which allows prisoners to remain for years in jail without conviction. Even British papers like the *Times* and the *Manchester Guardian* have commented on this and advocated that this procedure in the Indian criminal courts should be drastically changed. While the trial was going on questions were repeatedly asked in the British parliament drawing attention to this scandalous delay. Appeals were made to governments both in England and India by labour leaders and other political organizations to withdraw the prosecution. But all this was of no avail. Another effect of the trial and punishment of these men has been the creation of an impression that the holding of certain political opinions which the authorities consider

> as wrong is punishable. These men no doubt held opinions similar to the objects of the communist international, but the evidence of overt acts of sedition in pursuance of these views is meager...This Meerut trial has again demonstrated that a very strong case exists for a radical reform in India of the substantive law in regard to offences against the state.

It is reported that even President Roosevelt showed interest in the case. Muzaffar Ahmad wrote in 1966:

> Prof. Harold Laski told Dr. Katju [Defence Counsel] in England that, when he had been in America, President Roosevelt, who had invited him to dinner, had raised the subject of the Meerut Conspiracy Case and had enquired why the Case was being protracted for such a long time. Prof. Laski also told Dr. Katju that he could use this information in his argument before the Court.

After the sentences were reduced drastically by the High Court on appeal the *Manchester Guardian* commented on August 4, 1933:

> The drastic revision by the Court of Appeal of most of the Meerut sentences will be welcome news to all who have followed this four and a half years' trial...In the first place, the fact that a proportion of no less than one-third of the defendants have had their trial sentences completely reversed on appeal is a startling commentary both on the earlier findings and on the wisdom of the Government of India's action in starting this prosecution at all. As to the remainder who are still found guilty, the Appeal Court's estimate of the seriousness of the offences is sufficiently indicated by its great reduction of the sentences imposed on them at the trial. Those who started this prosecution will get

> little satisfaction out of the result of the appeals. Here are nine men—and there are three others who were acquitted at the earlier stage—who, after being kept in the gaol for four years without bail, are now adjudged to be innocent. If they should now raise a demand for compensation, will the Government be able, in equity or desire, to resist it? But how does one compensate a man for the loss of four years of his life? The only thing we can do—and we ought to do it—is to see that there is no repetition of such a blemish on British justice as the Meerut trial.

Similar comments were made by other British newspapers as well.

The entire Meerut Conspiracy Case received an extra-ordinary amount of international attention and no doubt it caused some embarrassment to the British Government who initiated it and allowed it to continue for four and a half years.

The distinctive features of the Meerut Conspiracy Case described in the above pages certainly make it plain why the case is considered a unique instance of a state trial in modern Indian history. It was the longest and the costliest trial of its kind. To a great extent the trial was shaped and designed by the Government of India for certain definite purposes. Bail was refused to the accused in order to keep what were considered to be the more "dangerous" and "troublesome" elements of the left-wing leaders out of the Indian political scene for a long as period as possible. Jury trial was disallowed so that the conviction of the accused would be made certain. The line of argument followed by both the prosecution and the defence as well as the nature of the evidence produced and statement made on both sides would hardly be admissible in any ordinary British court of justice. Indeed, the political character of the case has no parallel in Indian history. Finally, considering the fact that none of the thirty-two accused enjoyed any international reputation or fame as Mahatma Gandhi or Jawaharlal Nehru did, the extraordinary amount of international attention which the case received puts it into a special category of historical significance.

(Courtesy—Meerut Conspiracy Case and The Left-wing in India, Pramita Ghosh Pub-Papyrus-2-Ganendra Mitra Lane, Calcutta, 1978).

Poster found on the Walls of the City of Lahore after Saunders' Murder

"This killing of J. P. Saunders was only to avenge fully the murder of Lala Lajpat Rai. It was indeed a sad and shameful episode that so mean a fellow like J.P. Saunders should dare to deliver blows on the chest of the old and most respected person worshipped by a nation of thirty-five crores of Indians. That was indeed an affront to the nation. By that insult of the Indian Nation, the foreign power had as if thrown a challenge to the self-respecting and brave sons of the soil. This reply will surely convince the people and the foreign power that the Indian Nation is indeed not yet deed or spiritless to bear such insults. The people of Bharat have fresh blood flowing in their veins. Young India is up and ready to guard the honour of the nation even at the stake and sacrifice of life.

"Beware, you Tyrant of Government!

"Do not hereafter try to touch the provoked feelings of the people that are already exploited and harassed. Hold your devilish hands: Remember that in spite all your laws and endeavours to keep us disarmed a flood of pistols and revolvers will always flow into the hands of the youth of the country. Though it may be admitted that no armed revolution can be accomplished with a sprinking of arms yet they will indeed be enough to wreak vengeance for the repeated national insults which the administration indulged in from time to time. Our so-called national leaders may condemn and reproach our actions, and the foreign government may try their utmost to crush our organisation. But we want to make it clear here that we shall ever be ready to safeguard our national honour and to teach lessons to all the foreign aggrandisers. We shall never permit the cry of revolution to languish even under the encirclement of opression and suppression all around; bear in mind that even with the noose knot of death round our necks, we shall always shout and cheer 'Long Live Revolution'.

"We are really sorry that we had to kill a human being. But the man whom we had to shoot down was a part and parcel of such cruel, mean and unjust administration and of a foreign power that we had no alternative but to overthrow him. This man is killed only in his capacity as a representative of the British power in India. British power is undoubtedly the most tyrannical one in the world."

"We again repeat that we are sorry that we had to shed human blood. But it becomes inevitable to shed blood on the altar of revolution, which will end all exploitation of man at the hands of man."

Long Live Revolution Sd/-Balraj,
11 December 1928. *Commander: Punjab HSRA*

Hindustan Socialist Republican army

'It takes a loud voice to make the deaf hear' with these immortal words uttered at a similar occasion by a valiant French anarchist martyr, do we strongly justify this action of ours. Without repeating the humiliating history of the past ten years of the working of the Reforms and without mentioning the insults hurled down upon the head of the Indian nation through this house, the so-called Indian Parliament, we want to point out that while the people are expecting some more crumbs of reforms from the Simon Commission and are even quarrelling over the distribution of expected bones, the government are thrusting upon us new repressive measures like the Public Safety and Trade Disputes Bills while reserving the Press Bill for the next session. Indiscriminate arrests of labour leaders working in the open field clearly indicate whither the wind blows.

In these extremely provocative circumstances the Hindustan Socialist Republican Association in all seriousness and realising its full responsibility have decided and ordered its army to do this particular action so that a stop be put to this humiliating force and to let the alien bureaucratic exploiters do what they wish but to make them come before the public eye in their mailed form. Let the representatives of the people return to their constituencies and prepare the masses for the coming revolution and let the government know while protesting against the Public Safety and Trade Disputes Bills and the callous murder of Lala Lajput Rai, on behalf of the helpless Indian masses, we want to emphasise that you can kill individuals but you cannot kill ideas. Great empires crumbled but all the ideas survived. The Bourbons and the Czars fell while revolutions marched triumphantly ahead.

We are sorry to admit that we who attach so great sanctity to human life, we who dream of a very glorious future when men will be enjoying perfect peace and full liberty, have been forced to shed human blood. But sacrifice of individuals at the altar of great revolution that will bring freedom to all rendering exploitation of man by man impossible, is inevitable.

Long live Revolution
Sd/- Balraj
Commander-in-chief

Copy of the written statement filed by Bhagat Singh and B. K. Dutt in the court of the Sessions Judge, Delhi in the Assembly Bomb Case on 8 June 1929.

We stand charged with serious offences and at this stage we explain our conduct.

The following questions arise:

1. Were bombs thrown into the Chamber, if so, why?
2. Is the charge as framed by the lower court correct or otherwise?

To the first half of the first question our reply is in the affirmative but some of the so-called eye witnesses have perjured themselve and since we are not denying our liability to the extent and as such as it is our statement about them be judged for what it is worth. By way of illustration, we may point out that the evidence of Sergeant Terry regarding the seizure of pistol from one of us is a deliberate falsehood, for neither of us had a pistol at the time we gave ourselves up.

The other witnesses who dispose to having seen bombs thrown by us, have not scrupled to tell lies, patent on the face of them. It has its own moral for those who aim at judicial purity and fairplay. At the same time we acknowledge the fairness of the Public Prosecuter and the judicial attitude of the court so far.

In our reply to the next half of the first question, we are constrained to go into some details to offer full and frank explanations of our motive and circumstances leading up to what has now become a historic event. When we are told by some of the Police officers who visited us in the jail that Lord Irwin in his address to the joint session of the two houses after event in question, described it as an attack directed against no individual but against a constitution itself, we readily recognised that the true significance of the incident had been correctly appreciated.

We are next to none in our love for humanity and

so far from having any malice against any individual, we hold human life sacred beyond words; we are neither perpetrator of dastardly outrages and therefore a disgrace to the country as the pseudo-socialist Dewan Chamanlal is reported to have described us, nor are we lunatics as the *Tribune* of Lahore and some others would have it believed.

Serious Students of History

We humbly claim to be no more than serious students of history and conditions of our country, and human aspirations and we despise hypocrisy.

Our practical protest was against the institution which since its birth has eminently displayed not only its worthlessness, but its far reaching power for mischief. The more we have pondered, the more deeply we have been convinced that it exists only to demonstrate to the world the Indian humiliation and helplessness and it symbolises the overriding domination of an irresponsible and autocratic rule.

Time and again the national demand has been pressed by the representative of the people, only to find waste paper basked as its final destination. solemn resolutions passed by the House have been contemptuously trempled under the foot on the floor of the so-called Indian Parliament. Resolutions regarding the repeal of repressive and arbitrary measures have been treated with sublime contempt and government measures and proposal rejected as unacceptable by the elected members have been restored by a stroke of the pen.

In brief, in spite of earnest endeavour, we have utterly failed to find any justification for the existence of an institution which despite all pomp and splender organised with the hard earned money of the sweating millions of India is only a hollow show and a mischievous make-believe.

And alike have we failed to comprehend the mentality of our public leaders who help to squander public time and money on so manifestly a stage-managed exhibition of India's helpless subjection. We have been ruminating upon all this, as also upon the wholesale arrests of the leaders of the Labour movement when the introduction of The Trade Disputes Bill brought us into the Assembly to watch its progress and the course of the debate only served to confirm our conviction that the labouring millions of India had nothing to expect from an institution that stood as a menacing monument to the strangling power of the exploiters and the serfdom of the helpless labourers.

Finally an insult which we considered inhuman and barbarous, was hurled on the devoted heads of the representatives of the entire country and the starving and struggling millions were deprived of their primary rights to the sole means of their economic welfare.

None who has felt like us for the dumb-driven drudges of labourers could possibly witness the spectacle with equanimity, none whose heart bleeds for those who have given their life blood in silence to the building up of the economic structure of the exploiters of whom the Government happen to be the biggest in the country, could repress the cry of the soul-agonising anguish which is so ruthlessly wrong out of our hearts. Consequently bearing in our minds the words of late Mr S. R. Das once the Law Member of the Governor General's Executive Council, which appeared in the famous letter he had addressed to his son to the effect that the bomb was necessary to awaken England from her dreams, we dropped bombs on the floor of the Assembly Chamber to register our protest on behalf of those who had no other means left, to give expression to their heart-rending agony. Our sole purpose was 'to make the deaf hear' and to give the heedless timely warning.

Others have as keenly felt as we have done and from under the seeming illness of the sea of the Indian humanity a veritable storm is about to break out. We have hoisted a 'danger signal' to warn those who are speeding along without heeding the great dangers ahead. We have only marked the end of an era of Utopian non-violence of whose (8 Jume, 1929) futility the rising generation has been convinced beyond a shadow of doubt. Out of our sincerest goodwill and love for humanity we have adopted this methods of warning to prevent untold sufferings which we like millions of others elearly foresee.

Utopian Non-Violence

We have used the expression 'Utopian Non-Violence' in the foregoing para which requires some explanation. Force when aggressively applied is 'violence', and therefore, morally unjustifiable. But when it is used in the furtherance of a legitimate cause it has its moral justification. Elimination of force at all costs is Utopian and the new movement which has arisen in the country and of which we have given a warning is inspired by the deeds which guided Guru Govind Singh, Shiviji, Kamal Pasha and Riza Khan, Washington and Garibaldi, Lafayetti and Lenin. As both the alien government and the Indian public leaders appeared to have shut their eyes and closed their ears against the existence and voice of this motive we have felt it our duty to sound the warning where it could not be unherard.

Our Intentions

We have so far dealt with the motive behind the incident in question and now we must define the extent of our intentions.

It cannot be gainsaid that we bore no personal

grudge or malice against anyone of those who received slight injuries or against any other person in the Assembly. On the contrary we report that we hold human lives sacred beyound words and would sooner lay down our own lives in the service of humanity than injure anyone else. Unlike mercenary soldiers of imperialist armies, who are disinclined to kill without compunction, we respect, and in so far as it lies in us, attempt to save human life. And still we admit having deliberately thrown bombs into the Assembly Chamber. Facts, however, speak themselves and intention should be judged from the result of action without drawing upon hypothetical circumstances and presumptions. Despite the evidence of the government expert, the bombs that were thrown in the Assembly Chamber resulted in slight damage to an empty bench and few slight abrasions in less than half a dozen cases. While the government's scientist ascribed this result to a miracle we see nothing but precisely scientific process in it all. The first two bombs exploded in vacant spaces within the wooden barriers of desks and benches. Secondly, even those who were even within two feet of the explosion, for instance, Mr Rau, Mr Shankar Rao and Sir George Schuster were either not hurt or only slightly scratched. Loaded with an effective charge of Potassium Chlorate and sensitive Picrate the bombs would have smashed the barriers and laid many low within same yards of the explosion. Again had they been loaded with some other high explosive, with charge of destructive pellets or derts, they would have sufficed to wipe out a majority of the members of the Legislative Assembly. Still again we could have flung them into the official box chockfull with people of note. And finally we could have embushed Sir John Simon, whose luckless commission was hated by all reasonable people and who was sitting in the presidential gallery at the time. All this, however, was beyond our intention and the bombs did not do more than what they were desired to do and the miracle consisted of no more than a deliberate aim which landed them is safe places.

We then deliberately offered to bear the penalty for what we had done and to let the imperialist exploiters know that by crushing individuals they cannot kill ideas. By crushing two insignificant units the nation cannot be crushed. We wanted to emphasise the historical lesson that Letters de Catchet and Bastilles could not crush the revolutionary movement in France. Gallows and Siberian mines could not extinguish the Russian revolution. Can ordinances and Safety Bills snuff out the flames of freedom in India? Conspiracy cases trumpeted up or discovered and incarceration of all young men who cherish the vision of the greater ideal cannot check the march of revolution, But timely warning if not unheeded, can help to prevent loss of life and general suffering. We took it upon ourselves to provide this warning and our duty is done.

What is Revolution?

Bhagat Singh was asked in the lower court as to what he meant by revolution. In answer to that question, we would say that revolution does necessarily involve sanguinary stifes nor is there any place in it for individual vendetta. It is not the cult of the bomb and the pistol. By "Revolution" we mean that the present order of things, which is based on manifest injustice must change. Producers and labourers in spite of being the most necessary element of society, are robbed by their exploiters of the fruits of their labour and deprived of their elementary right. On the one hand the peasants who grow corn for all starve with their families. The weaver who supplied the world markets with textile fabrics cannot find enough to cover his own and his children's bodies. Masons, smiths and carpenters, who rear magnificent palaces live and perish in slums; on the other hand, capitalists, exploiters, parasites of society squander millions on their whims. These terrible inequalities, and forced disparities of chances are heading towards chaos. This state of affairs cannot last and it is obvious that the present order of society is merry-making on the brink of a Valcano and the innocent children of exploiters no less than the millions of the exploited are walking on the edge of a dangerous precipice. The whole edifice of this civilisation, if not saved in time, shall crumble. Radical change is, therefore, necessary and it is the duty of those who realise this to organise society on a socialistic basis. Unless this is done and the exploitation of man by man and of nation by nation which goes masquerading as imperialism, is brought to an end, the suffering and carnage with which humanity is threatened today cannot be prevented, and all talk of ending wars, and ushering in an era of universal peace is undisguised hypocrisy. By revolution, we mean the ultimate establishment of an order of society which may not be threatened by such breakdown and in which the sovereignty of the proletariat should be recognised and as a result of which the world federation should redeem humanity from the bondage of capitalism and the misery and peril of wars.

Fair and Loud Enough Warning

This is our ideal, with this ideology for our inspiration, we have given a fair and loud enough warning. If, however, it goes unheeded and the present system of government continues to be an impediment in the way of the natural forces that are swelling up, a grim struggle must ensue involving the overthrow of all obstacles and the establishment of dictatorship of the proletariat to pave the way for the consummation of the ideal revolution. Revolution is the inalienable right of mankind. Freedom is the imprescriptible birth-right of all. The labourer is the real sustainer of society. The sovereignty of the people is the ultimate destiny of the workers. For these ideals and for this faith we shall welcome any suffering to which we may be condemned. To the altar of this revolution we have brought our youth as incense, for no sacrifice is too great for so magnificent a cause. We are content to await the advent of revolution.

Long Live Revolution.

(Courtesy—J. N. Sanyal—Sardar Bhajat Singh, Allahabad–1931)

Nangla (Khulna) Conspiracy Case 1910

A big case, the Khulna Conspi-racy Case, was started against a dozen yourgmen on the omnibus charge of being members of a conspiracy to wage war against the King. After the preliminary enquiry a Special Tribunal of the High Court started proceedings on July 18, 1910. Judgment was delivered on August 30, 1910, in which five men were sentenced to transportation for seven years, three to five years', two to three years' rigorous imprisonment. Only one was acquitted.

Nasik Conspiracy

The murder of the District Magistrate of Nasik on December 21, 1909, was followed by vigorous investigations into the secrets of the organisation responsible for the death of Jackson. It was found that it was the outcome of a deep-seated conspiracy that imparted strength to the hands of the persons involved in direct action.

No less than thirty-eight men were hauled up before the court in what is known as the First Nasik Conspiracy Case. It transpired in evidence, mainly confessions, that the members of the *Mitra Mela*, started in 1899 by Vinayak Savarkar and changed to *Abhinaw Bharat* (or Young India Society) in 1904 were responsible for the outrage where a Browning pistol, brought by Chhatrabhuj Amin from London was used.

The aim of the Association was revolution, unalloyed, where the model and the methods of Russian secret societies were to be adopted. The whole organisation was to be divided into small groups, one individual unit would not know the members of any other, the connecting link being the accredited head of the organisation. The members were bound by oaths of secrecy individually and collectively when a whole group was concerned.

It was the endeavour of the Government to rope in (Ganesh) Vinayak Savarkar into the conspiracy so that he might be put out of the way for as long a period as the law allowed. It was not difficult for the prosecution with the resources at its disposal to secure evidence to establish connection with the other accused and Vinayak Savarkar.

The judgment of this historic trial was delivered on December 24, 1910, in which (Vinayak) Savarkar was sentenced to transportation for life. There were thirty-eight accused most of whom were convicted and sentenced to different terms of imprisonment.

From the pamphlet entitled *Bande Mataram* produced in the trial it was evident that the immediate aim of the organisation was assassination of officials, so that the cause of independence might speedily advance.

A few sentences from the document were sufficient to disclose its purpose. It ran as follows:

"Terrorise the officials, English and Indian, and the collapse of the whole machinery of oppression is not very far. The persistent execution of the policy that has been so gloriously inaugurated by Khudiram Bose, Kanai

Lal Datta and other martyrs will soon cripple the British Government in India. The campaign of separate assassinations is the best conceivable method of paralysing the bureaucracy and or arousing the people. The initial stage of the revolution is marked by the policy of separate assassination."

The judgment in the case gives an inkling into the working of the organisation and Vinayak's share of responsibility in the matter:

> There was evidence that there existed an association under Ganesh Vinayak Savarkar named *Mitra Mela* which was established prior to 1906. Membership was offered after closest scrutiny and under heavy oath about secrecy in matters related to the Association. Small groups of young men working with the common object were attached to the parent body. Literature was published, for disseminating sedition suggesting methods for preparations for war. Instructions were issued for the purchase and storing of weapons in the neighbouring countries to be used when opportunities should occur. It also suggested

"opening of many very small but secret factories at some distance from one another for the manufacture of weapons clandestinely in the country seeking independence and the purchase by secret societies of weapons in other countries to be secretly imported in merchantships."

About Savarkar the Judges remarked:

"We find the accused guilty of the abetment of waging war by instigation, by the circulation of printed matter inciting to war, the providing of arms and the distribution of instructions for the manufacture of explosives."

(*Courtesy*—Kalicharan Ghosho—
Roll of Movement)

Second Nasik Conspiracy Trial 1911

A Second Nasik Conspiracy Case charged Savarkar with the abetment of murder of Jackson, the Collector of Nasik. The trial opened on January 23, 1911, in which it was contended by the prosecution that the pistol used in the outrage was one of those twenty which Vinayak had been able to send clandestinely to India. It was, therefore, not a difficult matter to find the accused guilty of abetment and Vinayak was awarded on January 30, 1911, a second term of transportation for life.

It may be interesting to note that the two Savarkar brothers had the unique distinction amongst Indian patriots to pass jointly a big portion of their prison life in the Cellular Jail in the Andamans—aptly called "the Indian Bastille." The elder brother, Ganesh, was convicted on June, 9, 1909, for composing and publishing a book of patriotic verses, entitled *Laghu Abhinav Bharat Mela*, with a sentence of transportation for life, a punish-ment reserved for the gravest offences under the Criminal Law of the land.

The Lahore Conspiracy Cases of a later period have been dealt with at appropriate places.

(*Courtesy*—Kalicharan Ghosho—Roll of Movement)

Peshawar Conspiracy

British imperialists did not want communism to take roots in India. It began to do propaganda that Indian traditions go against any form of communist ideology. It united the propertied classes that supported British imperialism wholehog. British rulers were determined from the very beginning not to allow communist ideas to penetrate into India through air, land or sea.

But new ideas, specially communist ideas, cannot be imprisoned or hanged by the neck till they are dead as they have no necks. No walls, however high, can prevent their entering any country if they are true to life and heave of life. That is why communist ideas began to enter India in seen or unseen ways.

Influenced by Hijrat movement, many muslim youths left the Punjab and Sindh and went to muslim countries in the summer of 1920—Afghanistan and Iran—to fight against British imperialists for the restoration of the Khilafat in Turkey. The allied powers had designed to partition Turkey, thus reducing the position of the Caliph to a virtual non-entity. The Khilafat movement exhorted young men to escape from British tyrrany by migrating to Turkey to fight for their Caliph.

They were very shabbily treated by the Afghan government. They were denied food, asked to eat from their own pockets. The atmosphere was very suffocating. They felt imprisoned and wanted to flee from there. They crossed the Hindukush mountain, suffering great hardships and reached the Soviet Union where under the influence of the October Revolution and its achievements they studied communism and became communists and a number of them got together to form the first Communist Party of India in Tashkent.

Inspired by the new perspective given by the Russian revolution, they decided to return to India in small groups to work for the Indian revolution. On their way back, they were arrested on the borders and lodged inside jail.

We have studied the British imperialist policy of hatred and hostility towards communism. The British Indian government had planted spies among the muhajirs and received reports from them about the activities of the muhajirs who had crossed over into Soviet Russia and had remained there for some time. They had gathered information about their activities in Tashkent and Moscow. As soon as they began to come back into Punjab in batches or singly, they were arrested and conspiracy cases were launched against them.

These conspiracy cases were launched, not on the basis of any concrete action of theirs in the British Indian territory in the Punjab against the British raj but on the basis of having come into contact with Soviet ideology and the Russian revolution. It was pure and simple communist thought which these muhajirs had learnt in Soviet Russia which the British India rulers were prosecuting in their courts of justice (?)

The British rulers did not want to take any chance by allowing the muhajirs to move about freely in the Punjab, talk about the victorious Soviet revolution and what it was all about. They arrested them as soon as they set foot in the Punjab and cooked up conspiracy cases against them and passed barbarous sentences on them. What for? For having communist ideas.

The first conspiracy case judgement was given on 31 May 1922 and that last one ended in 1927. In between this period about five bolshevik (or Moscow) conspiracy cases were launched and heavy sentences were pronounced against the accused. For instance Akbar Khan was given seven years rigorous imprisonment including three months in solitary confinement; Mohammed Hussain, five years rigorous imprisonment including 3 months in solitary confinement; and Ghulam Mehboob (Peshawar) five years rigorous imprisonment including three months in solitary confinement. This was the second case tried by the session judge Fraser who delivered the judgement on 27 April 1922.

Shaukat Usmani was arrested on 9 May 1923. The *London Times* on 12 May 1923 wrote malignly about 'Bolshevik activity in India' saying that an alleged agent of Moscow had been arrested and conspiracy case had been started against him under Section 121-A (waging war against the king-emperor to overthrow him) and to impress the world against communists it wrote: Proscribed literature and suspicious correspondence have been found with him. The authorities are taking drastic action against the bolshevik agents. And it further added:

> Of late most striking activity has been intensified not so much by direct agents as by extremist politicians who have imbued bolshevik notions, and have seen in bolshevik propaganda useful and effective means of carrying on agitation against the government."

The *London Times* spearheaded the anti-communist propaganda in the world. Next day on 13 May it reported under the headlines 'Red Agent in India sent for trial'. His arrest would lead to revelations in regard to Soviet propaganda in India. He had been touring the country, organising groups and disseminating bolshevik propaganda. The documents recovered indicate that he had been receiving instructions constantly in regard to plans for propaganda and also financial help from bolsheviks outside India. He would be tried in Peshawar.

The allegations levelled against Shaukat Usmani were all cooked up, fabricated and unfounded. This was pure propaganda stuff, as usual, without any real basis, as the trial also proved.

Shaukat Usmani was individually tried in a supplementary case and sentenced to two years' rigorous imprisonment under the bombastic Section 121A. The *London Times* and its ilk knew how to make a mountain out of a mole hill.

The main conspiracy charge was against (1) Abdul Majid, (2) Habib Ahmad, (3) Rafiq Ahmad, (4) Feroze Din Mansur, (5) Sultan Ahmad, (6) Gauhar Rahman, (7) Mian Akbar Shah Khatak as coaccused. The judge on 18 May 1923 sentenced the first five to one year's rigorous imprisonment each and the latter two to three years' rigorous imprisonment each. Ghulam Ahmad Khan and Fida Ali had turned approvers i.e. traitors and hence were pardoned and released.

A number of returnees got demoralised and gave up politics. It was very difficult to work in the reactionary landlord dominated Muslim majority territory now in Pakistan. But a good chunk remained loyal to Marxism and continued working despite financial hardships and now and again suffering imprisonment. They were Mir. Abdul Majid, Feroze Din Mansur, Shaukat Usmani, Fazal Ilahi Qurban and Gauhar Rahman.

Feroze Din Mansur died in harness and Abdul Majid is still alive.

(*Courtesy*—Sohan Singh Josh—The Great Attack—Meerut Conspiracy—PPH. N.Del. 1979)

Tinnevelly Conspiracy Case-1911

About midday on June 17th, 1911, Mr Ashe, the District Magistrate of Tinnevelly, was shot in the presence of his wife in a railway carriage at Maniyachi Junction in the Tinnevelly District by a young Brahmin named Vanchi Aiyar, a clerk in the Travancore Forest Department, who committed suicide a few minutes later. Mr Ashe died about 30 minutes after he was shot. The assassin was accompanied by his brother-in-law, named Shankara Krishna Aiyar, who ran away and escaped but was afterwards arrested and sentenced to four years' imprisonment on the body of Vanchi Aiyar the following letter in the Tamil language was found:—

"The *mlechhas* of England having captured our country tread under foot the *Sanatam Dharam* (orthodox religion) of the Hindus and destroy it. Every Indian is trying to drive out the English and restore Swarajya and the Sanatan Dharma. Our Rama, Shivaji,

Krishna, Guru Govind and Arjun ruled over our land protecting all religions, but now they are preparing to crown in this land George V, *a mlechha* who eats the flesh of cows. 3000 Madrassis have taken a vow to kill George V as soon as he lands in our country. To make known our intention to others, I who am the least in this company have done this deed this day. Every man in Hindustan should consider this his duty".

The disclosures made in the course of the investigation led to the Tinnevelly Conspiracy Case which was decided on 15th February, 1912, by a Special Tribunal of the Madras High Court. Out of 14 persons accused, nine were convicted by a majority of the court and five were acquitted. Of the nine who were convicted the finding of the court as against four was unanimous but Mr. Justice Sankaran Nair differed regarding the remaining five mainly on the ground that he did not consider that the evidence of the approvers had been sufficiently corroborated. The convitions were all under section 121-A, Indian Penal Code (conspiracy to wage war against the king), the court holding that the second charge of abetment of the murder of Mr. Ashe failed as the murder was not the direct result of the Conspiracy, although it might have been the result of the pernicious influence of the conspiracy on the mind of Vanchi Aiyar, the assassin. The first accused, Nilakanta Aiyar, was sentenced to seven years' rigorous imprisonment. Six of the persons convicted petitioned the High Court in revision (there is no appeal from the decision of a Special Tribunal and the petitions were rejected by a majority of the full bench, the there European Judges rejecting the petitions and the two Indians Judges dissenting.

(Political Trouble in India—1907-1917
by James Campbell Ker, 1917)

The Titagarh Compiracy Case–1935

During the year 1935, a very decisive blow was struck at the Anushilan Party in Bengal and Faridpur by the investigation and subsequent trial of what is known as the Titagarh Conspiracy case, which at the time of writing, has only just concluded. On the 27th December 1934 a house in Belgharia, Calcutta, was searched and a young *bhadralok* of Sylhet was arrested with suspicious letters and other decuments in his possession. From his possession notebooks and cyphers were recovered. Later, on information given in an anonymous letter that some suspicious youths and a young girl were staying at a house at Titagarh, the house was raided and the inmates arrested after a struggle. One of those arrested was Purannanda Das Gupta who had escaped from the Alipore Jail with Sitanath De during the trial of the Inter Provincial Conspiracy case. A pistol, cartridges and a mass of documents including formula for explosives and much cypher material were recovered together with a large quantity of chemicals suitable for the preparation of explosives...A protracted and careful investigation followed in the course of which no less than 171 persons were arrested. Of these, 33 were sent for trial before the special tribunal which began hearing the case in November 1935. Purananda Das Gupta, has been sentenced to transportation for life, Prafulla Sen to twelve years' rigorous imprisonment, and fifteen others to various terms of imprisonment.

(Political Trouble in India—1917-1937 by H. W. Hale—Allahabad, Chugh Publication, 1974; pp. 49-52)

❑❑❑